THE HEAVENLY MAN

CHRISTIAN SOLIDARITY WORLDWIDE

Christian Solidarity Worldwide is a human rights charity working all over the world on behalf of those who suffer repression. We promote religious liberty for all, with a special focus on the 250 million Christians persecuted for their faith worldwide.

CSW works all over the world . . .

- for *individual prisoners of conscience* like Irene Fernandes awaiting trial in Malaysia for her exposure of human rights abuses and those *falsely accused* of terrorism in Peru
- for *legislation that adheres to universal standards of religious freedom* such as in Central Asia where registration requirements have denied many their freedom to worship
- for *innocent civilians caught in the crossfire of conflict* such as in Indonesia, Sudan and Nigeria
- for *children in need* such as those in Russia where we operate a pioneering child foster care programme

CSW works to highlight these injustices through raising awareness, campaigning and advocacy. Our publications provide first-hand reports from over 30 countries worldwide, and our supporters are equipped to pray and to write campaign letters to strategic decision makers. Supporters also send cards and letters of encouragement to those in prison. Our staff based in Westminster and Brussels ensure that CSW briefings and urgent appeals reach key officials in the European institutions and foreign ministries as well as the British government. In addition CSW advocacy targets other governments and multi-laterals organisations including the United Nations. Where resources allow, CSW provides humanitarian assistance to those in need.

Proverbs 31:8 "Speak up for those who cannot speak for themselves."

Christian Solidarity Worldwide
PO Box 99
New Malden
Surrey
KT3 3YF

The Heavenly Man

The Remarkable True Story of
Chinese Christian Brother Yun

WITH PAUL HATTAWAY

MONARCH
BOOKS

Mill Hill, London & Grand Rapids, Michigan

Christian Solidarity Worldwide

Copyright © Brother Yun and Paul Hattaway 2002.
The right of Brother Yun and Paul Hattaway to be identified
as authors of this work has been asserted by them in
accordance with the Copyright, Designs
and Patents Act 1988.

First published by Monarch Books in the UK and USA in 2002
Concorde House, Grenville Place,
Mill Hill, London, NW7 3SA.
Reprinted 2003 (seven times), 2004 (three times)

Published in conjunction with
Christian Solidarity Worldwide

Distributed by:
UK: Marston Book Services, 160 Milton Park Estate,
PO Box 269, Abingdon, Oxon OX14 4YN;
USA: Kregel Publications, PO Box 2607
Grand Rapids, Michigan 49501.

USA ISBN 0 8254 6207 X

British Library Cataloguing Data
A catalogue record for this book is available
from the British Library.

Book design and production for the publishers by
Bookprint Creative Services
P.O. Box 827, BN21 3YJ, England.

Printed in the United States of America

CONTENTS

PREFACE

For more than one thousand years the gospel of the Lord Jesus Christ has spread its influence across China, through many ups and downs, victories and trials.

In 1949 persecution of God's people commenced and the churches have suffered from all kinds of attacks since. By 1958 the government had closed all visible churches. Mao's wife, Jiang Qing, told foreign visitors, "Christianity in China has been confined to the history section of the museum. It is dead and buried." In the 1970s a visiting Christian delegation from the United States reported, "There is not a single Christian left in China."

At the start of the Book of Genesis we read that the earth *"was formless and empty, darkness was over the surface of the deep, and the Spirit of God was hovering over the waters"*. *Genesis 1:2*. This was also the state of the Chinese church at this time. The church in China, at least on the visible surface, was dead. In those days nobody dared to proclaim, "Jesus is Lord." The church was stripped from top to bottom, and for all intents and purposes, had died.

"And God said, 'Let there be light,' and there was light. God saw that the light was good, and he separated the light from the darkness." Genesis 1:3. Thankfully we serve a God who knows

how to raise the dead! I believe God allowed the atheist government to destroy the old structure of the Chinese church so that he could rebuild it according to his own purposes. He started with little and has made it much!

The simple fact that the Chinese church has grown into a force tens of millions strong today is a sign not only of God's existence but also of his matchless power.

In the 1970s the Chinese church, like a rosebud that has been closed for a long time, started to open up and reveal its beauty and life to the world again. At that time a young man in southern Henan Province met the Lord Jesus Christ and committed his life to follow him as Lord and Master. God took hold of his life in a remarkable way.

Through nearly thirty years of testing, Brother Yun has seen the grace of the Lord poured out on his life, overflowing as a blessing to many. He is one of God's chosen leaders to this generation, a great fighter and faithful worker. Many signs, wonders and miracles have followed his ministry, attesting that he is an apostle of the faith (2 Corinthians 12:12). He is a man of impeccable integrity and character, a noble man, a good husband and father. The joy of the Lord is always Brother Yun's strength. His infectious smile can light up a whole room.

After I read Brother Yun's book my heart was deeply moved. I felt regret at not knowing this dear brother longer than the twenty years we have worked hand-in-hand in China.

I testify that every story in this book is true. I have personally witnessed many of the events described in these pages. I feel so honoured to be Brother Yun's closest friend and co-worker. Although he has always honoured me as a spiritual elder and respected me as my pastor, I feel a mutual respect. When I was married I asked Brother Yun to conduct the wedding service and offer the blessing.

I have read this book with a heart of gratitude to God and sincerely recommend it as a true testimony of the great things God has done in China's church.

Xu Yongze
Chairman of the Sinim Fellowship of House Church Leaders in China

FOREWORD

I joyfully read Brother Yun's entire book in one breath, feeling great excitement in my heart and soul. It seemed to take me back to those fervent times, and recalled many precious memories.

Brother Yun and I were born in the same region, went to the same church, and laboured together in the harvest. We cried, rejoiced and preached together, and were rejected together. We ate in the wind and slept in the open air, stuck together through thick and thin. We loved each other as blood brothers.

Yun and I worked together for many years until we were arrested in Nanyang. In the prison we were put in separate cells, but we cried out along the prison corridors, hoping our voices would be heard as a source of encouragement to each other. We tried to slip notes to strengthen each other in the faith.

Yun's testimony is written with blood and tears; his journey has been one that encountered many bitter struggles. Instead of complaining and grumbling, he learned to tackle all obstacles prayerfully, on his knees with God.

Chinese believers remember Yun as a brave man who often prays on bended knee, raising his hands in thankfulness to the Lord while tears stream down his cheeks. After many unbearable situations, God not only opened the iron gate of the prison for Yun, but is also using him as a blessing to both the Chinese and Western churches in this new century.

Brother Yun is gifted at making contact with believers from different church backgrounds, gently bringing them together in unity. Like a thread, God has used him to combine different coloured patches into a beautiful cloth. In recent years Brother Yun and I drifted apart as our paths took us in different directions, and I sometimes even reprimanded him from afar. Yet when I heard the reports of how God was using him and learned about the path he has faithfully followed, I could only admire him and blush with shame and self-reprimand.

In the Chinese church I have seen many of God's servants come with great power and authority, but with brother Yun I saw a servant of Jesus who always came in humility and meekness, reflecting the heart of the Son of Man, who did not come to be served, but to serve, and to give his life.

I pray you will enjoy and be challenged by this book as much as I was.

Zhang Rongliang
Fangcheng House Church, China

INTRODUCTION

On a warm September evening a small group of Christians gathered at Bangkok International Airport to welcome back Brother Yun. It had been more than eight months since we had seen his smiling face. In January 2001 he had been arrested. During the first few days of his incarceration the prison authorities almost beat him to death. Later he was sentenced to seven years in prison.

Occasional messages were carried out of the prison to his concerned friends around the world. One said, "God has sent me to be his witness in this place. There are many people here who need Jesus. I will be in this prison for exactly the length of time God has determined. I won't leave one moment early and I won't stay one moment too long. When God determines my ministry in prison is complete, I will come out."

Miraculously, in God's perfect timing, Yun was released after spending just seven months and seven days of his seven-year sentence.

Now we were gathered at the airport, hoping to see him arrive. Would he be sick, tired and quiet after his harrowing ordeal?

Suddenly Yun appeared in the arrival hall. He was none

of these things! His face was full of light and a wide smile stretched from ear to ear. "Praise God! Hallelujah!" were his first words. "Glory to God!" We held hands and bowed our heads in a prayer of thanksgiving, as bemused passengers hurried past us to their check-in counters.

Brother Yun is known throughout China as "the Heavenly Man". This nickname stemmed from an incident in 1984 when he refused to tell his real name to the authorities. Divulging his true identity would have endangered local Christians. In reply to the threats and beatings of the Public Security Bureau to reveal his name and home address, Yun shouted, "I am a heavenly man! My home is in heaven!" The local believers, who were still gathered in a nearby house, heard his shouting and knew he was warning them of danger. They all fled and avoided arrest.

As a mark of respect for his courage and love for the body of Christ, house church believers in China have called Yun "the Heavenly Man" to this day.

Yun is the first to admit that there are parts of him that are not heavenly! Like all of us, he struggles against temptation and weakness, and deeply realizes that, apart from the grace of Jesus Christ in his life, he amounts to nothing. He once told his wife Deling, "We are absolutely nothing. We have nothing to be proud about. We have no abilities and nothing to offer God. The fact that he chooses to use us is only due to his grace. It has nothing to do with us. If God should choose to raise up others for his purpose and never to use us again we would have nothing to complain about."

Oswald Chambers once wrote, "If you give God the right to yourself, he will make a holy experiment out of you. God's experiments always succeed." This is certainly true of Brother Yun. From the time he first met Jesus Christ, he has endeavoured to serve him wholeheartedly.

There are lessons and experiences from Yun's life that can greatly encourage Christians around the world as they seek to follow the Lord Jesus.

Brother Yun's testimony is one that reflects the faithfulness and goodness of God in his life. His is a story of how God took a young, half-starved boy from a poor village in Henan Province, China, and used him to shake the world. Instead of focusing on the many miracles or experiences of suffering he has gone through, he prefers to focus on the character and beauty of Jesus Christ. He wishes the whole world to know Jesus as he does, not as an historical, distant figure, but as an ever-present, love-filled, all-powerful Almighty God.

In researching this book I interviewed dozens of Christians in China who were eyewitnesses of, and completely verified, the events contained in the pages that follow. Interspersed throughout the book are short contributions from Deling (Yun's wife) and a few Chinese house church leaders. These insights will help the reader gain a different perspective – and a more complete picture – of some of the key incidents in Yun's life. Most of Deling's reflections were made while her husband was in prison for the sake of the gospel.

It has been said, "It is not great men who change the world, but weak men in the hands of a great God." Those who know Brother Yun can vouch that he is a humble servant of God who does not want any part of his life to bring glory to himself or man.

Brother Yun desires that his story would focus all attention and glory on the only true Heavenly Man – the Lord Jesus Christ.

Paul Hattaway

CHAPTER ONE

HUMBLE BEGINNINGS

My name is Liu Zhenying. My Christian friends call me Brother Yun.

One morning in autumn 1999, I awoke in the city of Bergen in western Norway. My heart was stirred and excitement bubbled up inside me. I had been speaking in churches throughout Scandinavia, testifying about the Chinese house churches and inviting Christians to join us as we evangelize all of China and the nations beyond. My hosts had asked me if I would like to visit the grave of Marie Monsen, a great Lutheran missionary to China who had been mightily used by God to revive the church in different parts of my nation from 1901 to 1932. Her ministry was especially effective in the southern part of Henan Province, where I come from.

Miss Monsen was small in stature, yet a giant in God's kingdom. The Chinese church was not only impacted by her words, but also deeply challenged by her sacrificial lifestyle. She was a fully committed, uncompromising follower of Jesus Christ, who showed us an example of how to suffer and endure for the Lord.

God used Marie Monsen in a powerful manner, so that many miracles, signs and wonders followed her ministry. She returned to Norway in 1932 to take care of her elderly

parents, and by then her work in China was complete. She
never returned to China, but her legacy of uncompromising
faith, unquenchable zeal and the necessity of changed hearts
fully committed to the cause of Christ lives on in the Chinese
church today.

Now I had the great privilege of visiting her grave in her
homeland. I wondered if any other Chinese Christian had
ever enjoyed the privilege I was about to enjoy. When she
came to our part of China there were few Christians and the
church was weak. Today there are millions of believers. On
their behalf I planned to offer thanks to God for her life.

Our car pulled up at the graveyard, situated on the side of
a hill in a narrow valley, with a river flowing through it. We
walked around for a few minutes, hoping to see her name on
one of the several hundred tombstones. Not being able to
locate Monsen's grave immediately, we strolled to the office
for help. The administrator was not familiar with her name,
so he looked in a book that lists the names of the dead who
are buried there. After flicking through the pages he told us
some news I found hard to believe, "Marie Monsen was
indeed buried here in 1962. But her grave was left untended
for many years, so today it is just an empty lot with no headstone."

In Chinese culture the memory of people who did great
things is cherished for many generations to come, so I never
imagined that such a thing could happen. The local believers explained that Marie Monsen was still held in high
regard and that they had honoured her memory in different
ways, such as by publishing her biography decades after she
died. But to me her unmarked grave was an insult that had
to be made right.

I was deeply grieved. With a heavy heart I sternly told the
Norwegian Christians who were with me, "You must

honour this woman of God! I will give you two years to con-
struct a new grave and headstone in memory of Marie
Monsen. If you fail to do this, I will personally arrange for
some Christian brothers to walk all the way from China to
Norway to build one! Many brothers in China are skilled
stonecutters because of their years in prison labour camps
for the sake of the gospel. If you don't care enough, they will
be more than willing to do it!"

*   *   *

I was born in 1958, during the Chinese leap year – the fourth
of five children in our family. I came into the world in an old
traditional farming village named Liu Lao Zhuang in
Nanyang County, in the southern part of China's Henan
Province.

Henan contains almost 100 million souls – China's most
populated province. Despite this fact, there seemed to be
many open spaces where I grew up – lots of hills to scale and
trees to climb. Although life was difficult, I also remember
times of fun when I was a little boy.

All of the 600 people in our village were farmers, and still
are to this day. Not too much has changed. We mostly culti-
vated potatoes, corn, and wheat. We also grew cabbages and
other kinds of root vegetables.

Our home was a simple structure of compacted dried
mud. The roof was made of straw. The rain always managed
to find the holes in our roof, while in winter the icy winds
never failed to blow through the gaps in our walls. When the
temperatures dropped to below freezing we burned leftover
corn husks to keep warm. We couldn't afford coal.

Often in the summer it was so hot and humid that we
couldn't bear to sleep inside our poorly ventilated home.

Beds were dragged outside and our whole family joined the rest of the village sleeping in the cooler air.

"Henan" means "south of the river". The mighty Yellow River dissects the northern part of the province. Its frequent floods have brought centuries of pain to people living along its banks. We knew this as we grew up, but to us northern Henan was a million miles away.

Our village nestled in the hills of the southern part of the province, safe from devastating floods and outside influences. We were only concerned with the next harvest. Our lives completely revolved around the cycle of ploughing, planting, watering and harvesting. My dad always said it was a struggle just to get enough food to eat. All hands were required in the field, so from a young age I was called into action helping with my brothers and sisters. Consequently, I didn't have the opportunity to attend much school.

In other parts of China, Henan natives have a reputation for being as stubborn as donkeys. Perhaps it was that stubbornness that prevented the Henanese from receiving Christianity when Protestant missionaries first brought it to our province in 1884. Many missionaries laboured in Henan without much visible success. By 1922, after almost forty years of missionary effort, there were a mere 12,400 Protestant believers in the entire province.

Those who accepted the religion of the "foreign devils" were ridiculed and ostracized by their communities. Often the opposition spilled over into more violent expressions. Christians were beaten. Some were even killed for their faith. The missionaries, too, faced great persecution. Missionaries were considered by many people to be tools of imperialism and colonialism, sent by their nations to gain control over the hearts and minds of the Chinese people while their governments raped the land of its natural resources.

The outrage against foreigners reached its peak in 1900, when a secret society called "The Boxers" instigated a nationwide attack against foreigners. Most were able to flee the carnage, but many missionaries were located in remote rural areas of inland China, far from the safety of the large coastal cities. The Boxers brutally massacred more than 150 missionaries and thousands of their Chinese converts.

Those brave souls who had come to serve our nation sacrificially and bring the love of the Lord Jesus Christ to us were slaughtered. They had come to share Christ and to improve our lives by building hospitals, orphanages and schools. We repaid them with death.

In the aftermath, some people thought the events of 1900 would be enough to scare missionaries off ever coming back to China.

They were wrong.

On 1 September 1901, a large ship docked in Shanghai Port. A young single lady from Norway walked off the gangplank onto Chinese soil for the first time. Marie Monsen was one of a new wave of missionaries who, inspired by the martyrdoms of the previous year, had dedicated themselves to full-time missionary service in China.

Monsen stayed in China for more than thirty years. For a time she lived in my county, Nanyang, where she encouraged and trained a small group of Chinese believers that had sprung up.

Marie Monsen was different from most other missionaries. She didn't seem to be too concerned with making a good impression on the Chinese church leaders. She often told them, "You are all hypocrites! You confess Jesus Christ with your lips while your hearts are not fully committed to him! Repent before it is too late to escape God's judgment!" She brought fire from the altar of God.

Monsen told the Christians it wasn't enough to study the lives of born-again believers, but that they must themselves be radically born again in order to enter the kingdom of heaven. With such teaching, she took the emphasis off head knowledge and showed each individual that they were personally responsible before God for their own inner spiritual life. Hearts were convicted of sin and fires of revival swept throughout the villages of central China wherever she went.

In the 1940s another Western missionary preached the gospel to my mother, who was twenty years old at the time. Although she didn't fully understand, she was deeply impressed by what she heard. She especially liked to sing the songs and hear the Bible stories shared by the small teams of evangelists who travelled around the countryside. Soon she started attending church and committed her life to Jesus Christ.

China became a Communist nation in 1949. Within a few years all missionaries were expelled, church buildings were closed, and thousands of Chinese pastors were imprisoned. Many lost their lives. My mother saw the missionaries leave Nanyang in the early 1950s. She never forgot the tears in their eyes as they headed for the coast under armed guard, their ministries for the Lord having abruptly come to an end.

In just one city in China, Wenzhou in Zhejiang Province, 49 pastors were sent to prison labour camps near the Russian border in 1950. Many were given sentences of up to twenty years for their "crimes" of preaching the gospel. Of those 49 pastors, just one returned home. 48 died in prison.

In my home area of Nanyang, believers were crucified on the walls of their churches for not denying Christ. Others were chained to vehicles and horses and dragged to their death.

One pastor was bound and attached to a long rope. The authorities, enraged that the man of God would not deny his faith, used a makeshift crane to lift him high into the air. Before hundreds of witnesses, who had come to accuse him falsely of being a "counter revolutionary", the pastor was asked one last time by his persecutors if he would recant. He shouted back, "No! I will never deny the Lord who saved me!" The rope was released and the pastor crashed to the ground below.

Upon inspection, the tormentors discovered the pastor was not fully dead, so they raised him up into the air for a second time, dropping the rope to finish him off for good. In this life the pastor was dead, but he lives on in heaven with the reward of one who was faithful to the end.

Life was not just difficult for Christians. Mao launched an experiment called the "Great Leap Forward", which led to a massive famine all over China. It was actually a great leap backwards for the nation. In my Henan Province it was estimated that 8 million people starved to death.

During these difficult times the small fledgling church in my home town of Nanyang was scattered. They were like sheep without shepherds. My mother also left the church. Over the following decades, having been completely starved of all Christian fellowship and without God's Word, she forgot most of what she had learned as a young woman. Her relationship with the Lord grew cold.

*   *   *

On 1 September 2001 – exactly one hundred years to the day since Marie Monsen first arrived in China to start her missionary career – more than three hundred Norwegian Christians gathered in the Bergen graveyard for a special prayer and dedication ceremony. A beautiful new headstone was unveiled in memory of Monsen, paid for by contributions from various churches, and individual Christians.

Monsen's picture and her Chinese name appeared on the headstone, which also stated:

MARIE MONSEN 1878 – 1962
MISSIONARY IN CHINA 1901 – 1932

When I told the believers in China that Marie Monsen's gravestone had been rebuilt, they were thankful and relieved.

We must always be careful to remember the sacrifice of those God has used to establish his kingdom. They are worthy of our honour and respect.

CHAPTER TWO

A HUNGER FULFILLED

"Listen to me, you islands; hear this, you distant nations: Before I was born the Lord called me; from my birth he has made mention of my name." Isaiah 49:1.

The Lord called me to follow him at the age of 16. The year was 1974, and the Cultural Revolution was still raging throughout China.

At that time my father was sick. He suffered from a severe type of asthma, which developed into lung cancer. The cancer then spread to his stomach. The doctor told him he could not be cured and would soon die. My mother was told, "There's no hope for your husband. Go home and prepare for his death."

Every night my dad lay in bed and could hardly breathe. Being a very superstitious man, he asked some neighbours to fetch a local Daoist priest to come and cast the demons out of him, as he believed his sickness was the result of upsetting the demons.

My dad's sickness sapped all our money, possessions, and energy. Because of our poverty I wasn't able to attend school until the age of nine, but then I had to drop out at sixteen because of my father's cancer. My brothers, sisters and I were forced to beg food from our neighbours and friends, just to survive.

My father had been a captain in the Nationalist army. Because he had fought against the Communists, he was hated by the other villagers and persecuted during the Cultural Revolution. He had killed many men in battle, and had nearly died himself. He had twelve scars from bullet wounds in one of his legs.

When I was born, my father named me "Zhenying", which means "Hero of the Garrison".

Dad had a fearsome reputation. Neighbours avoided him because of his violent temper. When the Red Guards came to accuse him during the Cultural Revolution he endured many severe interrogations and beatings. Drawing on his courage, he refused to confess any "crimes" and would not answer when they asked him how many men he had killed. He stubbornly preferred to be beaten or even killed than to tell them what they wanted to hear.

There were two sides to my father. Most people only knew that he was extremely tough and had a bad temper. This was true. He taught his children two main things: first, we must be cruel and hard towards others, and second, we must always work hard.

But I also remember his gentler side. He always tried to protect his wife and children from outside harm. Overall, I had a very good relationship with my dad.

We hoped my father would get better, but his condition worsened. My mother was under great pressure, facing the daunting prospect of raising five children alone. She didn't know what would happen to us if father died. Things were so hopeless that she even contemplated suicide.

One night my mother was lying on her bed, barely awake.

Suddenly she heard a very clear and tender, compassionate voice say, "Jesus loves you." She knelt down on the floor and tearfully repented of her sins and re-dedicated herself to the Lord Jesus Christ. Like the Prodigal Son, my mother came home to God.

She immediately called our family to come and pray to Jesus. She told us, "Jesus is the only hope for Father." All of us committed our lives to God when we heard what had happened. We then laid our hands on my father and for the rest of the night we cried out a simple prayer, "Jesus, heal Father! Jesus, heal Father!"

The very next morning my father found he was much better! For the first time in months he had an appetite for food. Within a week he had recovered completely and had no trace of cancer! It was a great miracle from God.

We experienced revival in our family and our lives took a drastic change. It was such a powerful time that today, almost 30 years after Jesus healed my father, all five of his children still follow God.

My parents were so grateful to God for what he had done that they immediately wanted to share the good news with everyone else in our village. In those days it was illegal to hold any meetings or public gatherings, but my parents came up with a plan. They sent us children to invite relatives and friends to our home.

People came to our home without knowing the reason why they'd been summoned. Many presumed Father must have died and so they came dressed for the funeral! They were amazed to see my dad greet them at the door, apparently in good health! When all our relatives and friends had arrived, my parents asked them all to come inside the house. They locked the door and covered the windows, and explained how Father had been completely healed by praying to Jesus. All our relatives and friends knelt down on the floor and gladly accepted Jesus as Lord and Master.

These were exciting times. Not only did I receive Jesus as my personal Saviour, but I also became a person who really wanted to serve the Lord with all my heart.

My mother had never learned to read or write, but she became the first preacher in our village. She led a small church in our house. Although my mum couldn't remember much of God's Word, she always exhorted us to focus on Jesus. As we cried out to him, Jesus helped us in his great mercy. As I look back on those early days, I'm amazed at how God used my mother despite her illiteracy and ignorance. The direction of her heart was totally surrendered to Jesus. Some of today's great house church leaders in China first met the Lord through my mother's ministry.

At first, I didn't really know who Jesus was, but I'd seen him heal my father and liberate our family. I confidently committed myself to the God who had healed my father and saved us. During that time I frequently asked my mother who Jesus truly was. She told me, "Jesus is the Son of God who died on the cross for us, taking all our sins and sicknesses. He recorded all his teachings in the Bible."

I asked if there were any words of Jesus left that I could read for myself. She replied, "No. All his words are gone. There is nothing left of his teaching." This was during the Cultural Revolution when Bibles could not be found.

From that day on I earnestly wanted to have a copy of my own Bible. I asked my mother and fellow Christians what a Bible looked like, but no one knew. One person had seen some hand copied Scripture portions and song sheets, but never a whole Bible. Only a few old believers could recall seeing Bibles many years before. The Word of God was scarce in the land.

I was so hungry for a Bible. Seeing my desperation, my mother remembered an old man who lived in another village. This man had been a pastor before the Cultural Revolution.

Together we started out on the long walk to his home. When we found him we told him our desire, "We long to see a Bible. Do you have one?"

He immediately looked fearful. This man had already spent nearly 20 years in prison for his faith. He looked at me and saw that I was so young and poor, with tattered clothes and bare feet. He felt compassion, but still didn't want to show me his Bible.

I don't blame him because in those days there were very few Bibles in the whole of China. Nobody was allowed to read any book other than Mao's little Red Book. If caught with a Bible, it would be burned and the owner's whole family would be severely beaten in the middle of the village.

The old pastor simply told me, "The Bible is a heavenly book. If you want one, you'll need to pray to the God of heaven. Only he can provide you a heavenly book. God is faithful. He always answers those who seek him with all of their heart."

I fully trusted the pastor's words.

When I returned home I brought a stone into my room and knelt down on it every evening for prayer. I had just one simple prayer: "Lord, please give me a Bible. Amen." At that time I didn't know how to pray, but I continued for more than one month.

Nothing happened. A Bible didn't appear.

I went back to that pastor's house again. This time I went alone. I told him, "I've prayed to God according to your instructions, but I still haven't received the Bible I want so much. Please, please show me your Bible. Just a glance and I will be satisfied! I don't need to touch it. You hold it and I will be content just to look at it. If I could copy down some of the words I will return home happy."

The pastor saw the anxiety of my heart. He spoke to me again, "If you're serious, then you should not only kneel down and pray to the Lord, you should also fast and weep. The more you weep the sooner you'll get a Bible."

I went home, and every morning and afternoon I ate and drank nothing. Every evening I ate just one small bowl of steamed rice. I cried like a hungry child to his heavenly Father, wanting to be filled with his Word. For the next one hundred days I prayed for a Bible, until I could bear it no more. My parents were sure I was losing my mind.

Looking back years later, I would say this whole experience was the most difficult thing I've ever endured.

Then, suddenly one morning at 4 a.m., after months of begging God to answer my prayers, I received a vision from the Lord while kneeling beside my bed.

In the vision I was walking up a steep hill, trying to push a heavy cart in front of me. I was heading towards a village where I intended to beg for food for my family. I was struggling greatly, because in my vision I was hungry and weakened by constant fasting. The old cart was about to roll back and fall on me.

I then saw three men walking down the hill in the opposite direction. A kind old man, who had a very long beard, was pulling a large cart full of fresh bread. Two other men were walking on each side of the cart. When the old man saw me he felt great pity and showed me compassion. He asked, "Are you hungry?" I replied, "Yes. I have nothing to eat. I'm on my way to get food for my family."

I wept because my family was extremely poor. Because of my father's sickness we'd sold everything valuable to buy medicine. We had little to eat, and for years we'd been forced to beg for food from friends and neighbours. When the old man asked me if I was hungry I couldn't help but cry. I'd never felt such genuine love and compassion from anyone before.

In the vision the old man took a red bag of bread from his trolley and asked his two servants to give it to me. He said, "You must eat it immediately."

I opened the wrapping and saw there was a bun of fresh bread inside. When I put the bun in my mouth, it instantly turned into a Bible! Immediately, in my vision, I knelt down with my Bible and cried out to the Lord in thanksgiving, "Lord, your name is worthy to be praised! You didn't despise my prayer. You allowed me to receive this Bible. I want to serve you for the rest of my life."

I woke up and started searching the house for the Bible. The rest of my family was asleep. The vision had been so real to me that when I realized it had only been a dream I was deeply anguished and I wept loudly. My parents rushed to my room to see what had happened. They thought I had gone crazy because of all my fasting and praying. I told them about my vision, but, the more I shared, the crazier they thought I was! Mother said, "The day hasn't dawned yet and no one has come to our house. The door is firmly locked."

My father held me tightly. With tears in his eyes he cried to God, "Dear Lord, have mercy on my son. Please don't let him lose his mind. I'm willing to be sick again if it will prevent my son from losing his mind. Please give my son a Bible!"

My mother, father and I knelt down and wept together, arm in arm.

Suddenly I heard a faint knock at the door. A very gentle voice called my name. I rushed over and asked through the locked door, "Are you bringing the bread to me?" The gentle voice replied, "Yes, we have a bread feast to give you."

I immediately recognized the voice as the same one I had heard in the vision.

I quickly opened the door and there standing before me were the same two servants I had seen in the vision. One man held a red bag in his hand. My heart raced as I opened the bag and held in my hands my very own Bible!

The two men quickly departed into the still darkness.

I clutched my new Bible to my heart and fell down on my knees outside the door. I thanked God again and again! I promised Jesus that from that moment on I would devour his Word like a hungry child.

Later I found out the names of those two men. One was Brother Wang and the other Brother Sung. They came from a village far away. They told me about an evangelist whom I'd never met. He had suffered terribly for the Lord during the Cultural Revolution, and had nearly died while being tortured.

About three months before I received my Bible this evangelist had received a vision from the Lord. God showed him a young man to whom he was to give his hidden Bible. In the vision he saw our house and the location of our village.

Like many Christians at the time, the old man had placed his Bible inside a can and buried it deep in the ground, hoping a day would come when he could dig it up and read it again. Despite this vision, it took the evangelist a few months before he decided to obey what the Lord had told him to do. He asked two other Christian men to deliver it to me. They then walked throughout the night to reach my home.

From that moment on I prayed to Jesus with faith-filled prayer. I fully trusted that the words in the Bible were God's words to me. I always held the Bible. Even when I slept I laid it on my chest. I devoured its teachings like a hungry child.

This was the first gift I ever received from God in prayer.

*   *   *

DELING: Around the same time God was preparing my husband for a life of gospel service, he was also calling me to himself and preparing me to be Yun's partner. I was born in 1962 in Nanyang County, Henan Province, in a village called Yenzhang. Yun's village was located a few miles away.

My family was extremely poor. With seven children, we hardly had any clothes to wear or food to eat.

When I think back to my childhood I remember times of happiness mixed with times of struggle for survival. Our field was more than a mile from our house, so we had to walk there and back every day, carrying heavy tools and farm implements. We also had to lead our animals there and back each day.

We children were given the chore of carrying the harvested cotton back to our house in two heavy baskets, suspended by a pole. We slipped and slid in the mud. Sometimes it took more than an hour just to make it home with our loads. It was heavy and back-breaking work.

My life was dominated by my struggle with haemophilia. If I cut myself, the blood would not stop flowing for a long time. I seemed to be forever wrapping my feet and hands in old rags to stem the bleeding.

Because of the incredible pressure she was under, my mother became mentally ill. During the daytime she seemed quite normal but at night-time we often heard her talking to herself, laughing and crying. She would sometimes talk to the wall as if it was another person.

After my mother believed the gospel, the peace of God gradually conquered her and restored her sanity. This was a powerful witness to our family and neighbours.

I first came to Jesus because of my terrible physical affliction. My neighbour, a Christian lady, gave me a simple promise: "If you believe in Jesus, he will heal you."

At the age of 18 I committed my life to Jesus Christ.

The very first night as a believer I was taken to my first house church meeting. The Public Security Bureau came and we all had to escape on foot through the darkness. This was my very first introduction to what it would be like following the Lord!

A few days after I was baptized I received a clear vision from the Lord while I was sleeping. A person led me to a lake that contained perfect crystal-clear water. I was told to wash my hands and feet because I had been totally wounded by my sickness. In the vision I dipped my scarred hands and feet into the water and I saw how my skin was completely healed and renewed. When I awoke the next morning I discovered my skin was like a newborn baby's skin! What had happened to me in the vision actually happened while I was sleeping!

I have never suffered haemophilia again to this day.

Because of this great miracle the Lord was very real to me. Even though our lives were difficult and we faced persecution every day, I committed myself to follow Jesus regardless of the cost.

Two other young women came to the Lord at the same time as me. We attended meetings together. These were in different parts of the district so we often had to walk more than an hour to get there. After the meetings I often had to walk home by myself. This was quite dangerous because it was so dark and there were evil men and wild dogs out late at night.

God worked a great miracle to protect and help me in those early days. Many nights as I walked home I could see a light about ten metres ahead of me on the path, as if someone was carrying a lamp, showing me the way I needed to take. In the pitch dark I often lost my way, but then I'd see the light, like a small star, showing me the way to get back on the right path. The light wasn't constant; it just appeared whenever I was heading in the wrong direction.

Because of many experiences like this, my faith grew quickly.

CHAPTER THREE

"GO TO THE WEST AND SOUTH"

Every day from morning to late evening I read the Word of God. When I had to work in the fields I wrapped my Bible inside my clothing and took every opportunity to sit down and read. At night-time I took my Bible with me to bed and laid it on my chest.

In the beginning, reading my Bible wasn't easy because I had only received three years of education. Furthermore, my Bible was in the traditional Chinese script, while I had learned to read simplified characters. I found a dictionary and painstakingly looked up one character at a time as I advanced through the Bible.

Finally I finished reading through the whole Bible, so I started to memorize one chapter per day. After 28 days I had memorized the whole Gospel of Matthew. I quickly read through the three other Gospels before proceeding to the Book of Acts and started to memorize it.

One morning at around 9 a.m. I was reading the first chapter of Acts. I started meditating on the verse in Acts 1:8, *"But you will receive power when the Holy Spirit comes on you; and you will be my witnesses in Jerusalem, and in all Judea and Samaria, and to the ends of the earth."*

I wasn't sure who the Holy Spirit was. I ran and asked my

mother. She couldn't explain. She simply said, "I've already told you all I can remember. Why don't you pray and ask God for the Holy Spirit just like you prayed for your Bible?" My mother was illiterate and so she had a shallow knowledge of the Bible. She had learned only to recite a few verses she'd heard from other believers.

This was a defining moment in my life. I had a desire for God's presence and power, and now I realized how important it is to know God's written Word.

I prayed to the Lord, "I need the power of the Holy Spirit. I am willing to be your witness." After the prayer God's spirit of joy fell upon me. A deep revelation of God's love and presence flooded my being. I'd never enjoyed singing before but many new songs of worship flowed from my lips. They were words I had never learned before. Later I wrote them down. These songs are still sung in the Chinese house churches to this day.

I began to wait on the Lord for his guidance, and a wonderful thing happened. One night around 10 p.m. – before my parents had gone to bed – I had just completed a time of prayer and had memorized Acts chapter 12. As I lay down on my bed I suddenly felt someone tap my shoulder and heard a voice tell me, "Yun, I am going to send you to the west and south to be my witness."

Thinking it was my mother speaking, I jumped out of my bed and went to my parents' room. I asked her, "Did you call my name? Who tapped me on my shoulder?"

My mother said, "Neither of us called for you. Go back to sleep." I prayed again and climbed into bed.

Thirty minutes after again lying down I heard a clear voice that urged me, "Yun, you shall go to the west and to the south to proclaim the gospel. You shall be my witness and will testify on behalf of my name."

Immediately I got up and told my mother what had happened. She told me to go back to sleep and asked me not to be so excited. She was concerned I was losing my mind again!

I knelt down and prayed to the Lord, "Jesus, if you're speaking to me, then I am listening. If you're calling me to preach your good news, then I'm willing to obey your call on my life."

Around four o'clock the next morning I received a dream from the Lord. I saw the same loving old man who had given me the bread in my previous vision. As he walked towards me he looked into my eyes and said, "You should face the west and south to proclaim the gospel and be the Lord's witness."

In my dream I also saw a large meeting with a multitude of people. The old man radiated great authority before the crowd. He told me, "You shall be my witness to them." I felt inadequate. In the meeting a demon-possessed woman came toward me. The old man said, "You should lay your hands on her and cast the demon out in Jesus' name." In the dream I did so. The woman struggled as if she was in the throes of death. Then she was completely set free from the demonic forces that controlled her. All the people were amazed because they had never seen such things before.

Suddenly in my dream a young man came out of the crowd and asked, "Are you brother Yun? Our brothers and sisters have been fasting and praying for you for three days. We hope you will come to our midst and preach the gospel to us. We desperately need you to come to our village."

The young man told me his name, age, and home village. I was moved and told him, "I shall go to your place tomorrow."

At daybreak I hurriedly called my parents and told them

I was going to preach the gospel because Jesus Christ had commanded me to do so. My mother asked me where I intended to go. I told her, "Last night the Lord spoke to me three times. He told me, 'Go west and south to preach the gospel.' I will be obedient to the heavenly call."

I knew that the dream I'd received was from God, so I was confident that things would happen just as they had been shown to me. I told my mother, "After I leave today there will be a young man come from the south. He is 24 years old. He will be wearing a white shirt and grey trousers with patches over both knees. Christians in his village have been praying and fasting for three days. They need me to come and witness for the Lord. This morning I met this man in my dream. I promised I would go with him to the west and south."

My mother didn't understand what I was talking about, so I told her plainly, "A young man named Yu Jing Chai will come to our house today. Please stay at home and welcome him. Don't let him leave until I return home."

That morning I left my home village and started walking toward the west. When I crossed a bridge I met an old Christian man whose name was Yang. He asked me where I was going. I replied, "This morning the Lord spoke to me three times. He wants me to preach the gospel to the west and south."

Brother Yang's heart was deeply moved. He said, "Right now I was on my way to see you. I was given the job to come and take you to the west, to Gao Village, so that you can share the gospel. The brothers and sisters there have heard how you prayed and received a heavenly book. We want you to come and share its words with us. We've been fasting and praying for you for three days. They sent me to come and take you to our midst."

When we arrived the whole village was busily working in the fields, as it was harvest time. But when Brother Yang told them, "This is the man you've been praying for," they all put down their tools and ran to us.

We went into a house. I sat down on the floor and everyone crowded around me. I was quite nervous because I had never spoken to a group of people before. Thirty or forty people were all staring at me, searching me with their eyes, and longing to hear God's Word. They were so hungry for the truth. There were already a few Christians in Gao Village but the majority of people had not yet believed.

I sat there with my eyes tightly shut and held the Bible up above my head. I declared, "This is the Bible. The angel of the Lord sent it to me in answer to my prayers. If you want to get a Bible, you will have to pray and seek God as I did."

They all looked at me in astonishment, with their mouths wide open. The way God had provided my Bible caused great wonder among them. They wanted me to teach them. At that time I didn't know what it meant to preach. I could only recite the Bible from the chapters I had memorized, so I recited the entire Gospel of Matthew out loud, from chapter 1 to 28.

I didn't know if the people understood what I was saying or not. In order not to lose my place or forget anything, I recited what I had memorized quickly, like a flowing river.

When I had finished I was filled with the Holy Spirit and sang some Scripture songs that I'd never learned before.

When I opened my eyes I saw how God's Word had captivated everybody. The Holy Spirit was convicting them of their sins. They all knelt down and repented with tears flowing down their cheeks. That night, even though I was just 16 years old, I learned that God's Word is powerful. When we share it with a burning heart, many people are touched. At that first meeting, thanks to the power of God, dozens of people had given their hearts to Jesus.

They pleaded with me to stay and continue to read the Bible. I told them, "God told me I must also go to the south to be his witness." This didn't please them and they wouldn't let me go! Therefore I stayed and recited the first twelve chapters of the Book of Acts to them. I promised that after I'd memorized more of the Bible I would return to their village and recite to them what I had learned.

As I got ready to leave Gao Village a young woman came up and asked me, "You said you are heading south. Where exactly are you going?"

I told her, "There's a man in the south named Yu Jing Chai. I promised him this morning I would go with him to his village." This woman was surprised and asked me if I knew him.

I replied, "Yes, I know him."

She asked, "Where did you meet him?"

I explained, "I met him in a dream that the Lord gave me this morning."

She started to weep in front of me and said, "Yu Jing Chai is my brother!"

This sister had been the first believer in her family. She had then led her mother and brother to the Lord. Although they now lived in separate places, the three of them had been fasting and praying for me for three days. The Lord had put it all together as only he can. The Holy Spirit was working in such a wonderful way.

The people of Gao Village lovingly said goodbye to me with many tears in their eyes.

As I left the village to go home, something amazing happened. Gao Village is about six kilometres from my village. Most of the way is along narrow trails, so it can take up to

two hours to walk. Because I knew Yu Jing Chai was probably waiting for me in my house, I decided to run home so
that he wouldn't have to wait long for me.

As I ran I recited Bible verses out loud, and didn't pay
much attention to where I was running. Suddenly, even
though I didn't feel anything or notice anything happen, I
found myself entering my home village without any time
passing! What should have taken a few hours took just a few
moments.

This experience is difficult to explain, but it was unforgettable. I believe God performed a miracle like that when he
translated Philip in Acts 8:39–40, "... *the Spirit of the Lord suddenly took Philip away ... Philip ... appeared at Azotus and travelled about, preaching the gospel in all the towns.*"

When I got home my mother was filled with joy. She didn't
even call me by my name, but called me Samuel. She cried,
"Samuel, Samuel, the young man you told me about this
morning, Yu Jing Chai, came to visit. He was dressed just like
you told me." I asked her where he was but she told me he had
already left. I exclaimed, "Oh Mother, I asked you to make
sure he wouldn't leave! I promised him in my dream that I
would go and preach the gospel in his village."

My mother told me, "Don't worry! Be patient and let me
finish speaking. When this dear boy visited this afternoon I
knew he was the young man you told me about this
morning. His name really was Yu Jing Chai. When I asked
him if his name was Brother Yu he was very surprised and
wanted to know how I knew his surname. I then asked, 'Are
you Yu Jing Chai?' He became frightened and begged to
know how I knew his full name. I asked, 'Have you come to
ask my son to go with you to the south to share the gospel?' "

Brother Yu was astonished and asked, "How do you
know?"

My mother explained, "Brothers and sisters have already fasted and prayed for three days that my son will come and preach the gospel to you. My son already promised he would go with you. But he went to the west this morning and will be home by sunset. Will you please sit down and have a drink of water?"

When Yu heard my mother's words, he was so happy he turned around and ran home. He was in such a rush that he even forgot to take his straw hat! He promised he'd return at sunset to get me.

At that moment, right as the sun was about to set, Yu Jing Chai entered our yard. He was covered in sweat from the long run. He looked exactly as I'd seen him in my dream the previous night. I took his hand and told him, "You are Brother Yu, and you and others have been praying for three days for me to come. I met you this morning in my dream. Jesus loves you. I will come with you."

We hugged each other and cried together. My mother no longer doubted my sanity. After she laid hands on us and blessed us we walked into the darkness toward his village to the south. When we arrived I again quoted all the Bible verses I had memorized to the people.

The fire of the gospel in our area started to burn that day. Not only did it burn to the west but also to the south. Later we encountered much persecution and suffering for the faith, but in those early days everything was sweet and wonderful.

God poured his Spirit out to many desperate souls. Like thirsty men in the desert, they gleefully drank in the water of God's Word. Even though I was just a teenager, the Lord enabled me to lead more than 2,000 people to Jesus in my first year as a Christian.

In those early days my understanding of "the west and

south" was limited to those areas near my home village. Gradually, by the Lord's grace, that territory has expanded over the years to include the whole of China and even to nations outside China.

*　　*　　*

When I first shared at Gao Village the Lord gave me Scripture songs to sing before the people. They wrote down the words so they could remember them.

One of the songs was taken from the Gospel of Matthew where Jesus tells us if someone strikes us on the right cheek, we should turn our other cheek to him as well. Another song taught how we are to rejoice greatly when we are persecuted for the sake of the gospel. Yet another song explained how we should never be like Judas and deny our Master.

After so many people came to Jesus at once, it caught the attention of the authorities. All the Christians in Gao Village were arrested and taken to the police station. The officers demanded to know, "Who brought the name of Jesus to you? How did you all come to believe in this superstition?"

The believers were filled with overwhelming joy. The only thing they would say was, "We won't be like Judas! We won't betray our Lord Jesus!"

The officers started to beat them and they rejoiced even more. They said, "Please, sir, hit us on the other side of the face as well!" The Christians were laughing and rejoicing.

The officers grew tired of beating them and finally said, "You Christians are all crazy!" After a final warning, they sent them all home.

CHAPTER FOUR

GOD BLESSES MY WHOLE FAMILY

I thank God that he saved my whole family.

My father went home to heaven a few years after being miraculously healed of cancer.

I was grieved and happy at the same time. Grieved because I'd lost my father at such an early age, yet happy that the Lord had saved him. God had used my father's illness to bring our whole family to the foot of the cross.

My mother was just like Anna the prophetess. She *"worshipped night and day, fasting and praying." Luke 2:37.*

I thank God, because he not only gave me wonderful parents, but a very virtuous wife. The Bible asks, *"A wife of noble character who can find? She is worth far more than rubies. Her husband has full confidence in her and lacks nothing of value. She brings him good, not harm, all the days of her life." Proverbs 31:10–12.*

By God's grace he found such a wife for me!

Deling chose to marry me because of her love and obedience to the Lord. Our mothers were the matchmakers. Deling's mother is a very sincere and honest woman who loves God.

The first time Deling and I met I told her, "God has chosen me to be his witness and to follow him through great hardships and the way of the cross. I don't have any money and am always being pursued by the authorities. Do you really want to marry me?"

She answered, "Don't worry, I will never let you down. I will join with you and together we'll serve the Lord."

We went to the marriage office together. After answering some questions we wrote our names on the registration form. The clerk asked Deling to leave and wait outside for me. I was then told to go to a separate room. The clerk had realized my name was on the Public Security Bureau's "Wanted" list. Several officers came and arrested me.

This was the beginning of our life together, but Deling never gave up on me and has never regretted the life the Lord has called her to. She has chosen to walk the way of the cross.

Throughout our marriage Deling has been under tremendous pressure from her own family, from the community, from the authorities, and from every side, but she has remained completely faithful. She decided to stand with me, and has even experienced suffering in prison for the Lord.

I couldn't have asked for a better wife and partner!

A few days after our wedding my wife and I took a bus to attend an important leadership meeting. Outside the station the leader of the Religious Affairs Bureau from my home district recognized me. He grabbed me by the collar and said, "Be still. You cannot go anywhere. You will come with me to the Public Security Bureau (PSB) office." He also took hold of Deling's handbag.

Suddenly the Spirit of the Lord urged me to run! I shouted to Deling, "Run!" and I jumped out of the grip of the officer before he knew what was happening. He dropped the bag and chased me. As he ran he shouted, "Spy! Stop the spy!" Pandemonium broke out in the bus station. I jumped over a wall and slipped away from the crowd. It was a miracle. People said later the wall was far too high for a person to jump over.

In the commotion Deling also escaped.

The PSB retrieved my wife's handbag and found the address of the meeting place. They went there and arrested several of the leaders who had already gathered for the meeting.

*　　*　　*

DELING: Let me tell you how I first met Yun. After I became a Christian we visited a nearby village where once a year they held a large baptismal service. I was due to be baptized as a new believer.

It was November so it was already very cold. The baptism started around midnight for security reasons. We figured the PSB would never get out of their cosy beds in the middle of the cold night to arrest us, but we were wrong. Around one o'clock in the morning the PSB came and more than one hundred Christians were arrested.

Brother Yun was the one who had been baptizing the new believers, including me. The PSB ordered us to get into two lines so they could register our names and identify each one of us. Yun was also in line, but when they weren't paying attention he slipped away. It was as though God blinded the eyes of the officers and they just couldn't see him.

I had seen Yun a few times previously because meetings were held in his home on Sunday nights, but this experience at the baptismal service left a lasting impression on me. I thought he was a little bit crazy!

According to our custom, our marriage was completely arranged by our respective mothers. After my mother was healed and saved, she felt she had to find a preacher for me to marry. Yun was the only unmarried preacher in the whole area! My mother visited Yun's mother and together they arranged for us to get married.

This decision cost my mother dearly. When she announced to my family that I was to marry a preacher, my father and brothers were furious. To them, marrying a preacher was worse than marrying a beggar. They knew Yun had no money so he would not be able to give any gifts or money to my family as a bride price. They tried everything they could to stop it, but my mother held firm.

In those days this was how marriages were arranged in our part of China. These days more young people make their own decision about whom they will marry, although many marriages are still arranged.

Even after our engagement my family made sure I didn't have anything to do with Yun, so even though his village was just 1.5 kilometres from mine, we didn't have another chance to meet or talk before the wedding. Yun's father passed away before we were married, before I had a chance to meet him.

I was just a child, aged 18, when our wedding day arrived. My mother told me Yun was a very poor preacher but I should marry him, so I didn't question it. I had no idea what marriage meant. I had no way of knowing what the future would hold. I was just a young wide-eyed girl, very simple and innocent.

Before the wedding Yun and I went to the marriage registry office to apply for our marriage licence. After we'd completed the formalities I waited outside for a long time but Yun didn't come out. I decided I couldn't wait for him any longer and returned home.

Only later was I told that when Yun wrote his name in the registry office, the clerks noticed that he was wanted by the PSB for being an illegal preacher, so they arrested him on the spot! They already knew he had been preaching the gospel all over the province.

This was the start of our life together! Because of the delay when he was arrested, it took a little more than one year from the time we were engaged to the time Yun and I were married.

Our wedding day took place on a nice sunny day on 28 November 1981. Elder Fu presided over the ceremony, which was held in Yun's home. There were more than twenty tables set, and eight to ten guests were seated at each table, so about 200 people came. According to our culture, the wedding took place at the groom's home and neither of my parents were permitted to attend. My brothers and sisters, and all of Yun's family and relatives were present.

I remember there was preaching and then Elder Fu blessed us and suddenly we were married!

On our honeymoon we travelled to a meeting in another place. A sister was travelling with us also. When we were just outside Nanyang City the leader of the Religious Affairs Bureau in our home district recognized Yun. He grabbed my husband by the collar.

This sister and I rushed into the ladies' toilet and began to rip up Yun's Bible and some other Christian books, because we knew he would get into big trouble if they discovered his books had come from overseas.

That man started to shout out all the crimes Yun had supposedly committed, and in the excitement Yun brushed him off and ran away. I caught up with him later in the day.

Three or four months after we were married, we were together in a meeting about 30 kilometres from our home. Yun had been arrested but managed to escape from custody, so from that time he became a wanted man and was unable to return home. He therefore went on the run, preaching the gospel all over China.

Brother Xu introduced us to Zhang Rongliang for the first time and Yun teamed up with Zhang. Xu and Zhang led different house church networks but Brother Xu told my husband, "You go as a representative of our movement, make friends and be a blessing to Zhang's group."

The stress of having my husband on the run from the police, and the daily pressures of life were too much for me at that time. Around that time I conceived but after a few months I suffered a miscarriage. We lost a baby boy.

It was very stressful to go to the train station or bus station and see "wanted" posters on the walls with pictures of my husband, a fugitive of the law.

It has certainly been an interesting time being married to Yun! The womanly instincts in me have often craved for a more settled existence and a structured family life, but persecution has usually made this impossible.

CHAPTER FIVE

THE PATH OF PERSECUTION

The church in our area started to grow in grace and in number as God radically saved many people and sent them out as soul winners. Soon, however, opposition arose against us. Because so many people were believing in Christ the authorities became aroused. Before us, there had never been a Christian in our entire village.

My mother was identified as the leader of our church and was persecuted by the authorities. They placed a large dunce hat on her head and paraded her through the streets. She was forced to attend "re-education" classes, to "help her reform her incorrect views".

After I took over as leader of our church the pressure diverted off my mother and onto me. The authorities frequently came to question her about my whereabouts, but she usually just ignored them and pretended not to understand a word they said! After a while they left her alone, thinking she had lost her mind.

At the age of 17 I was arrested for the first time for preaching the gospel. In the years to follow we were often arrested and interrogated by the Public Security Bureau.

Instead of weakening us, the persecution just made us stronger. The more pressure there was, the more fire and love there was to spread the gospel. We were like the children of Israel while they were enslaved in Egypt, *"But the more they were oppressed, the more they multiplied and spread; so the Egyptians came to dread the Israelites." Exodus 1:12.*

In 1977 my father died. He had been weak and malnourished for some time, and finally, at the age of 66, he passed into the presence of God. The cancer the Lord had healed him from in 1974, however, never returned!

His funeral was very emotional for me. Even though I knew he was saved and in heaven, I missed him terribly. He was totally supportive of my ministry, and was proud of me, always encouraging me to serve the Lord with all my heart.

By the winter of 1978 we started to baptize people for the first time. The only safe way was to cut a hole through the ice on the river and baptize the new believers in the freezing water during the night while the police were sleeping. On many occasions we baptized hundreds of people in the rivers and streams of southern Henan. Sometimes the Lord did a miracle so that nobody felt the freezing water. Some even commented that the water had felt warm!

In the late 1970s multitudes of people were coming to the Lord daily. They were in great need of training and being established in the faith. Even though I was just in my early 20s, I was seen as a mature leader and one of the old Christians because I had come to the Lord in 1974!

The year of 1980 was a phenomenal year for the church in Henan. We remember it as the year when God constantly did outstanding miracles and divine healing, and the words of Jesus came supernaturally to many people. That wonderful year saw tremendous growth in the church. Later, many of the converts from 1980 became leaders of God's church throughout China. Henan Province became the Galilee of China, where many of Jesus' disciples come from.

In one meeting in the Nanyang area hundreds of people – Christians and unbelievers alike – saw a vision of a beautiful boat floating on a sea of clouds above the meeting place. Many sinners repented and gave their lives to Christ as a result of this sign and wonder.

In Fen Shuiling ("Watershed Hill") village, also in Nanyang, an unbeliever was dying after a protracted illness. His family had never heard the gospel. One evening Jesus appeared to that man and said, "My name is Jesus. I have come to save you."

Fen Shuiling village is situated in a remote mountainous area where preachers had not yet visited. It had no church or pastor, so when I first visited there I was surprised to find the gospel had spread to many villages and that dozens of families had put their faith in Christ. Jesus himself had preached the gospel to them! These new believers were now hungry to receive teaching from his Word.

In December 1980, a few weeks before Christmas, the devil used a new way to try to tempt and deceive us. Instead of torture and force, he started to use subtle suggestions and sly trickery. The government called a gathering of 120 religious representatives from all over our county. Muslim, Buddhist, Daoist and Christian leaders were all invited to attend.

At that time we didn't know anything about the Three-Self Patriotic Church that the government was forming. "Three-Self" stood for the movement's three guiding principles: Self-Propagating, Self-Supporting, and Self-Governing. Most Christians considered it a good thing, and rejoiced that a new day appeared to be dawning when believers could worship freely without interference or persecution. I went to the meeting completely open to the idea of joining the new church, and was even open to the possibility of being a leader for our area if that was what God wanted.

The meeting was organized through the joint co-operation of the local Religious Affairs Bureau (RAB) and the PSB. In that meeting they intended to select the committee members and the chairman for each religion. The chief of the RAB invited me to the meeting because I had a reputation for proclaiming the gospel and also because I owned a Bible.

More than 90% of the delegates wanted me to be the chairman of the Christian Association, but a few publicly slandered me, saying I was a false pastor because I had never attended a seminary.

One man named Ho was my main accuser, because he wanted the job of chairman for himself. He claimed to have believed in Jesus since he was in his mother's womb! It was well known, however, that Ho had denied the Lord during the Cultural Revolution and that he believed in an extremely liberal man-centred theology.

During the meeting Ho proudly announced that he was a better-qualified pastor than I because he had attended a seminary and had also studied in a missionary school before 1949. He assured the delegates that he was the right person to take care of the affairs of the church in our area.

Ho said the government should oppose my co-workers and me, because we went everywhere illegally preaching the gospel, healing the sick, and casting demons out of people. He said we should be stopped because we disturbed the social order and threatened peace and stability.

In the meeting this man started shouting at me in anger. I kept quiet for as long as I could, but then I felt the fire of God rise up inside me, like Jesus when he confronted the money-changers in the temple.

When Ho had finished his speech the PSB leader stood to his feet and urged him to continue to speak out against the "false Christians such as Yun". Gleefully rubbing his hands together, the leader said, "Please tell us everything you know about how Yun and his co-workers have disturbed the social order. Confess the dirtiness of your Christianity. Tell us how these false pastors are trying to destroy our nation."

Ho felt honoured and rose to his feet again. He proudly declared, "We true Christians have many complaints against false Christians like Yun."

I felt so angry that this man had spoken slander and disgraced God's church in front of unbelievers. I could contain myself no longer. I stood up on my chair and commanded him in the name of Jesus Christ to shut up!

The meeting was in an uproar. I was filled with the Holy Spirit and with mighty words from the Lord I proclaimed, "This meeting does not please God!" I pointed my finger at those people who claimed to believe in Jesus. "You shame-faced people will be judged by the Lord. The Bible says believers and unbelievers should not be yoked together. How can light and darkness dwell together? God's church has no communion with idols. The Lord and his church will judge you!"

Before I finished my words some Christian brothers and sisters came with tears in their eyes and pulled me down to my seat, pleading with me to stop before I got myself into deep trouble.

The PSB and the religious leaders were infuriated. They stood on their feet and banged the table with their fists. They threatened me, "Who do you think you are that you can disrupt this meeting? You will never be allowed to attend another meeting like this again!"

As soon as I heard those words I stood up again and declared, "I'm leaving now. Don't you ever invite me to a meeting like this again!"

This is how the Lord led me to give my life for the gospel

in China, and to work for the growth of the house churches. From that day on I clearly understood that the kingdom of God can never mix with politics. The ultimate, stated aim of Marxist teaching is the complete eradication of all religion. The pure bride of Christ can never be controlled by an atheistic government or led by men who hate God!

The true church is not an organization controlled by the rules of men but a holy collection of living stones with Jesus Christ as the cornerstone.

As I walked away from the meeting hall I felt as free as a bird. A new song came into my heart:

> *Since the day I left home I've carried my cross*
> > *Running to the ends of the earth for Jesus*
> *I've shared in the sufferings of my Lord*
> > *Proclaiming the gospel through eyes of tears*
> *Many times through the wind and rain*
> > *Tears have fallen down my cheeks*
> *Many things burden my heart*
> > *But Jesus' love keeps leading me*
> *His love and grace encourage me*
> > *Keeping me perfectly from day to day.*

I prayed, "Lord, where can I go? Lord, what will my future hold?"

The Lord immediately reminded me from Jeremiah 1:5–8 *"'Before I formed you in the womb I knew you, before you were born I set you apart; I appointed you as a prophet to the nations.' 'Ah, Sovereign Lord,' I said, 'I do not know how to speak; I am only a child.' But the Lord said to me, 'Do not say, "I am only a child." You must go to everyone I send you to and say whatever I command you. Do not be afraid of them, for I am with you and will rescue you,' declares the Lord."*

Over the ensuing weeks and months the Lord started to teach me to know the difference between his church and the Three-Self Church in China.

We knew the government had only created the Three-Self Patriotic Movement, and allowed "open, legal" churches in a bid to control Christians and to promote their own political agenda inside the churches.

We see the Three-Self believers as caged birds. Yes, they are able to sing to the Lord, but their environment is controlled and their wings are clipped. They are free to sing only within the restrictions imposed on them. In the house churches we enjoy the freedom to fly around wherever God leads us and to sing from the depths of our hearts. We have been released from the cage and we never intend to return!

It is a known fact that birds confined in cages have a hard time reproducing. This is also true of most believers confined within the Three-Self Church structure. House church Christians love to be free, to roam around the country wherever the Lord leads them, and to proclaim the gospel to all people. Reproduction has been occurring at a rapid rate!

We know there are many true followers of Jesus attending the government-sanctioned church in China today. I personally know many of them and have grown to appreciate them. It's not with the caged birds in the Three-Self churches that we have a problem, but with the corrupt leadership and the political power used to control people.

These leaders have severely restricted what Three-Self Church pastors and members are allowed to do. Ministry is not allowed without their permission. Evangelism is discouraged. All outreach to children is strictly banned. They even decree that certain parts of the Bible cannot be preached, such as the Second Coming of the Lord Jesus. They are not allowed to teach on divine healing, or the deliverance of demons. The entire Book of Revelation is banned!

In the house churches we simply couldn't adhere to such control and interference. We believe that Jesus is the head of his church, not the government. We broke away from the Three-Self Church and took a firm stand against all attempts to bring us under its control.

In response, the authorities in China launched a long-running "bird-hunting" season. They cannot stand those free birds who refuse to come under their control. Sometimes they manage to trap birds and cage them behind iron bars, but even within those cages the free birds have laid eggs and reproduced, winning many souls to the Lord in prison.

At this time I started my career of "fleeing evangelism". That is, we preached the gospel and then had to flee from one place to another being pursued by the police, just like Jesus had told his followers to do: *"When you are persecuted in one place, flee to another." Matthew 10:23.*

In July 1981 I narrowly escaped going to prison after I was arrested while leading a meeting of 120 house church believers. As the police car drove me to the station the tyre deflated and I was able to escape into the night. That night as I lay down on the wet ground I cried out to God, "Why are they treating us like this? Why can't you protect us?"

The Holy Spirit reminded me of two Scriptures:

"To this you were called, because Christ suffered for you, leaving you an example, that you should follow in his steps." 1 Peter 2:21.

"Although the Lord gives you the bread of adversity and the water of affliction, your teachers will be hidden no more; with your own eyes you will see them. Whether you turn to the right or to the left, your ears will hear a voice behind you, saying, 'This is the way; walk in it.'" Isaiah 30:20–21.

The Lord again reminded me of his call to preach the

gospel to the west and south. God's grace is sufficient for me, and his ways are higher than ours. We must submit ourselves to God and embrace whatever he allows to happen. Sometimes there are times of peace, other times struggle and persecution. But both are from the Lord, to mould us into the vessels he wants us to be.

At the time most of our co-workers couldn't go home because the police were searching for them. If they returned home they would be arrested immediately. Therefore they fled to different counties and towns to preach the gospel.

Even my own wife couldn't go home. The police went to our homes and confiscated all our belongings. Our ministry became nocturnal. We met in the night-time and slept during the daytime, so that our chances of being identified were minimized.

We all received much encouragement from the example left for us by the early church. We realized what was happening to us was not new. Multitudes of believers had suffered similar trials over the centuries and yet had patiently endured to the end.

The Word of the Lord comforted and strengthened our hearts. *"Remember those earlier days after you had received the light, when you stood your ground in a great contest in the face of suffering. Sometimes you were publicly exposed to insult and persecution; at other times you stood side by side with those who were so treated. You sympathized with those in prison and joyfully accepted the confiscation of your property, because you knew that you yourselves had better and lasting possessions." Hebrews 10:32–34.*

For many centuries the gospel struggled to gain a foothold in the stubborn land of China. Our soil was too rocky to accept the root of the gospel, but in his time God accomplished his purposes and established his church. Suffering, persecution and imprisonment made his gospel rapidly spread throughout China. If our lives had been more comfortable we'd probably have stayed in our home villages. But because we were always fleeing to new places the gospel spread to many areas that had never heard it.

The PSB posted a warrant for my arrest. I was charged with "Disturbing the Social Order". Every bus and train station noticeboard, and hundreds of telegraph poles and walls carried "wanted" notices and pictures of us. The PSB placed plain-clothed officers in all public places to search for us.

I was arrested on several different occasions at this time, but the Lord allowed me to elude capture and escape each time.

On one occasion we held a large meeting in a barn on a remote farm. The Holy Spirit moved so powerfully that the believers couldn't help but stay up to worship God all through the night. One night I needed to sleep. To get away from the barn, where the singing was very loud, I decided to lie down in the cornfield some distance away from the meeting place.

I was fast asleep when the PSB arrived and started to arrest the other leaders. They were herded into vehicles and taken to the police station for questioning. Somehow they knew I had been speaking and they were eager to find me. They were told I was asleep somewhere but nobody knew I was in the field.

The officers searched all the rooms and buildings but couldn't find me. Then they got the idea that if they turned off the loud diesel generator they might be able to locate me in the stillness of the night.

Soon they heard a noise coming from the cornfield. I was snoring loudly!

The officers' steel-capped boots woke me. However,

because I was sleeping and wasn't in the barn, the authorities couldn't prove I was involved in the meeting so they had to let me go.

These incidents were the first of many years of trials and suffering. The Lord started to teach us how to walk along the path of persecution.

*   *   *

DELING: In the early 1980s none of us had a Bible. Between all of our hundreds of church members we had just one New Testament. A little later we started to receive Bibles as a result of Operation Pearl, when foreign Christians boldly brought one million Bibles into China on a boat. The Bibles we received were all wet and we had to dry them in the sun and separate the pages, but we didn't care. These gifts were more precious than gold!

In those days, when Yun took a stand against the government-controlled church, I received a vision from the Lord. In this vision I saw myself walking towards a mirror on a wall. When I looked into the mirror I saw that I had two Bibles stacked on top of my head.

In the vision I discovered that I was able to fly like a bird. I was so free! I landed on a rock, with the Bibles still sitting on my head. As I stood there on the rock a large number of evil men and women hissed at me and threw dirt at me. They wanted to devour me, but I could safely fly away in the Spirit at any time I needed to.

The Lord showed me that this was the kind of life I would experience with my husband. On one hand we would be free in the Spirit, yet on the other hand we would have many enemies who wanted to destroy and persecute us. We would be able to fly in the Spirit but any time we landed we would experience this kind of life.

It was a clear revelation about my life to come. I didn't understand this vision at the time, but as the years have unfolded I've seen that it has happened exactly as the Lord showed me.

CHAPTER SIX

"THE GOD OF PETER IS YOUR GOD"

In 1983 a crime wave exploded across China, with rampant murders, kidnappings, extortion and prostitution. The government saw they were losing control and launched an anti-crime campaign. Hundreds of criminals were publicly executed.

Unfortunately, the house churches were also considered illegal by the government because of our refusal to register with the Three-Self Patriotic Movement (TSPM), so we became targets in the campaign. Unregistered Christians were labelled "spiritual pollutants" by the authorities and the TSPM. Hundreds of house church leaders were rounded up and sent to prison labour camps. In Henan many believers were executed for their faith in Jesus.

During this wave of terrible persecution, Brother Xu shared with me some important thoughts. He said, "The future of our Chinese house churches needs careful consideration. We should be faithful in small things while believing for big things from God. We have to learn whatever the Lord wants to teach us from his Word, from life, from our experiences, and from our sufferings. Therefore we should initiate a prayer effort and look to God's mercy and revelation. Let's set up training centres and take the gospel to all parts of our nation. We need to be better prepared to equip the troops in order to establish God's Church."

Brother Xu wrote a booklet called *Building up the Chinese House Church*. In this booklet he outlined seven main biblical principles that we should focus our activities on. I thanked God that we now had a more definite plan for the house churches to march forward. Until that point we didn't really have a nationwide plan to win all of China. From 1983 until today the gospel has spread and thousands of workers have been sent to strategic unreached areas.

Being obedient to the guidance of the Holy Spirit, we turned our focus on Shaanxi Province, which had received little gospel witness. The few rural churches there were in great need of solid teaching and encouragement. Shaanxi is the home of Xian, China's ancient capital city. The province had a reputation for being more resistant to the gospel than most other Chinese provinces.

When I joined a prayer meeting in Henan, the leaders told me they had received a letter from the Shaanxi church, begging us to send workers into their midst to train them how to plant new churches. They told me, "For the last few days we've been fasting and praying about their request. Brother Yun, we believe God wants you to go to the west, to Shaanxi. We want you to take two of our co-workers immediately to Shaanxi. Although these two sisters have no preaching experience, you can teach them on the way. They are warriors of the gospel, wholeheartedly dedicated to saving souls."

Before we left for Shaanxi that evening we asked God to prepare the hearts of the people to receive his Word. While praying, I suddenly saw a terrible vision that shook my soul. The others told me I startled them when I shouted out, "Hallelujah! Jesus' blood has overcome you!"

Everyone stopped praying and asked me what the matter

was. With sweat on my brow I told them, "I saw a terrible evil vision. A black, heinous creature came after me. It had a horrible twisted face. It pressed me down on the ground and sat on my stomach so I couldn't get up. With one of its hands it grabbed my throat and started choking me. With its other hand it grabbed some steel pliers and tried to shut my mouth with them. I could hardly breathe. Then I saw a great strong angel fly toward me. With all my strength I poked my fingers into the eyes of the evil creature. It fell to the ground, and I was carried away to safety by the angel. I shouted, "Hallelujah! Jesus' blood has overcome you!"

After telling what I'd seen, we prayed and shared the Lord's Supper together. We committed ourselves to the care of the Lord. The three of us – the two young sisters and I – arrived in Shangnan County in Shaanxi. Shangnan is an isolated mountainous district in the extreme south-east of the province. Most of the impoverished people there had never seen outsiders before.

The local believers were informed of our arrival and three days of meetings were hastily arranged. Leaders from several counties gathered. On the first day I shared the history of the cross throughout church history and mission. On the second day, around 1 p.m., I lost my voice. The believers suggested I take a rest and let my co-workers share in my place. I asked Sister Juan to preach on the salvation of the cross.

Neither of these two women had spoken in public before. They'd never even stood in front of a crowd! Sister Juan was so nervous she fell down on her knees and cried. Her Bible fell to the ground. Everyone had compassion on her and prayed for her.

I was taken to a room so I could rest. When I lay down I meditated on the message I'd shared that morning.

Suddenly I heard a loud noise! Several PSB officers kicked down the door to my room. They grabbed me and held me down on the bed. One officer lay on me, pinning me down with his weight. With one hand he held me by the throat. With his other hand he reached into his pocket and pulled out his ID card. He shouted, "I come from the Public Security Bureau. Where do you come from?"

Immediately I remembered the vision I had seen of the dark monster.

Two other PSB officers took a rope and tightly bound my arms behind my back, as well as binding the rope around my chest, back and waist. One of the officers noticed a red wooden cross that was attached to the wall, with the words "For God so loved the world" inscribed on the horizontal piece of the cross. On the left and right were written, "He hung on the cross" and "He took our sins upon himself."

The officers read those words and laughed loudly. They tore the cross from the wall and tied it to my back with the ropes. Then they started to kick me furiously. Blows rained down on my legs, arms, chest and ribs.

The owner of the house came and knelt down before the officers, begging them to release me. He said, "This man is a good man. He's done nothing wrong. Please arrest me in his place."

The officers kicked and pushed him out of the room, shouting, "You can never pay this man's debt."

For the first time I had the honour of literally bearing the cross of Christ on my body! They triumphantly marched me off, bloodied and bruised, to Shangnan township. I was reminded of the verse, *"For it seems to me that God has put us apostles on display at the end of the procession, like men condemned to die in the arena."* 1 Corinthians 4:9.

When the townspeople saw me bound with rope and that

I was carrying a big red cross, a story began to circulate that "Jesus from Henan" had come. Many people crowded around to witness this remarkable sight.

As I was paraded through the streets, a police car drove slowly in front. Through a loudspeaker they proclaimed, "This man came from Henan to preach Jesus. He has seriously disturbed the peace. He has confused the people. Today the Public Security Bureau has captured him. We will punish him severely."

I was made to kneel down in the dirt while officers punched me in the chest and face and repeatedly kicked me from behind with their heavy boots. My face was covered with blood. The pain was unbearable and I nearly lost consciousness as I lay on the ground.

They lifted me up and made me stagger down another street. They were determined to make an example of me to as many people as possible.

I lifted up my head and caught glimpses of people in the crowd. Some pitied me and wept. When I saw this it really strengthened my faith. When I had the chance, I softly told one woman, "Please don't feel sorry for me. You should weep for the lost souls of our nation."

When the onlookers heard my voice they cried even more loudly. I was paraded through the streets for half a day. When night fell they took me into a big courtyard inside the police station.

They didn't loosen my ropes, but they did take the wooden cross off my back. They locked me inside a large interrogation room. I noticed the door was made of iron and the windows had iron bars on them.

Some evil-faced officers came in. They questioned me with great gravity in their voices. The Lord spoke to my heart, "In the hidden place your Father shall protect you."

They shouted at me, "Where exactly do you come from?" "Henan," I replied.

Then I remembered that I was a wanted man in Henan. I didn't want to tell them the name of my home county or town because I would get many believers into trouble, so I shut my mouth and determined not to answer any more of their questions.

I felt that God wanted me to pretend I was crazy, like David had done in the Bible. I lay down on the ground and acted insane. I rolled my eyes back in their sockets and spat like a madman. I didn't say a word. The PSB were frightened and were convinced I was crazy.

Many spectators had crowded outside the window and looked in.

One officer went to another room and made a telephone call to Henan, to try to find out who I was from the authorities there. The other interrogators went with him to hear what was said. They left me alone in the room and shut the door. I was still tightly bound by rope so they saw no chance I could escape. The onlookers also gave their attention to the telephone call, and crowded outside the window of that room to listen.

At that moment, with everyone's eyes off me, the Holy Spirit spoke to my heart, "The God of Peter is your God." I remembered how angels had opened the prison gates for Peter to escape. *"Are not all angels ministering spirits sent to serve those who will inherit salvation?" Hebrews 1:14.*

The rope that bound my arms behind my back suddenly snapped by itself! I didn't tear the ropes off, but kept them loosely in place. I decided to try to escape, and if caught I would claim I was trying to go to the toilet. With my arms still positioned behind my back, I used my mouth to turn the door handle and I walked out of the room!

At that moment God gave me faith and courage. I reminded myself that the blood of Jesus Christ protected me. I walked through the middle of the onlookers in the courtyard. Nobody stopped me or said anything to me! It was as though God had blinded their eyes and they didn't recognize who I was.

I walked through the courtyard to the toilet block in the northern part of the compound, about 30 feet away from the interrogation room. As quickly as I could, I pulled off the rope from around my body. My hands, arms and shoulders were still numb from being bound by rope for so long.

Because the front gates had been locked, the only way out of the compound was over an eight-foot high cement wall. The wall had sharp glass embedded in the top. I stood there for a moment, stared at the wall and prayed, asking the Lord to heal my hands and body.

I decided to try to leap over the wall. I saw no other choice. I was trapped and at any moment the officers would come and grab me. What happened next is not possible from a human perspective, yet God is my witness that what I am about to tell you is the truth.

First I pulled myself up onto the wall as high as I could manage. I looked over the top and saw that on the other side was a ten-feet-wide open septic tank.

As I hung grimly onto the side of the wall, all of a sudden I felt as if somebody hoisted me up and threw me over! I jumped so far that I even cleared the septic tank! A Scripture came to mind, *"With your help I can advance against a troop; with my God I can scale a wall."* 2 Samuel 22:30.

The God of Peter wonderfully helped me leap over the wall and escape! I believe the same angel I had seen in my vision helped to lift me up.

Darkness had fallen in the mountains. I ran blindly through the hills and forests. I had no idea where I was heading, but just sought to put as much distance between the police station and myself as I could.

As I ran I spoke out the Psalms with a thankful heart to the Lord, *"Even in darkness light dawns for the upright, for the gracious and compassionate and righteous man. . . . Surely he will never be shaken; a righteous man will be remembered forever. He will have no fear of bad news; his heart is steadfast, trusting in the Lord. His heart is secure, he will have no fear; in the end he will look in triumph on his foes."* Psalm 112:4,6–8.

Many times as I ran through the darkness I slipped over, but God guided me with his abundant mercy. After several hours I'd climbed over two mountains and crossed a river. Suddenly in the darkness I heard someone shouting, "Brother Yun, where are you going?"

A man approached me and asked, "Brother Yun, why do you look like this?" He saw the blood and scars on my hands and cried, "What has happened to you?"

It was about midnight. I couldn't see who it was, so I asked him quietly, "Do you believe in Jesus? Do you know me?"

The man replied, "Yesterday and this morning I attended your meeting, but this afternoon when you lost your voice I ran back to my farm to do some work."

He hadn't heard about the arrests earlier that day. In God's provision he had enabled this man to leave the meeting just minutes before the PSB came. This brother was a hard-working farmer who had many chores to attend to each day. He was working in the field at midnight, spreading fertiliser on his crops, trying to catch up with the time he had lost while attending the meetings.

I told him, "I was captured by the PSB this afternoon but the Lord has rescued me from their hands. He helped me escape over the police station wall. Where am I? Can you help me?"

This dear brother told me, "Come to my home and change your clothes."

"No!" I protested. "There's no time. The most important thing is that you take me to see my co-workers and your church leaders."

This brother's farm was a long way from our meeting place. He immediately put his load on the ground and led me down a very narrow pathway until finally we came to the house where I'd been arrested the previous afternoon.

When we arrived we heard people loudly praying. They were crying out for me before the Lord, interceding for my release. When they saw me they could scarcely believe their eyes! They were amazed that the Lord had rescued me from the hands of evil men. They changed my wet clothes, bathed my scars, and lovingly wiped the blood from my face and hands.

I encouraged the Shaanxi believers. I prayed for them and placed them in the merciful hands of God. I taught them, *"We must go through many hardships to enter the kingdom of God."* Acts 14:22. They confidently told me, "We will continue by obeying the words from the Bible."

Everyone wept.

Before daybreak, after a final prayer, the three of us left that place and went to another destination by car. The embarrassed authorities searched everywhere for me but couldn't find me. A few days later we safely returned home to Henan.

Our trip to the west was a journey of tears and marvellous protection from the hands of evil men. We were truly dependent on God's mercy, poured out in response to the many fervent prayers of the brothers and sisters.

When I arrived back in Henan I met Brother Xu, Brother Fu, and my dear wife. When I saw them I quoted the

Scripture, "*We do not want you to be uninformed, brothers, about the hardships we suffered in the province of Asia. We were under great pressure, far beyond our ability to endure, so that we despaired even of life. Indeed, in our hearts we felt the sentence of death. But this happened that we might not rely on ourselves but on God, who raises the dead.*" 2 Corinthians 1:8–9.

Brother Fu was excited to see me. He said, "A few days ago during our prayer meeting your wife had a vision. A voice said, 'Yun has been arrested in Shaanxi. He needs a great miracle to get him out.' We told the church and everyone immediately fasted and prayed for you."

After hearing these words I wept tears of thankfulness for God's love and mercy.

*   *   *

Let me tell you what happened to the two young women who accompanied me on the trip to Shaanxi. Sister Juan was so nervous that she had broken down and cried when I first asked her to teach at the meeting.

God has done a wonderful work in the hearts of those sisters. They both decided to remain single so they could dedicate themselves more fully to the work of the Lord. Today, Sister Juan is one of the top leaders of the Born Again house church network. She is as bold as a lion, full of faith and courage!

*   *   *

DELING: Our lives were becoming more and more unsettled at this time. Part of me longed to have a stable family life, to have a normal daily routine with my husband at home alongside me.

When we made a firm commitment to follow Jesus regardless of the cost, we didn't really understand what that would involve! 1983 was a terrible year for persecution in China. Hundreds of house church leaders were hunted like criminals and sent to prison. We were forced to run from the authorities. It was a very tense and stressful time for all of us.

At this time my husband went to Shaanxi Province, preaching the gospel in an area where we'd never sent workers before. Yun had been gone a few days when the Lord spoke to me in a vision and told me he'd been arrested, but that the Lord was going to help him escape.

The vision greatly encouraged me. I realized how much God is in control. We had no telephones and no way of communicating, but the Lord communicated for us!

I was so happy and relieved when I saw my husband's face again! He looked in bad shape. He'd been hit around the head and hair was torn from his scalp. His whole body was covered in scars and purple bruises, but he was safe. When we heard what had happened and how the Lord of Lords helped him to escape in such a miraculous way, we were so thankful and full of praise to Jesus.

This experience helped me have confidence that whatever Yun would go through was in God's hands and according to his will.

CHAPTER SEVEN

GOD WANTS ALL OF MY HEART

For months we lived like hunted animals, never knowing where we would sleep at night or when we might be hauled away by the authorities.

The government and the Three-Self Patriotic Movement have fooled many Christians around the world by insisting there is freedom of religion in China, freedom for people to choose. They boldly claim Christians are no longer persecuted for their faith.

My own personal experiences – as well as those of thousands of other house church believers – are quite the opposite. On one occasion when I was arrested the authorities let me choose whether I wanted to be shocked with an electric baton or whipped with a rope. They mocked me and said, "This is your free choice."

There is "freedom" of religion in China only if you're willing to do, say, live and worship exactly as the government instructs you. Anyone who desires to live a godly life and obey all of Jesus' teachings will soon find out how much freedom there really is.

For weeks after I was beaten in Shaanxi I continued to bleed from my mouth. While I was recovering, our church decided to send me to the south, to Hubei Province.

On this trip we experienced many miracles. By the power of the Holy Spirit there were many divine healings.

Because of the efforts being made by the authorities to catch us in that place, my co-workers were very concerned for my safety. They relocated me to northern Hubei.

We slept in caves and fled on foot from one place to another. Our clothes were torn and our hair unkempt. People were disgusted by us and considered us *". . . the scum of the earth, the refuse of the world". I Corinthians 4:13.*

I spent much time in the northern part of Hubei. Many miracles took place and the gospel was spread to thousands of people. This grabbed the attention of the PSB and the government in the whole border area of Hubei and Henan went on the alert.

The storm of persecution soon came upon us.

Posters were plastered all over the streets of each town, stating that all illegal house churches would be crushed and the leaders arrested. Loud speakers blared all over the countryside, stating that the pastors from Henan were illegal and would be arrested.

Announcements were also made over the radio. People were warned not to listen to us and to tell the authorities if they knew where we were.

We were conducting a meeting in a believer's home outside Heping town in northern Hubei Province. A cold wind blew from Siberia in the north, causing the temperature to plummet to well below freezing.

News came to us that Brother Enshen had been sentenced to prison just that morning. The situation was so tight, and the risks so great that even our Christian hosts decided they couldn't accept us in their home that night. They knew they would go to prison for many years if caught hosting us. The mother of the family knelt down and begged us to leave.

I spoke to her and asked, "We are strangers being chased by the police. Can you at least lend us a ragged old blanket so we can spend the night in the wet and cold?" She replied, "If you are caught, the PSB will see that the blanket is from our house, and we'll be in big trouble."

Finally, without hope and without even a blanket, my co-workers and I left the house. We walked in the darkness shivering, hungry, wet and cold. Several dogs emerged and howled at us in a mocking tone. It was so dark I couldn't see my fingers when I stretched my hand in front of my face.

Even our own brethren had rejected us.

This is the way God chose to train us, so that we would cry out and trust only in him for protection and provision. We cried to the Lord with many tears.

The freezing wind lashed us. Zhang Rongliang, myself and the other co-workers walked on, trying to keep warm. We sang songs through gritted teeth. After wandering for a while we came across a haystack in a field. We dug a hole into the straw to escape from the bitterly cold wind, but there was room for only one person. One sister crawled into the haystack. Brother Zhang and I continued to walk on in the dark. We tried to warm ourselves by wrapping an old torn sack around our bodies.

We jogged two kilometres until we came to a large fish-pond. All night the PSB searched the village for us, but we were huddled in a bush next to the pond. After midnight the temperature plummeted even further. The wind blew more fiercely and it started to rain. Icy sheets of rain cut us like nails, right to the bone. Our teeth chattered and our empty stomachs groaned. Brother Zhang and I clung to each other, trying to keep warm.

We knelt down on the embankment of the pond and prayed, "O Lord, for the sake of the precious blood you shed on the cross, please have mercy on our nation. Please disperse the dark clouds over China."

At about four o'clock I felt so discouraged that I walked to a spot by myself and cried out to the Lord. Suddenly, in the cold, I received a clear vision from the Holy Spirit.

The sky was filled with darkness. A great sandstorm rose up from the desert and engulfed me. I heard the roll of thunder, but there was no rain. Suddenly I saw a great flood coming from the north. A wall of water raced towards me to carry me away. I cried out, "O God, save me!"

Then in the vision I saw a huge jar, about three feet (one metre) tall. It floated in front of me. I grabbed the jar and jumped inside as quickly as I could. Immediately an umbrella fell from the sky onto the top of the jar. I held the umbrella above my head as torrential rain bucketed down, but I was dry. The flood waters swept me away. Rocks and debris knocked the jar around, but I was safe.

While in the jar I lifted my eyes and saw how brothers and sisters from many parts of China were being arrested, beaten and imprisoned by the police. I saw this terrible wave of persecution but I was completely helpless to save them. I just cried out.

After my vision ended I complained bitterly to the Lord, "Why do you have no strength to protect me or the other believers? I know that I will also be arrested. I will fall into the hands of the PSB. I have a mother and a wife. Why are you treating me like this?"

Despite my anger, the Lord didn't answer me.

I could not return home because I would be arrested. I couldn't help my brothers and sisters who were being tortured all across China. I felt so frustrated. I couldn't go forward and I couldn't go back.

The Lord used these circumstances to show me that he

wanted all of my heart to be totally committed to him. In my desperate condition a new song began to form in my mind:

As long as I live, I will only love my Lord
With all my heart, strength and mind, I will only love my
  Lord
Regardless of what happens, I will only love my Lord
In all my actions and words, I will only love my Lord.

In times of humility and learning, I will only love my Lord
In times of joy and gladness, I will only love my Lord
Whether I face hunger or if I'm full, I will only love my Lord
I am his in life or death, I will only love my Lord.

The Lord has sacrificed his life for me
My deep sin has been pardoned
I have dedicated all my life to him
I will only love my Lord.

I shared what I had seen in my vision with Brother Zhang. I told him, "We must leave this place now. The Lord will protect us. He'll be our shelter." We continued our journey without even waiting for dawn to come.

I had a deeper understanding that no matter what situation would come my way, I would be in the hands of the Lord, and he would rescue me. I started to march ahead again, according to God's calling.

I felt ashamed and guilty for how I'd complained to the Lord, but he was patient and loving to me, not treating me as I deserved, but gently helping me like an eagle tending her baby chicks.

*   *   *

DELING: In the early 1980s we enjoyed sweeter fellowship and closer unity than ever before. The pressure meant we had to rely on the Lord and on each other for our very survival. The love of the brethren brought great comfort to my heart. At this time we also witnessed the greatest number of miracles in our ministry for the Lord. Supernatural visitations, divine healings, and people being delivered of demons were common occurrences.

Despite the hardships – or rather because of them – the church experienced rapid growth. Revival fires from the Lord ignited all across China.

Some remarkable incidents took place that led multitudes of people to the salvation of the cross.

In my village of Yenzhang a Communist Party secretary named Zhang had persecuted and tortured Christians for years. Like the Apostle Paul before he met Jesus, Zhang seemed to delight in destroying the church.

One brisk winter evening my mother, Brother Fu, some co-workers, Yun and I went to Yenzhang village. We visited a Christian family and prayed for them. About thirty Christians gathered so we decided to have a meeting.

A neighbour overheard our worship and made a report to the Party secretary, Mr. Zhang. He sent a team of Public Security Bureau officers to the house. They came with batons and ropes to arrest us and take us to the local police station.

The Party secretary had a brother who lived in a nearby village. This man had a mental illness. At exactly the same time that the PSB were dispatched to break up our meeting, the devil put a murderous spirit into the mind and heart of the secretary's brother. That insane man grabbed his 80-year-old mother and murdered her by cutting off her head with a rusty knife. He then threw her corpse into a latrine outside the house.

Brother Fu was leading the singing when the officers ran into the courtyard of the house where we were meeting. The police kicked in the door and beat Brother Fu severely with their batons. For what seemed like an eternity they tortured the elderly man until he was almost dead. They then bound his unconscious body tightly with ropes. There was nothing we could do but pray for our beloved pastor.

They threw Yun's mother to the ground and viciously kicked her. As they were about to bind her with rope they noticed some young people in the meeting. They used the ropes to bind them instead and took us all back to the station.

That night they left us in the cell, intending to deal with us at daybreak. During the night a chilling report came to the secretary, "Your younger brother has killed your mother! Your mother's body has been found lying in the latrine with her head cut off!"

The secretary ran home and forgot about persecuting us. In the morning we heard the news and cried out to the Lord to have mercy on the secretary and his family, that they might repent and receive forgiveness.

When the secretary reached his home he found his brother lying on his bed. He asked him, "Where is our mother?" He replied, "I've already killed her and thrown her body in the latrine." The secretary shouted with great anger, "Why have you done this terrible thing?" The insane man replied, "Why have you been persecuting the Christians? Because you have persecuted them, I have killed our mother." He then pulled out the long rusty knife and tried to attack his own brother, but was prevented from doing so by the PSB officers who had accompanied Zhang. They bound him and took him to the police station.

The PSB and all the people in the area believed this incident was the judgment of God on Zhang's family for persecuting Christians. The authorities left the believers alone from that time on. This incident amazed everyone in the village. They all confessed, "Jesus truly is the living God." The entire village became Christians and received baptism.

All the Christians showed genuine love and compassion to the secretary and his family for their loss. The family was deeply touched and they all humbly received Jesus. I was reminded of the Scripture, "And we know that in all things God works for the good of those who love him, who have been called according to his purpose." Romans 8:28.

Many of the new Christians from Yenzhang village made commitments to serve the Lord wholeheartedly. They decided to take the gospel to other areas that had never heard the name of Jesus before.

In various ways and through the spilling of much blood, the gospel spread rapidly during the struggles of 1983.

CHAPTER EIGHT

"BE STILL AND KNOW THAT I AM GOD"

"Because of my chains, most of the brothers in the Lord have been encouraged to speak the word of God more courageously and fearlessly." Philippians 1:14.

I thank God for his grace and calling to me. What great power he has for those who believe in him!

Despite the terrible season of persecution that was raging across China, Deling and I prepared to travel north. Together we sang a song based on the Apostle Paul's courageous declaration in Acts 20:22–24,

And now, compelled by the Spirit, I am going to Jerusalem
Not knowing what will happen to me there.
I only know that in every city the Holy Spirit warns me
That prisons and hardships are facing me.

However, I consider my life worth nothing to me
If only I may finish the race
And complete the task the Lord Jesus has given me –
To testify to the gospel of God's grace.

We continued meeting with believers, encouraging them and seeking the Lord for guidance. During one prayer time a servant of the Lord suddenly spoke a prophecy to us: "This time, when you and your wife go north, you will encounter danger. But no matter what happens, the Lord will be with you."

The next morning, before the sun rose, Deling and I took the bus towards Wuyang County in the north. We passed through many bus stations displaying posters with my name and picture, announcing that I was a dangerous criminal, a counter-revolutionary. The posters accused me of being the leader of an anti-government organization that stirred people up against state religious policies.

At one town we had to change our bus. I was wearing sunglasses to hide my eyes. Many people at the station had seen my picture and we overheard them discussing it. One man said, "The person who helps catch this fugitive will receive a great reward from the government."

My wife and I had an unspoken joy inside because we knew the Lord was our refuge. We felt so honoured to be wanted criminals as we walked hand-in-hand together for Jesus. It's a great honour to be humiliated for the name of the Lord.

We found the Christians in Henan were totally different from those in Hubei. They were all willing to risk their lives for us and to welcome us "criminals" into their homes. The more tense the situation, the more they earnestly desired to show their love and respect to God's servants.

Onward we marched. A meeting was arranged at a certain village. We were led by the Holy Spirit to sing a powerful song called *Martyrs for the Lord:*

From the time the church was birthed on the day of Pentecost
The followers of the Lord have willingly sacrificed themselves
Tens of thousands have died that the gospel might prosper
As such they have obtained the crown of life.

Chorus:
To be a martyr for the Lord, to be a martyr for the Lord
I am willing to die gloriously for the Lord.

Those apostles who loved the Lord to the end
Willingly followed the Lord down the path of suffering
John was exiled to the lonely isle of Patmos
Stephen was stoned to death by an angry crowd.

Matthew was stabbed to death in Persia by a mob
Mark died as horses pulled his two legs apart
Doctor Luke was cruelly hanged
Peter, Philip and Simon were crucified on a cross.

Bartholomew was skinned alive by the heathen
Thomas died in India as five horses pulled his body apart
The apostle James was beheaded by King Herod
Little James was cut in half by a sharp saw.

James the brother of the Lord was stoned to death
Judas was tied to a pillar and shot by arrows
Matthias had his head cut off in Jerusalem
Paul was a martyr under Emperor Nero.

I am willing to take up the cross and go forward
To follow the apostles down the road of sacrifice
That tens of thousands of precious souls can be saved
I am willing to leave all and be a martyr for the Lord.

When we finished singing the whole meeting place was shaken. There was a great sound of weeping. I stood up to speak about suffering for the Lord. The Holy Spirit fell upon us and we earnestly interceded for our nation. We re-dedicated ourselves to fight for the Lord.

After the meeting brother Zhen, a humble and faithful brother, knelt down in the courtyard after everyone else had gone to sleep, and continued to pray for our nation. The Holy Spirit clearly told him, "Within three days there are people among you who will be bound and beaten for me. Some will even lay down their lives for me."

After he told me this I felt the Lord was speaking to me personally. I whispered a prayer, "O Father, I'm willing to suffer for your Name."

My wife and I prayed together and we felt she needed to return home to comfort the families of our many workers who had been imprisoned. I waved goodbye to her as the local believers took her to the bus station.

For all three days of our meeting the snow kept falling. Some of the older homes in the village collapsed from the weight of the snow on their roofs. The whole village was blanketed with ice and snow, but everyone in the meeting was on fire for the Lord.

At midnight on the third day, 17 December 1983, the meeting concluded. The hosts had prepared warm water to wash everyone's feet. I washed my co-workers' feet with my tears. Then they urged me to sit down. They took off my socks and washed my feet with their tears, before gently putting my shoes back on again. Our meeting was in a place called "The Village of Love". How true it had turned out to be!

We split up to go to the homes of different believers to rest. Before we left, Brother Zhang took off his big winter scarf and gave it to me.

Just after we left the meeting place about a dozen men carrying flashlights confronted us at the outskirts of the village. They shouted, "Who are you? What is your business here?" Our co-workers knew something was wrong so they turned around and ran. I also turned to run but it was too late.

One man, wielding an electric baton, ran to me and shocked me with hundreds of volts of electricity. I was immediately thrown backwards into the snow. Excruciating pain surged through my entire body.

They kicked me with their steel-capped boots and struck me with their pistol handles. Another four brothers were arrested with me. At that moment I heard a gentle voice from above that simply said two words to me, "I know!"

I realized this was the familiar voice of my Lord Jesus, who many centuries before had told the persecuted believers in Smyrna, *"I know your afflictions and your poverty – yet you are rich! I know the slander of those who say they are Jews and are not, but are a synagogue of Satan. Do not be afraid of what you are about to suffer. I tell you, the devil will put some of you in prison to test you, and you will suffer persecution for ten days. Be faithful, even to the point of death, and I will give you the crown of life." Revelation 2:9–10.*

My Lord knew what I was going through and he knew everything I would have to endure. I was greatly encouraged!

Brother Zhen's prophecy came into my mind, and all the pain left me. One officer demanded, "What is your name? Where are you from? How many workers do you have? Where are they? Speak now! Tell the truth!" He leaned forward and spoke more threateningly than before, "Tell me the truth. If you lie, I'll skin you alive!"

Suddenly I felt tense inside as I realized many brothers and sisters still in the meeting place were in danger of being found. The only thought I had in my mind was how I could raise an alarm so they would know trouble was at their door.

The Holy Spirit immediately reminded me of the story when King David feigned insanity when he met Abimelech.

I shouted in a loud voice, "I am a heavenly man! I live in Gospel village! People call me Morning Star! My father's name is Abundant Blessing! My mother's name is Faith, Hope, Love!"

The officers kicked me violently then dragged me to my feet. They shouted, "What nonsense are you shouting? We asked you where you're from and who your co-workers are!"

At that moment I was facing the east. I told them, "They're in that village over there." I shouted again with a loud voice, "I've been caught by the Security Police!"

The officers shoved me and ordered me to take them to find my co-workers. "Take us. If you're lying we'll skin you alive!" they grimly threatened.

I walked ahead of them and shouted in a loud voice, "I've been arrested by the Security Police! I don't know where the meetings took place because I'm a heavenly man! I'm not from this earth!"

I shouted louder and louder, hoping my co-workers would hear my voice and escape before they too were arrested.

From that day to now, completely unknown to me at the time, I was given the nickname "the heavenly man" by believers in China. As you can see, I didn't ask for this name, for I'm just a weak human vessel, but this is how I came to be known by this nickname.

Instead of fleeing when they heard my shouting, many of the brothers and sisters came out to see what was going on! They were more concerned for me than for their own safety.

I led the officers through the snow, towards the village to the east. They grabbed me and demanded, "Quickly, tell us which house! Take us in!"

I pretended to be confused and shouted, "Oh, it's not this village. I'm mistaken! My co-workers are in another village!"

They threw me to the ground, beating and kicking me. Again the baton was used to electrocute me. I would surely have died if the Lord had not protected me.

Some brothers and sisters were silently following us at a distance. When they saw the punishment I was given they were filled with grief and started to pray. The officers noticed them.

I didn't want to place the believers at risk so I shouted again, "I'm a heavenly man. I don't know where the meeting was. I don't know any of you who are following us. The heavenly man will never become a Judas! I only know the Master from heaven!"

The brothers and sisters realized I was warning them. They turned around and fled.

The officers were furious because I had tricked them. The four co-workers and I were pushed into the back of a tractor that had been brought to transport us to Wuyang City. We were tied together with one rope like cattle going to slaughter. Standing in the back of the tractor, I sang in a loud voice:

First comes blood, then the anointing oil
First we must be clean then we receive blessing from the Lord
First we must experience Calvary, then will come Pentecost.

Cross, cross, forever my glory
His blood has washed my sins away
Only through the blood of Jesus.

The five of us were placed in a prison cell inside the police station. The temperature was well below freezing. There was no heating at all, and they had taken my coat and thrown it in the snow. We shivered and our limbs turned blue. We almost fell unconscious. Our frozen handcuffs cut like knives into our swollen wrists.

I used the handcuffs to knock on the door and the iron windows. As I looked around I saw a broken wooden box in the corner of the cell. Inside was an old drum. I beat the drum with my handcuffs and made a loud noise. At the top of my voice I sang Psalm 150:

Praise the Lord.

Praise God in his sanctuary;

Praise him in his mighty heavens.
Praise him for his acts of power;
Praise him for his surpassing greatness.
Praise him with the sounding of the trumpet,
Praise him with the harp and lyre,
Praise him with tambourine and dancing,
Praise him with the strings and flute,
Praise him with the clash of cymbals,
Praise him with resounding cymbals.

Let everything that has breath praise the Lord.
Praise the Lord.

The more I sang the more I was filled with joy. I stood up and praised the Lord. Gradually my frozen hands and feet regained feeling and I wasn't cold any more. The four brothers knelt down on the floor and earnestly prayed for China. The piercing wind whistled loudly outside, but inside our cell weeping and the groans of intercessory prayers were heard.

The guards were greatly incensed by my drumming and singing, but they didn't want to get out of their warm beds to stop me. The five of us encouraged and strengthened one another throughout the night. Just like Shadrach, Meshach and Abednego, we learned that where the Spirit of the Lord is, there is liberty, whether in a freezing prison cell or a fiery furnace. Hallelujah!

The next morning the guards opened the cell door and took us out into the yard. There was a thick layer of snow on the ground. They released the handcuffs from my four brothers. They told them, "You must clear all the snow in the yard. But this crazy 'heavenly man' will not have his handcuffs removed. Last night he created an uproar and kept us awake with his singing and drumming."

The chief guard waved his electric baton in front of my face and said, "Now is the time for you to wake up!" He ordered me to kneel down before him. I loudly protested, "I will not kneel down before you. I will only kneel down before my God!"

He arrogantly stated, "I am your Lord! I am your God! If you kneel down before me I can release you immediately."

I spoke angrily to him, "In the name of Jesus, you are not my God! You are just an earthly officer. My Lord is in heaven. I am a heavenly man."

He turned on the power switch on his baton and snarled, "If you are a heavenly man then you won't be afraid of this electric baton. Come! Use your hands to take hold of it!"

Several guards grabbed my arms and forced me to stretch out my hand. In an instant I was stung with hundreds of volts of electric current, like the sting of a scorpion or as if a thousand arrows had pierced my heart. Feeling I was about to pass out, I cried out, "Lord, have mercy on me!"

Immediately the electric baton malfunctioned! They couldn't get it to work!

I opened my eyes and stared at the guard who'd dared to

call himself "God". He was terrified. Despite the temperature, he was sweating! He turned and ran away as fast as he could!

The four brothers had witnessed this event and when they saw the guards force my hand on the baton they prayed God would have mercy on me.

The next morning the five of us were shoved into a van. They took us to the prison in Wuyang.

When I entered the prison yard on the way to the cell I knew there must be many Christian brothers inside that prison because of the wave of persecution against the church. In a bid to encourage them I shouted out, "A heavenly man has been sent to prison. I'm not like Judas! I will not betray the Lord!" After we arrived the guard locked me in the same cell as Brother Zhen and ten other men.

Some minutes later I was in my cell when I heard the prison gate open. Some more believers were being brought in. The guard on the gate asked one Christian, "Are you a heavenly man, or are you an earthly man?"

The brother said, "I don't know what you're talking about." The guards wanted to know which of the Christians were like the heavenly man they had just brought in, and which were not.

This brother finally answered, "I'm a man from the earth, not a heavenly man."

The guard said, "Because you're just an earthly man, tonight I will put you in the cell of a heavenly man."

When he entered the cell I was kneeling down in prayer. I stared at him with great intensity. My spirit was so angry because he'd denied being a believer in order to make it easy on himself.

With great fervency I shouted, "You should say No! No! No! to the devil!"

I stood up and continued to shout, "You must say No! No! No! to the devil!"

While he watched, I used my right forefinger to trace the word "No!" on the cement wall. I pressed my finger against the rough wall so hard that it became numb and started to bleed. With the blood from my own finger I wrote this sentence on the wall: "No! No! No! Don't be afraid! Don't trust in man, trust only in Jesus."

When this brother saw these words written with my own blood he felt great shame and conviction for compromising his testimony. He bowed his head and wept tears of repentance. After his release from prison he became a leader of the church in his locality.

Several old Christian women living nearby heard of our arrest. In the night they trudged through the snow to bring us their best blankets and coats. One of the old sisters even hobbled through the snow on her crutches; such was her love for the family of God!

When they arrived at the prison they told the guard they had brought these gifts for the heavenly people. The guard asked, "For whom?"

They replied, "For the heavenly people."

I was staying in the cell closest to the prison office, so I could hear all of this. My heart was filled with thanksgiving when I heard of their love. I cried out, "I am a heavenly man!" so that those dear sisters could hear my voice.

The next morning the guards had exchanged the old sisters' gifts. They threw a tattered blanket into my cell and kept the good blankets and clothes for themselves. The women had also brought me a new pair of boots, but a guard stole them for himself. The blanket I received was old and ragged, but those sisters' love gave me great faith and courage.

There were dozens of Christians in that prison, and we all

endured terrible beatings and torture for the Lord. God granted us special patience and wisdom in dealing with our persecutors.

The prison authorities liked to entice some of the rough prisoners to beat up other prisoners. They offered to make their sentences lighter and bribed them with promises of better meals if they agreed to do their dirty work for them.

At mealtimes we were served a tiny bowl of mouldy, mashed sweet potato paste mixed with radish. Once a week we were given a *mantou* – a small steamed bread bun. All of the prisoners were nearly starving, so this was a real treat.

One evening after I received my precious *mantou* I knelt down, closed my eyes, and gave thanks to the Lord with the *mantou* in my upraised hand. While my eyes were still closed one of the other prisoners came and snatched my bun from me.

One of the guards saw the man take my *mantou* and hide it in his shirt-pocket. The guards beat him mercilessly and ordered the other prisoners to beat him too. They then forced him to kneel down inside the urinal, smearing his head with human waste.

Like brute savages they held the man's head in the urinal until he nearly drowned.

I felt so guilty! I wept loudly and uncontrollably because of what had happened to my fellow prisoner.

I cried out to the Lord, "O God, have mercy on me! Have mercy on me! Please forgive me!"

The next morning the guards took me out from the cell and practised martial arts on my body. They kicked and punched me to the ground and ordered several other prisoners to stamp on my chest and private parts. Blood gushed from my mouth. I was dizzy and in great pain. I was sure I was going to die.

Up until that time Brother Zhen and I – though we shared the same cell – pretended we didn't know each other. If the prison authorities knew two Christians were encouraging each other they would be furious.

But when Brother Zhen saw what had happened to me in the yard, he rushed over to me, cradled my body in his arms, and cried, "Heavenly man, my dear brother!" He used his sleeves to wipe the blood from my nose and mouth.

Brother Zhen served me like an angel. He always encouraged me with words of hope from the Scriptures. All the other prisoners and guards sensed he had a kind and merciful spirit so they liked him.

A few days later the PSB sent a car to collect him and take him back to his home town for sentencing. They shouted, "Zhen, get ready. It's time for you to leave."

Brother Zhen hated to leave me. We wept and knelt in prayer together on the floor.

"Leave in peace," I told him.

This man of God was taken away from our prison and from our lives.

Although Brother Zhen had left, his teaching remained. Some of the prisoners began to say to each other, "We need to believe in Jesus." As a result, those criminals no longer treated me cruelly.

One young prisoner was an unbeliever, though his mother was a Christian. He stayed in my cell for a few days and found I wasn't mad like the guards had told him I was. He said to the other prisoners, "Yun is not crazy. He's a man who has paid a great price for his faith in God."

He took off his coat and gave it to me out of love and compassion. The next day the young man was released from the cell and given a job in the kitchen. A little while later he was allowed to go home and he became a committed disciple of Jesus Christ.

During those days in prison I was interrogated many times. They sensed that they had caught a "big fish" but couldn't find out my true identity. They used every technique they knew to try to find out where I came from, so that they could go after my co-workers. I foiled their plans by refusing to answer their questions. I could never implicate the brothers and sisters in my home church.

Because I wouldn't reveal my identity, the authorities in Wuyang County sent a letter to every other county in Henan, asking them to come and see if I was from their area. Several PSB officers from other counties came and left disappointed that I wasn't who they thought I was. The prison telephoned all over the province trying to identify me.

Finally, more than five weeks after my arrest, I was identified. At around 8:30 a.m. on the morning of 25 January 1984, PSB officers from Nanyang County came and immediately recognized me. They were overjoyed. They told me, "You're good at fooling the police here with your feigned insanity, but you don't fool us! Even if you lost your skin we'd still be able to recognize you. You've escaped from us many times and made us look stupid, but you won't escape this time!"

They slapped me and handcuffed me behind my back. They said, "Let's go! We're taking you back to Nanyang and will deal with you when we get there."

The Nanyang officers thanked the local PSB for taking care of me and threw me into the back of their van. They handcuffed me to a steel rail above my head that ran down the centre of the van. After closing the doors they beat me with their fists and with batons, severely wounding me.

As they drove throughout the day on the bumpy roads my handcuffs cut into my wrists so that blood splattered everywhere, covering the walls of the van. The handcuffs cut so deep that my wrist bones were exposed. I was in such agony I could hardly breathe. I was about to fall unconscious because of the pain and loss of blood.

I cried out to the Lord and said, "Jesus, I can no longer endure. Why are you allowing me to be tortured like this? Please receive my spirit now."

The guards travelling in the back of the van switched on an electric baton when they heard me praying and jolted me with shocks. The pain was too severe for me and I felt my heart and my brain were going to literally explode from my body.

Again I cried to the Lord, "God, have mercy on me. Please receive my spirit now."

The word of the Lord came to me clearly, "The reason you suffer is so you can partake in the fellowship of my suffering. Be still and know that I am God. I will be exalted among the nations. I will be exalted in the earth."

In my proud heart I'd been thinking that I was important to the church, that they needed me to lead them. Now, I vividly understood that he is God and I am but a feeble man. I realized that God didn't need me at all, and that if he ever chose to use me again it would be nothing more than a great privilege.

Suddenly the fear and pain left me.

The police van finally entered the streets of Nanyang, my home town. They slowed down. I could see through the windows that posters had been plastered on every wall along both sides of the street, announcing, "Celebrate and warmly congratulate the Public Security Bureau! The Christian counter-revolutionary Yun, who has clothed his

criminal activities in the cloak of religion, has been appre-
hended!"

"The arrest of the counter-revolutionary Yun is good news
for the people of Nanyang!"

"Down with the reactionary Yun and his fellow workers!
Resolutely strike down all illegal Christian meetings led by
Yun!"

The guards turned their siren on so they could boast to the
people of their great achievement in catching me. The news
of my arrest spread quickly and people rushed after the van
to see me.

But I was no longer afraid. The Lord had already told me,
*"Do not be afraid of what you are about to suffer. I tell you, the devil
will put some of you in prison to test you . . . Be faithful, even to
the point of death, and I will give you the crown of life."* Revelation
2:10.

CHAPTER NINE

THROUGH THE VALLEY OF DEATH

"Dear friends, do not be surprised at the painful trial you are suffering, as though something strange were happening to you. But rejoice that you participate in the sufferings of Christ, so that you may be overjoyed when his glory is revealed. If you are insulted because of the name of Christ, you are blessed, for the Spirit of glory and of God rests on you." I Peter 4:12–14.

During my long painful van journey back to Nanyang the Lord continually comforted me by saying, *"Be still, and know that I am God." Psalm 46:10.*

When the police van arrived at the Nanyang prison gate, they took my handcuffs off the steel rail and pushed me out of the back of the van onto the frozen ground. A bitterly cold blizzard was blowing from the north. My face and hair were drenched with blood. My eyes were blackened and my face swollen. I had no shoes on my feet and the handcuffs had cut deeply into my wrists.

They took me into a large interrogation room where a dozen PSB officers were waiting to see what kind of a person I was.

When they first saw my small frame, my swollen bloodied face, and my unkempt hair sticking out, they laughed loudly at me and mocked, "What? You are the heavenly man?"

The chief officer looked at me with disgust in his eyes. He asked, "Are you Yun? Are you the Yun who's been running all around the country causing trouble? Today you belong to us. Don't you dare ever try to escape from us. The law has finally caught up with you!"

The man second in charge of the PSB arrogantly boasted, "We have a net covering the heavens that is without any holes. You could never escape the long arm of our law! Yun, you have lost the fight today. Your co-workers are already in our hands. Even your fellow criminal Mr. Xu Yongze is under our control. Your church is totally finished. You have completely failed. You are an enemy of our country and an enemy of the Party."

When I heard these words I felt great anger inside. A spirit of faith spoke from within me, "The gospel grows through hardship and will spread throughout the world. The truth will enter everyone's heart. Truth is always truth. Nothing and no one can change that. It will always conquer."

The officers stared at me with total disdain. One man, wearing a sinister smile, leaned forward and whispered, "Yun, haven't you experienced enough suffering yet? Do you want us to 'entertain' you some more?"

I bowed my head and said nothing. He continued, "You should be aware how serious your crimes are. The policy of our government is to treat you well if you confess your crimes openly and honestly. But if you lie and don't co-operate we'll treat you harshly!"

In my heart I felt strong. I was determined to obey God and not man. I meditated on the Scripture, *"The Lord is my light and my salvation – whom shall I fear? The Lord is the stronghold of my life – of whom shall I be afraid?" Psalm 27:1.*

The deputy leader spoke again, "Even though you've committed so many serious crimes against our nation, we will have mercy on you and give you a way out. If you honestly report, in detail, about all your work, your co-workers, and the activities of your movement over the years, I guarantee we will release you immediately and you can go home to be with your wife and mother for the New Year festival."

He thought I was an uneducated peasant, so he tried to trick me with big words and with government policy. It was just seven days before the start of the Lunar New Year holiday.

When the deputy leader spoke, I inwardly wanted to say these words, "You guarantee my release if I confess all my 'crimes'? I guarantee you will die and go to hell if you don't repent of your sins and believe in Jesus Christ."

However, I held back those words and said the following, "For the last few days I've been tortured, beaten, and almost starved to death. Sometimes I couldn't even breathe because of the pain inflicted on me. I haven't eaten properly for a long time. Now you want me to tell you everything I've done for years. How can I do that in my present condition? Please give me time to think, rest and recuperate. When I've finished reflecting on my past I'll let you know."

The officers were impressed by my logic. They thought my request was reasonable so they let me go back to the cell to think over my activities. They asked me, "When will you be ready?" I replied, "I'll let you know the very moment I'm ready."

I was taken to the number two prison cell, passing through four iron gates. Encircling the prison was a high red-brick wall topped by electric wire. Armed guards closely watched the prisoners from watchtowers at all four corners of the prison wall.

As I settled into my new home the Holy Spirit reminded me of these verses: *"Do not be afraid of those who kill the body but cannot kill the soul. Rather, be afraid of the One who can destroy both soul and body in hell."* Matthew 10:28.

"Everyone who wants to live a godly life in Christ Jesus will be persecuted." 2 Timothy 3:12.

"Consider it pure joy, my brothers, whenever you face trials of many kinds, because you know that the testing of your faith develops perseverance." James 1:2–3.

Again the Lord spoke to me, "Be still and know that I am God."

I began to understand that the presence of God was my refuge. I knew I was about to face a great fiery trial. There was no way I would ever be like Judas and turn against my brothers and sisters. I'd rather be skinned alive than reveal the names of my precious co-workers.

I decided to lean upon God's Word and fast and pray in order to face the storm clouds gathering on the horizon. I needed to follow Jesus' example when he fasted in the desert to overcome the devil's temptations.

"Who shall separate us from the love of Christ? Shall trouble or hardship or persecution or famine or nakedness or danger or sword?" Romans 8:35.

On my first day in Nanyang prison I concluded that God wanted me to fast and pray for the advance of the gospel, that thousands of souls would experience salvation, and that the house churches throughout China would be victorious.

I started to fast in my cell on the evening of 25 January 1984. Immediately the sense of hunger attacked me. More and more temptation came. I was so hungry I could hardly stand it.

Immediately my commitment was sorely tested. That night

the chief prison warden wanted to show his compassionate side in celebration of the upcoming New Year, so he allowed the prisoners to have better food than their usual rancid meals. Each man was given one *mantou* along with some pork soup and a stick of celery.

To the starving prisoners this was truly a lavish feast. The smell of the food floated down the hallways before we saw it. When it arrived the prisoners gobbled it up like ravenous wolves and literally licked their bowls clean.

The devil reasoned with me, "There's only one New Year's holiday each year. You should eat a little bit of good food now while you have the chance." I very nearly surrendered to the temptation.

From the time of my capture in north-east Henan I'd eaten very little, and had lost weight. I was hungry, bruised and battered. I decided I would eat, but immediately a word from the Lord came to me, *"Submit yourselves, then, to God. Resist the devil, and he will flee from you." James 4:7.*

I prayed, "Spirit of hunger, leave me now in the name of Jesus Christ."

I gave my soup, *mantou*, and celery back to the prison warden and told him, "Please share my portion with all the men in this cell."

The hunger pains immediately left me.

Food was the god of the criminals in that prison. Because I'd surrendered my portion they began to think well of me and started to treat me nicely. After they finished scoffing down their meal my cell mates wanted to know why I'd been arrested. They asked, "Why is a nice person like you in this place?" I told them it was because I was a chosen vessel of the Lord.

They asked me if I could sing them a song. I began to sing,

The north wind blows, but the southern breeze will arise
In everything God's will is done
The north wind is bitterly cold, but it will not last long
Soon the warm southern breeze will arise.

Chorus:
Be patient and wait, be patient and wait
The Lord will make everything beautiful in his time
When the time has come, when the time has come
Abundant grace will overflow to you.

You who are burdened with sorrow, don't sigh any longer
The Lord will undertake for you
If the Heavenly Father does not permit it
Who can do anything to you?

All my fellow prisoners loved to listen to this song. Some understood the words and some didn't. They all believed in fate – that we can't change what will happen to us during our lives. I told them that God controlled all things, not fate, and that our lives were determined by him and by the choices we make to obey or disobey his Word. I used this opportunity to tell them what the Bible says, *"Just as man is destined to die once, and after that to face judgment, so Christ was sacrificed once to take away the sins of many people; and he will appear a second time, not to bear sin, but to bring salvation to those who are waiting for him."* Hebrews 9:27–28.

I urged the prisoners to repent and accept Jesus as their Saviour.

After speaking for about half an hour I had great pain in my head and chest because of the beatings I'd received. Even while I was sharing, my head throbbed and my chest felt it would collapse.

I knew the Lord wanted me to rest, so I told my cell mates,

"I'm willing to share more with you about Jesus, but I can't speak now because I have a great pain in my head and chest. My God has told me I need to rest and be still. From this day on, therefore, I won't eat any food or drink any water. Instead, I will give my portion to all of you. Please don't report this to the guards, because if they know they won't let me give my meals to you."

Everyone was overjoyed with my offer, because in the prison the men were cruelly treated and the food was horrible. Their stomach was their god, and food their master.

On 29 January 1984, I was taken for interrogation again. The presiding judge said, "We've already given you some days to think. We want you to speak now. If you're honest we will let you go home and you can reunite with your family."

I told him, "I've been involved in so many activities that I haven't been able to think about them all in these few days. I don't want to ruin your holiday celebrations by causing you unhappiness, so please give me some more time to think."

The two main judges looked at each other and told me, "Yun, you're an understanding person. We'll let you go back to your cell, but after the New Year festival you'll have to give us a very clear confession."

After I returned to my cell the Lord gently told me, "You shall rest. Do not be afraid. Just submit to me. Do not look upon circumstances, do not look upon yourself, and do not look to others. Pray more and you shall see my glory."

Day and night I meditated on the Word of God, on all that is holy and edifying. I thought of the great men and women of the Bible who had suffered for their faith.

I considered how Jesus had willingly submitted himself to God's will, and had endured the wrath of sinful men. I thought about Joseph and his experiences in Egypt, Daniel in the lion's den, and about Stephen as he was being stoned to death. I meditated on what Paul had written during his times of incarceration, and of Peter's imprisonment and miraculous escape in the twelfth chapter of Acts. They were like clouds of witnesses surrounding my thoughts. Their example cast away the fears and burdens from my heart.

In those days I was just like a baby sleeping in the arms of his mother, peacefully suckling at his mother's bosom.

God purified my heart. I held no hatred or malice against those who had treated me so cruelly. I lived in close fellowship with the Lord. I realized that everything that had happened to me was the result of God's will alone. This enabled me to genuinely love the souls of those bad men who had attacked and tried to destroy me. I felt very meek and gentle. My spirit was full of joy and thanksgiving as I magnified the Lord.

I told the Lord I would not speak a single word to anyone until the day I saw my family again. I didn't want to speak because the Lord had told me I should rest and trust only in him.

For day after day, week after week, I didn't eat or drink a thing. The Lord himself was my sustenance. I know that it's medically impossible to live more than a few days without any water, but *"What is impossible with men is possible with God." Luke 18:27.*

I never stopped to think that the fast was a miracle, and I never knew it would go on so long. All I knew was that God had told me to rest and to meditate on Jesus. This is what my mind and heart was wholly focused on during the fast. After the first few days I didn't think about food or water again. Day by day my spirit communed closer with Jesus. My own sinfulness diminished as the presence and light of the Lord was magnified in my spirit.

I learned the literal truth of Jesus' teaching, *"Man does not live on bread alone, but on every word that comes from the mouth of God." Matthew 4:4.*

For his glory, God had instructed me to fast. It was not merely my idea or something that man could plan. I was able to fast like this, without a crumb of food or a drop of liquid, only because God wanted me to. It was undertaken out of obedience to his command, not as a sacrifice in a bid to please him. *"To obey is better than sacrifice." 1 Samuel 15:22.*

Time quickly passed. On 11 February I was interrogated again. I'd become so weak that I had to be carried into the interrogation room by a fellow prisoner. My eyes were tightly shut and I just lay on the floor, motionless.

The officers asked me several questions but I didn't open my mouth. They thought I was pretending so started whipping me with a leather whip.

The prisoner who had carried me there jumped to his feet and protested, "From the day Yun entered prison he has suffered severe pains in his head and chest. He hasn't eaten anything for more than ten days." There was nothing my persecutors could do except order me to be carried back to my cell.

All the other prisoners in my cell witnessed these events. They saw that I didn't eat or drink a thing. Most of the time I just lay down in the corner of the cell and said nothing. My hands were tightly manacled for much of the time. The prisoners started to wonder how I could continue to live without eating or drinking anything. As the days and weeks passed my fellow prisoners started to discuss among themselves, "What does this man's life stand for?"

My body was getting smaller and weaker, but my spirit was enlarged and strong.

From 25 January to 2 March 1984, I had not eaten or drunk anything.

On the evening of the 38th day of my fast, the devil tempted me, "Yun, Jesus fasted 40 days. How can you as a servant do more than the Master? Are you going to fast longer than Jesus? Will you try to outdo your Master?" Suddenly dark clouds filled my heart. I had never experienced such desperation. I was in an intense spiritual battle.

It was as if thousands of demons surrounded me and attacked me with all their strength. I felt discouraged and hopeless. I was so weak in my body and mind that I even contemplated suicide. I hadn't spoken for so long that when I tried to pray out loud I discovered my voice had become a faint whisper. I asked, "God, what shall I do?" At that time the Lord didn't say anything to me, but I knew he was watching over me. I asked, "Lord Jesus, why are you allowing me to be buffeted like this? Please receive my spirit."

After a long night of struggle I again came before the Lord. He told me, *"I know your deeds. See, I have placed before you an open door that no one can shut. I know that you have little strength, yet you have kept my word and have not denied my name."* Revelation 3:8.

When I heard these words my heart was filled with joy! I felt like a little boy whose father has taken a stand for him against bullies. "Yes, Lord, you know my deeds!" I cried.

God's voice impacted me like thunder from heaven. My tears burst forth. That moment I had a powerful vision. I saw a series of iron gates open, one after another.

A multitude of men and women from various nationalities, arrayed in beautiful colourful clothing, were worshipping together before the Lord. My heart filled with light and strength. God gave me a joyful spirit. In the vision I sang to the Lord with a loud voice, *"I will praise the Lord all my life; I will sing praise to my God as long as I live."* Psalm 146:2.

The vision continued and I saw my life as a boy flash in

front of me. It was like a curtain being pulled back and I clearly saw that from birth God had called me to himself.

In the vision I exclaimed, "Lord, I don't have any chance to go out and preach the gospel. Even if you opened the gates of the prison this very moment, I'm so weak that I couldn't even crawl out of the door."

But the Lord revealed his will to me through two Scriptures that I hadn't paid special notice to before this time, *"For God's gifts and his call are irrevocable"*, Romans 11:29, and *"I tell you the truth, anyone who has faith in me will do what I have been doing. He will do even greater things than these, because I am going to the Father." John 14:12.*

The Lord released the pain in my heart and dispelled the darkness from my soul. Like living water welling up inside me, a spirit of joy filled my heart.

I felt I had passed through the valley of death. The Lord had sustained me.

I continued to fast.

The devil continued to put many bad thoughts into my mind. He asked me, "Who will take care of your family when you die? Where is your God? Has he forsaken you and left you to die?" I meditated on God's Word to counteract these attacks, such as Micah 7:8–9,

Do not gloat over me, my enemy!
Though I have fallen, I will rise.
Though I sit in darkness,
The Lord will be my light.

Because I have sinned against him,
I will bear the Lord's wrath,
Until he pleads my case
And establishes my right.

He will bring me out into the light;
I will see his righteousness.

*   *   *

DELING: After my husband was arrested there were many brothers and sisters who helped me every day. Of course I had the burden and the pain of having my husband imprisoned while I was pregnant, but the believers eased the weight of my burden and it wasn't a terribly dark experience for me. The unbelievers in our village constantly tried to put me down but I paid no attention to them.

Yun was brought back from Wuyang to Nanyang in a van. He was tortured at the local police station for eight months. All the reports we received indicated that his sentence was going to be one of two things: execution or life in prison. Even Yun's own brother said his crimes were so severe that he would be executed.

The believers outside the prison heard that Yun was suffering terribly, and that he had taken a stand of uncompromising trust in the Lord. Some people who were allowed to visit their relatives in prison passed on rumours to us about a miracle man inside the facility who lived without eating. Many people around town were talking about this strange event.

Thousands of house church Christians continued to pray and fast for my husband day and night. Meanwhile the churches continued to grow. Great miracles and signs and wonders took place regularly, causing thousands to be added to the body of Christ.

The devil tried to tempt me through my relatives. The wife of my elder brother came to my house and advised me to divorce Yun and find another man while I was still young. Others also placed pressure on me to divorce him, especially when it was believed he would be put to death anyway.

I refused to listen to them.

Many Chinese preachers have been forsaken by their wives while they were in prison for the gospel. One brother, Li, was sentenced to many years in prison. The moment the sentence was read out in the courtroom his wife stood up and shouted, "I divorce this man!"

I didn't want to do such a thing.

CHAPTER TEN

THE FIERY TRIAL

"We are hard pressed on every side, but not crushed; perplexed, but not in despair; persecuted, but not abandoned; struck down, but not destroyed. We always carry around in our body the death of Jesus, so that the life of Jesus may also be revealed in our body." 2 Corinthians 4:8–10.

During the fast I was very weak in my body, yet my spirit was alert and I continued to trust in the Lord. I knew that his grace was sufficient for me.

Because of what God had told me, I kept fasting longer than 40 days. I continued to pray constantly and sought God's forgiveness and mercy for my family, our church, our country, and for myself. I often quoted Psalm 123:1–2, *"I lift up my eyes to you, to you whose throne is in heaven. As the eyes of slaves look to the hand of their master, as the eyes of a maid look to the hand of her mistress, so our eyes look to the Lord our God, till he shows us his mercy."*

In this way, God accepted my heart's desire to continue to fast and pray. I entered into a very intense spiritual war, the kind of which I'd never experienced before.

Let me take a moment to explain what it's like when I receive a dream or vision from the Lord. These don't happen

frequently, but usually only when there is something important or urgent God wants to impress on me. All the visions
I've received are very short, often lasting just a second or
two. Often a picture or scene flashes into my spirit and mind,
yet it is so vivid and real I know it's from the Lord.

As Christians we are not to live by any vision or dream,
nor should we seek after them. We must only live by the
Word of God and seek the face of Jesus. But we should also
be open to allow the Lord to speak to us in these ways if this
is how he wants to. Any vision or dream we receive needs to
be carefully weighed against the Scriptures, as nothing from
God will ever contradict his Word.

God spoke to people through dreams and visions all the
way through both the Old and New Testaments. In these end
times the Bible declares, *"I will pour out my Spirit on all people.
Your sons and daughters will prophesy, your old men will dream
dreams; your young men will see visions." Joel 2:28.*

Out of the various dreams and visions the Lord has given
me over the years, only once or twice have I received a vision
that I saw with my eyes open – an actual scene that was
visible to my eye and not just an inward impression. One
such vision happened on the 40th night of my fast.

I saw a great yellow sandstorm that had been whipped
up from the desert. It carried a swarm of millions of poisonous hornets, vipers, scorpions and centipedes. The wind
lifted the roof off my house. The foundations of my home
stood firm, even though the roof was lifted off and the
walls cracked. The poisonous creatures started to attack
me.

At that moment, in my vision, I turned around and saw a
naked prostitute. She opened her shirt to expose herself, and
called out for me to come to her for refuge. I was confused.
On one hand I longed to flee from the painful creatures that

were stinging me, yet I didn't want to run into the arms of a prostitute.

I wondered what I should do. Suddenly, in my vision, my mother appeared in front of me. Her face was shining and peaceful. She lovingly said, "My son, lie down quickly." She gave me a large loaf of bread and instructed, "Son, eat it immediately."

Those thousands and thousands of hornets, snakes, scorpions and centipedes continued to attack my body. I couldn't stand the pain any longer and shouted, "Lord, help me!" My own voice awakened me from the vision. I found it was already midnight and I was still in the prison cell.

The experience was so real to me that I could hardly believe it had only been a vision.

Later that night after I had gone to sleep I received another dream from the Lord. This one was brief and I didn't comprehend its meaning. I saw myself carried away to a white-walled room. White sheets surrounded me. A man dressed in white clothes told me, "Stretch your hand out on the sheet." When I did so, a red bloody handprint appeared on the sheet. I didn't understand how it got there because there was no ink or anything else on my hand.

When I woke I couldn't figure out what this dream meant, but I knew the Lord would show me in due time.

I put my hand on Brother Li, who was next to me in the cell. I whispered, "Tomorrow I'm going to have another trial and I will suffer more for Jesus. Please pray for me." Brother Li mumbled something and fell back to sleep.

At about 9 a.m. the next morning I heard a voice calling, "Bring Yun out!" The steel hinges on our cell door creaked open.

Brother Li carried me to the interrogation room because I was too weak to walk. Li was a new Christian. Before he came to the Lord he was known as a violent man and a ruth-less robber. He was assigned to watch me closely, and to report everything I did to the guards. I knew the government had placed Li in my cell as an informant.

After living with me for some time he realized I was just a Christian pastor. He saw the consistency of my life and wit-nessed God's sustaining power during my fast. He saw that I lived what I taught and was not a criminal. One day as Li carried me back to the cell he leaned forward and whispered, "I now believe in your Jesus." He became my very dear brother.

Before the interrogation began I sensed the Lord was standing beside me and was my strength and joy, as the Psalmist wrote, *"I have set the Lord always before me. Because he is at my right hand, I shall not be shaken. Therefore my heart is glad and my tongue rejoices; my body also will rest secure."* Psalm 16:8–9.

The more I meditated on God's grace the more faith I received.

As Brother Li carried me he prayed under his breath, for I had told him a great trial awaited me. The officers directed him to place me on the ground. They told Brother Li to sit down and wait.

That day two new officers came to interrogate me. I refused to talk. I just closed my eyes and lay down. One of the men kicked me and shouted, "Yun, you will speak today!" The other officer forced my eyelids open and said, "Look around, Yun! We have methods to deal with people like you. If you don't want to speak we'll make you!"

This time they had brought various instruments of torture with them, including whips and chains.

Another officer approached me with an electric baton. He turned the voltage up to the highest level and struck my face, head and various parts of my body with it. Immediately my body was filled with overwhelming agony, as if a thousand arrows had pierced my heart.

The Holy Spirit encouraged me with three Scriptures from the Bible: *"He was oppressed and afflicted, yet he did not open his mouth; he was led like a lamb to the slaughter, and as a sheep before her shearers is silent, so he did not open his mouth."* Isaiah 53:7.

"To this you were called, because Christ suffered for you, leaving you an example, that you should follow in his steps." 1 Peter 2:21.

"Blessed is the man who perseveres under trial, because when he has stood the test, he will receive the crown of life that God has promised to those who love him." James 1:12.

By meditating on the Word of God, the Lord strengthened me to endure. I realized any suffering I was to go through was nothing compared to what Jesus had suffered for me, and that no pain I could ever experience was beyond the understanding and compassion of the Lord Jesus. *"For we do not have a high priest who is unable to sympathize with our weaknesses, but we have one who has been tempted in every way, just as we are — yet was without sin."* Hebrews 4:15.

The Lord didn't allow me to feel as much pain as I should have. The officers stood on my hands and my feet, electrocuting me again and again. They pulled my eyelids, lips, ears and other body parts to humiliate me.

I still refused to speak. I was a half-dead pile of skin and bones lying motionless on the cold cement floor.

Realizing their approach wasn't working, one officer suddenly changed his attitude and adopted a "silk glove" method. He said, "Stop! Wait a minute! Yun, I'll give you another chance. This day, if you admit your crimes against the government, we'll release you if you agree to attend a Three-Self Church. We can even let you become the Chairman of the regional branch of the Three-Self Patriotic

Movement! We'll stop investigating your previous crimes and will forgive you."

He kicked me again and asked, "Yun, did you hear what I said? Do you accept my offer? Answer me immediately!"

Before I opened my mouth to answer, I was reminded of the vision of the prostitute trying to lure me to safety.

Suddenly my spirit was taken away from my body and I saw the vision again of the snakes, scorpions, hornets and centipedes that had attacked and almost killed me as I lay on the ground. I realized why God had shown me the vision the previous night.

The officers tried brutality, then seduction, in an attempt to conquer me, but the Lord enabled me to repel their efforts.

Seeing their methods were not producing the desired results, they instructed Brother Li to carry me to the prison's medical clinic.

A short, fat man dressed in white entered the room and told the four guards who had accompanied me, "Please leave me alone as I examine Yun." After they left the room the doctor told me, "Yun, if you won't talk, I can make you talk." He smiled with an evil grin. "This needle will help cure you of your problem. It will make you talk."

The guards were called back in. They spread my hands and feet and held me down on the bed. Then they separated my fingers and held them palm-down on a wooden board. The doctor took a large needle, labelled number 6, from his bag. Starting with my left thumb, he jabbed the needle under my fingernails one at a time.

I can't describe how I felt. It was the most excruciating agony I've ever experienced. Intense pain shot through my entire body. I couldn't help but cry out. Lapsing between consciousness and unconsciousness, I couldn't tell if I was in my body or separate from my body.

By the time the doctor reached my middle finger the Lord mercifully allowed me to faint and not feel the pain being inflicted on me.

When I awoke I had no feeling in either of my hands or fingers. I felt a terrible surging pain running through my entire body. Despite the cold weather I was covered in sweat from head to toe. I understood the dream I'd received from God of my red handprints on the white sheets.

Later on Brother Li told me he didn't know what had happened. Forced to wait outside at the other end of the corridor, he'd heard the doctor shout, as he started to torture me, "Yun, take your stubborn mind and go and see your God!"

When Brother Li heard me scream like a wounded animal he could do nothing but pray for me, so he bowed his head and asked God to preserve my life.

After I returned to the cell the other prisoners asked what was wrong with me. Brother Li fell on his face and sobbed uncontrollably. When he managed to compose himself he explained what had taken place. They all felt pity for me. Even those hardened criminals had tears in their eyes when they heard what had happened.

Thank God he protected and preserved me through these trials. I knew that God was using the wrath of evil men to accomplish his purposes in me, to break down my self-centredness and my stubbornness. He taught me how to wait on him, how to patiently endure hardship, and how to love the family of God in a more real way.

After these tortures I felt just like David described in Psalm 102:4–5, *"My heart is blighted and withered like grass; I forget to eat my food. Because of my loud groaning I am reduced to skin and bones."*

Even though the officers and doctor had stabbed me, kicked me, and electrocuted me, they didn't get what they wanted. They were furious. After a few days they devised a new plan. One morning I heard the prison gates open. One of the men in my cell climbed to the window and looked out. He saw a few well-dressed PSB officers enter. They ordered the guards, "Bring Yun out!"

They ordered Brother Li to wrap my blanket around me and carry me out. A motor-tricycle with a sidecar was outside the prison gate, waiting to take me to the Nanyang Hospital, where a doctor examined me and concluded, "Yun does not have any serious medical problems except that he's badly dehydrated. We must give him an IV, so fluids can enter his body."

A nurse prepared two bottles of saline liquid for the IV. I closed my eyes and heard cameras clicking as the nurse inspected my arm. The doctor told the nurse, "He's too thin to find a vein. We'll just have to stab the needle into his arm." The doctors and nurses were acting for the reporters and cameramen who'd been called in to witness this staged performance.

They still couldn't find my vein so they made me lie down on a bed in the hallway. Many people walked past me and despised me. *"All who see me mock me; they hurl insults, shaking their heads: 'He trusts in the Lord; let the Lord rescue him. Let him deliver him, since he delights in him.'" Psalm 22:7–8.*

I was a pitiful and dreadful sight. Like the Apostle Paul said, *"We have been made a spectacle to the whole universe, to angels as well as to men. . . . Up to this moment we have become the scum of the earth, the refuse of the world." 1 Corinthians 4:9,13.*

Finally the nurse stabbed the needle into my arm muscle because she was frustrated at not being able to find a vein. The reporters were waiting and the medical staff had grown flustered by the delay. Two bottles were emptied into the muscle tissue of my arm. Immediately it swelled up and I was in great agony.

The doctors and nurses didn't care if I lived or died. They just did the performance for the newspapers to "prove" that the state had been concerned for me. The authorities were certain I would soon die and wanted to show they had tried to "help" me.

I was returned to the prison, where another session awaited me in the interrogation room. I closed my eyes but the officers again forced my eyelids open with their fingers. They played with me and mocked me, but they couldn't make me speak.

Two officers took me back to my cell. They threw me onto the cement floor, took away my blanket, and used two electric batons to electrocute and beat me again.

It was a dark hour for me.

My fellow prisoners had no pity on me this time. Earlier that day, while I was being tortured, prison officers had made a speech to my cell mates, telling them, "Yun is an evil man, an anti-government criminal. He knows he has committed serious crimes, so now he is pretending to be crazy. But we realize his plan. He has started a hunger strike to make our government look bad. But today the hospital has diagnosed no sickness, so from this day on we shall treat him according to his own devices. You prisoners need to be careful of this counter-revolutionary. His presence in your cell has brought bad luck to you all. You should separate yourself from Yun and report if you see something bad in him. Whoever does this the best will be rewarded with a more lenient sentence."

In this way the other prisoners (except Brother Li) were taught to hate me, so that they could be rewarded.

Among the other men in my cell were some serving life

sentences, and others sentenced to between ten and twenty years. They had great hatred in their hearts, and the offer of leniency was too much of a reward for them to ignore.

From that moment on it was difficult for me just to stay alive in the cell. If not for God's mercy and protection, I would surely have died.

There were now fifteen or sixteen prisoners in our small cell. They all did their excrement in the same toilet. They took my bedding and soaked it in the human waste. The smell was terrible.

The cell leader, who had been appointed by the guards, came and deliberately urinated on my face, and urged the others to do the same. So all the prisoners – except Brother Li – constantly urinated on me, laughing and mocking me as they did so. This was a great humiliation, but I was too weak to protest. I suffered in my heart, but I endured silently.

I thought of the words from 1 Peter 2:23, *"When they hurled their insults at him, he did not retaliate; when he suffered, he made no threats. Instead, he entrusted himself to him who judges justly."*

I also meditated on the promise of Jesus, *"Blessed are you when men hate you, when they exclude you and insult you and reject your name as evil, because of the Son of Man. Rejoice in that day and leap for joy, because great is your reward in heaven."* Luke 6:22–23.

The guards also started to treat the other prisoners more cruelly. In this way the men hated me even more, believing it was my fault their conditions were worsening.

Every day at a set time the other prisoners were allowed out to exercise in the yard. One afternoon I was also carried to the yard, where the guards instructed the men to throw me into a septic tank where the waste of all the prisoners was collected.

The guards urinated on me and tried to force me to pass

waste. But of course I hadn't eaten for so long that this was impossible. I was fading away almost to nothing. At that time I only weighed about 30 kg (66 pounds).

The guards electrocuted me again and again, and forced me to crawl like a dog through the human faeces. They kicked me with their steel-capped boots, forcing me to roll over into the excrement.

They even used their electric batons to stab me inside my mouth. I cannot easily describe the pain this caused. I thought my brain was going to explode. My mind and body shake even today when I think about those experiences. I longed to die to escape the pain.

Instead of trying to use my own words to describe how I felt, let me simply quote the words of the Psalmist, *"Many bulls surround me; strong bulls of Bashan encircle me. Roaring lions tearing their prey open their mouths wide against me. I am poured out like water, and all my bones are out of joint. My heart has turned to wax; it has melted away within me. My strength is dried up like a potsherd, and my tongue sticks to the roof of my mouth; you lay me in the dust of death." Psalm 22:12–15.*

I finally lost consciousness.

All the other prisoners witnessed these events. The guards wanted them to mock and humiliate me. Some did, but others couldn't handle the scene and wept bitterly.

My brother-in-law was in the prison at the same time as me, in a different cell. When he saw my condition, he ran out from the crowd and tried to help me. The guards electrocuted and kicked him, shouting, "Who do you think you are? Get out of here!" As soon as the current hit his body he collapsed on the ground.

By March 1984, the long winter was coming to an end and the snow had stopped falling, although the early mornings were still cold. I was shivering in the cold wind because I wore only rags and torn clothes that had been given to me by the other prisoners.

One morning the time came for the prisoners to go to the toilet, and they all lined up. I was so weak that I couldn't stand, so the guards made me lean against the wall.

I recalled the night I was arrested, when Brother Zhang, Brother Zhen and the other co-workers had lovingly washed my feet. I remembered the beautiful scarf Zhang gave to me, saying, "This scarf will keep you warm from the cold."

I felt as if my dear brothers and sisters were always with me, even in prison. I took great comfort as I thought about their sweet fellowship. I still had the scarf Brother Zhang had given me. I wrapped it around my waist to keep warm. In this way I felt I was still bound together with the believers.

That day I was left alone alongside the wall until sunset. Then Brother Li was told to pick me up and carry me back to the cell. When I entered I found the guards had not finished with me yet. They tore the scarf from around my waist. I had a small porcelain teacup from my family, which I had tied to the scarf. Many small blue crosses were painted on the teacup. It had given me strength for a long time. It reminded me of the cross of Jesus and also of my family's love.

The prisoners untied the teacup and threw it into the urinal. They also threw my scarf into the human excrement.

I felt such pain and anger. Struggling with all my strength, I crawled into the waste to retrieve my teacup. The prisoners urinated on my cup and on my hands. I grabbed my teacup and hugged it closely to my chest. I was so angry that they had tried to take away the last remaining earthly possession that was precious to me.

I wanted to strike back at them with my words, but the Lord stopped me and told me, *"Do not repay anyone evil for evil. . . . Do not take revenge, my friends, but leave room for God's wrath. . . . Do not be overcome by evil, but overcome evil with good." Romans 12:17, 19,21.*

I repented for the way I felt. I started to bless my fellow prisoners, especially those who insulted me the worst.

Less than two days later, God's wrath fell upon my cell mates and they started to itch from scabies. Their skin itched all over, so badly that it drove them crazy.

Brother Li and I were the only prisoners spared. Even though I had lain in human waste and been subjected to the vilest unsanitary conditions, the Lord made sure I wasn't afflicted by this disease.

The guards took every opportunity to watch me for a sign of weakness, but they saw I just lay there on my back and said and did nothing.

The prison authorities discovered that Brother Li had been secretly taking care of me in many ways. He had lovingly prevented the other prisoners from doing more harm to me, and had encouraged them to treat me kindly. Consequently, Brother Li was transferred to another cell. Now I was alone, without the fellowship of any other believers.

The guards took me and again threw me into the urinal. The prisoners urinated on my face. I wanted to cry out. Now I felt so alone. *"Scorn has broken my heart and has left me helpless; I looked for sympathy, but there was none, for comforters, but I found none." Psalm 69:20.*

The next morning the other prisoners awoke to find their bodies covered with red welts! They had a condition known as pustule. They couldn't bear the irritations. They scratched their welts until pus oozed out.

The afflicted prisoners couldn't sleep or lie down because they were so tormented by their need to itch.

The guards came to examine me. They tore off my under-garments to see if I had the disease. They thought the disease had originated from me because I'd spent so much time lying in human waste. They found I was the only prisoner free of the affliction!

My cell mates left me alone for a while and concentrated on relieving their discomfort. The leader of the cell was the most badly infected. His whole body was covered in spots, even his face. The other prisoners were afraid to go near him.

Because I was disease free, my cell mates moved my bed from next to the urinal to alongside the cell leader, to increase my chances of catching the parasites from him. It infuriated the prisoners and the guards that I wasn't suffer-ing the same affliction as the others.

One cell mate named Yu had watched me closely for many weeks. He came to me and lovingly covered my body with a blanket and was kind to me. He was a God-given replace-ment for Brother Li.

One night Yu came over to cover me. I reached out and took hold of his arm. I was so weak that my voice was almost unintelligible. He lowered his head to hear my whisper, "Yu, you must receive Jesus Christ as your Lord and Saviour." Right then, Yu silently received the Lord's salvation.

The leader of the cell, who had suffered so much from the disease, hated me even more when he saw I'd escaped the affliction. He took my blanket and used it for himself. In its place, he wrapped me in his own disease-ridden blanket, covered in blood, dirt and pus that had oozed from his sores. But the Lord protected me, and I still did not contract the disease.

The devil had attacked and threatened me through many evil men, but the Holy Spirit had made me strong in Jesus, even though my outer body was almost totally destroyed. My enemies had all been confounded.

The prisoners discussed among themselves how much longer I would live. Some said, "He will die within three days." Others said, "He will surely not even last tonight. I bet you he will die by the morning. If he survives the night I'll give you my *mantou*."

In this way they gambled with each other, but I didn't die. Those who gamble against God's servants will surely lose! I had placed myself in the hands of the Lord of justice. I was no longer living by my own strength, but by the grace of God.

The PSB were unable to extract any confession from my mouth to use against me. They were afraid that if I died they would have to give an account to the provincial authorities, so they were nervous.

The prison arranged for several nurses from the hospital to come. They used a tool to open my mouth and a bottle to force-feed soup to me, but I refused to swallow and let it run down onto the floor. Photographers were present. They took pictures as "evidence" the authorities had done everything they could to save me.

When the guards saw that I let the soup run down to the floor they mocked me and said, "Yun, we no longer care if you live or die. We couldn't care less. We've done everything possible to help you. You thought your hunger strike would affect our government, but now we hope that you die. When you die, it will be announced as suicide. We'll take your body and cremate it, and we'll be glad to be rid of you, you stubborn man."

CHAPTER ELEVEN

THE END OF THE FAST

During the wave of intense persecution in Henan, from the second half of 1983 to June 1984, our church encountered severe difficulties. Hundreds of workers were arrested.

I thank God that he gave me a mother who prays without ceasing. My mother prayed every morning and evening for the church and the leadership. She and the other believers cried out for God's mercy and revival, because the shepherds had been struck and the sheep were scattered.

In the evening of 1 April 1984, while kneeling in prayer, my mother saw a vision. It was very powerful to her, because at the time she was the midwife in our village.

In her vision a young woman was having a difficult time giving birth. Because she was malnourished, she was giving birth prematurely at seven months. A tiny baby boy was born. The girl's family and the midwife said, "This baby will not survive." So they placed the baby in a linen bag and intended to throw it away.

In the vision my mother walked forward and said, "Let me have a look inside the bag." She turned to the girl and assured her, "Your baby will not die." After she spoke, the baby transformed and became me. My mother was shocked and woke from the vision. She was overcome with emotion and cried aloud, "Father God, have mercy on my son!"

Then a very clear voice spoke to her: "Your son will not die."

Since the day I was put in prison, many friends and family members not only prayed for me, but they had tried to find out information from the PSB about my condition. No one was allowed to visit me.

They were told there was no chance I would live. Some were told I'd been sentenced to death, others that I would receive a life sentence. The news reached the ears of my wife and mother.

Deling's sister-in-law told her, "Go home to your mother and marry someone else as soon as possible. There's no chance Yun will ever come back home to you."

But thankfully the Lord helped my dear wife resist these temptations. She decided to stand firm and faithfully committed herself to the Lord.

At this time my wife received a dream, the very same night my mother received the promise that I wouldn't die.

In my wife's dream, she saw herself and my mother visiting me in prison. I was so skinny yet strong in the Lord's grace. I was full of joy and peace. In the dream I gave her a key. I firmly told her, "This key can open every door!" When Deling woke up she immediately realized that the Lord Jesus wanted her to use prayer to open every door of difficulty.

The next morning my mother and wife shared the vision and dream they had received. They were greatly strengthened in their faith. They knelt together and gave thanks to the Lord. They also shared the dream and vision with some of the other believers.

At that time there was just one church leader – Brother

Fong – who was not in prison. He visited my home and prayed all night, crying out to God for mercy and revival. The next day he told my family, "It's time to visit Yun in prison."

In China people cannot just visit prisoners whenever they like. They can go only when they receive an official invitation from the prison authorities.

The very next day my wife Deling received an invitation from the prison. This was no surprise to anyone, because my family had already received the invitation from the Lord!

More than 70 days had passed, and I hadn't eaten any food or drunk any water in all that time. Since the day I was imprisoned I hadn't received a single word from my family or my church.

My cell mates, despite their skin disease, didn't stop torturing me. I nearly believed the words from their mouths that I was going to die. Darkness and torment pressed against me. At that time I felt that an angel of the Lord surrounded me with his strength and kept me from dying.

On the 75th day of my fast, around 3 a.m., a brilliant light flooded my cell. In a vision I saw myself riding a bicycle along a road. On the handlebars of the bicycle sat a lovely seven-year-old boy named Xiao Shen. I knew this boy before I'd been arrested. Both his parents love Jesus.

In my vision, Xiao Shen said, "Uncle, let me sing a song for you!" He sang, *"Jesus said 'I am the way, the truth, the life. No one comes to the Father except through me.'"* John 14:6. I sang with him, louder and louder. I was full of joy! I felt as free as a bird!

In my vision I saw my body was still lying in the cell, but I was able to see through the prison walls to the outside world. I saw many different people with various skin colours. They came from numerous nationalities and diverse cultures. Some were kneeling and some standing. They all had their hands raised in prayer.

I tried to walk out and meet them, but suddenly the scorpions, hornets, snakes and horrible creatures came and attacked me again.

I was knocked to the ground. Slowly I opened my eyes and found I was cradled in my mother's arms. She held me tightly. My wife, sisters, and brothers were all grasping my hand and weeping out loud. I told them, "Jesus is the way, the truth and the life."

Then I awoke from my vision.

During the long fast, my days were full of struggle, miracles, dreams, visions, and revelation from the Lord. I experienced his strength every day. Although I had no Bible, I meditated on his Word constantly from the Scriptures I had memorized.

Although men tried every way possible to destroy me, they did not succeed. Now they tried another way. The authorities invited my family to the prison to try to get them to convince me to eat and talk. They intended to listen closely to what I said, hoping to gather a confession or some information they could use against me.

On 6 April 1984, the PSB sent officers to my home, instructing my mother and wife what they should say to persuade me to eat and talk. But the Lord had already warned my mother and wife, *"They come to you in sheep's clothing, but inwardly they are ferocious wolves." Matthew 7:15.*

The next morning, at eight o'clock on 7 April, my mother, wife, and six other relatives and co-workers arrived at the front gate of the Nanyang prison. The gatekeeper made them wait while the guards ordered Brother Yu to carry me to the interrogation room again. They tried to trick me, saying, "Yun, this is again your big opportunity. If you'll open your mouth and speak, all of this can be settled once and for all."

When I refused to answer them they again madly beat me with a whip and shocked me with an electric baton. I lost consciousness.

When I came to, I felt a very warm sensation flowing over my body, as if I was lying on a soft bed. I didn't know if I was alive or dead, awake or asleep. I felt warmth against my face as if someone was gently and lovingly caressing me.

I thought I was having a vision, but when I opened my eyes I saw I was in the arms of my mother! Beads of warm tears awakened me and her loving arms tightly comforted me. I saw my mother was in great anguish, as if a knife had cut into her heart.

Deling stood beside her. She couldn't believe her eyes at my physical condition. My wife spoke to my sister and said, "I tell you, this is not him. This is definitely not my husband!"

I was just a pile of skin and bones. Much of my hair had fallen out from being beaten and kicked. My ears had shrivelled. I had grown an unkempt beard and had messy hair. The patches of hair that remained were knotted together from my own dried blood. My whole appearance had changed because of the electric shock therapy.

My own wife could not even recognize me.

My mother knew it was me after she identified my birthmark. She wept aloud and cried, "This is my son! Lord, have mercy on us!"

When my wife realized this tiny human frame in front of her truly was her husband she almost fainted.

Suddenly the Lord increased my strength. A great power came over me. It's difficult to explain, but I felt as if my spirit had become one with my Heavenly Father. The Lord commanded, "Speak! This is your time!"

When I was about to open my mouth to speak, my sister's hand closed it. She knew the guards were listening. She knew I hadn't tasted food or water for more than 70 days, and was afraid I would receive more torture if I spoke.

I pushed my sister's hand away and cried out, "*Do not put your trust in princes, in mortal men, who cannot save.*" Psalm 146:3. "*It is better to take refuge in the Lord than to trust in princes.*" Psalm 118:9.

In the meantime I tightly gripped the hands of Brother Fong and fixed my gaze on him. I told him, "Brother, riches and honour cannot corrupt us. Threats and violence cannot affect us. Poverty and obscurity cannot divert our path. Be strong in God and look only upon the Lord Jesus Christ. My heavenly Father already told me you would come to visit me today."

The prison officers and guards didn't understand what was happening or what I was talking about. Everyone was weeping and wailing. When I tried to speak again my sister placed her hand over my mouth. I felt as if a great fire was locked in my bones, wanting to get out.

I held my mother's hand and told her, "Mother, your son is hungry! Mother, your son is thirsty! Mother, the autumn has ended and the cold winter has come. Why didn't you send any clothes to me?"

She wiped my tears and said, "Dear son, it's not because your mother doesn't love you. We sent you many clothes and things to eat, but none of them reached your hands. We asked other people to send you clothes and food, but the prison guards took them away too."

My family didn't understand that I wasn't referring to physical hunger and thirst. One of our co-workers heard me say I was hungry and thirsty, so she ran out of the prison to the nearest shop to buy some food and drink. I couldn't stop crying.

I spoke again, "Mother, I'm not hungry for earthly bread and water. I'm hungry for the souls of men. Mother, preach the gospel and save people, that is the only food that satisfies."

I cried out, *"My food is to do the will of him who sent me and to finish his work. Do you not say, 'Four months more and then the harvest'? I tell you, open your eyes and look at the fields! They are ripe for harvest."* John 4:34–35.

With tears in my eyes I said, "I've been fasting 74 days. This morning before dawn the Lord showed me in a vision that I would meet with you all. Dear mother, I was nearly beaten to death. If I die, I will die, but I will remain faithful to the Lord. Mother, did you bring the meat and blood of the Lamb?"

The sister returned from the shop with some crackers and a bottle of grape juice. When I saw this, I broke one cracker, blessed it, and handed it to my wife, mother, Brother Fong, and the other co-workers and relatives. From my broken heart I said, "This is the Lord's body, broken for you. Eat this in remembrance of him."

I then poured out some of the grape juice, "This cup is the blood of the Lord that was shed for us." Everyone bowed their heads and solemnly received the Lord's Supper.

This was my first food of any kind for 74 days. From 25 January to 7 April 1984, I ate and drank nothing.

I cried out loudly and held my loved ones. I said, "Mother, today may be the last time I take the Lord's Supper with you." I turned and kissed my wife. I told everyone, "My dear wife, mother, brothers and sisters, I will see you all in heaven."

Everyone burst into tears.

Brother Yun in China

My dear family, outside our house in Nanyang in 1993. I am holding Isaac, alongside my mother, little Yilin and Deling.

Two great gospel warriors in China: Xu Yongze, my dear brother and co-worker for more than twenty years, and his sister Deborah, on the Great Wall of China.

Zhengzhou Maximum Security Prison in Henan. This is the prison the Lord miraculously enabled me to escape from in 1997. In the background you can see two tall buildings with iron grills over the windows. The building on the right, second floor from the top, is where my cell was. During my escape, the Christian brothers ran to these windows and watched me walk across the courtyard and out of the front prison gate, the one with flags on it. A yellow taxi van picked me up and drove me to safety.

The front gate of the Zhengzhou Prison. When I escaped, these gates were standing open and I walked out!

My oldest sister hugged me and asked, "How can you leave your old mother and your young wife, to die for your own sake? Besides, your wife is pregnant. How can you be so cruel to her?"

My mother pleaded, "Son, your wife needs you. Your mother needs you. God's family needs you." She lowered her voice and whispered in my ear, "Listen to your mother. God has told me that you will not die. You must be strong and stay alive."

Under the Lord's protection we finished sharing with each other. The prison authorities seemed puzzled and confused. They heard our words but didn't understand what was happening.

I told my family, "Please fast and pray for me. I never became a Judas. I never denied the Lord or his people."

Then the officers returned to normal, as if they were waking from a dream. They banged their fists on the table and shouted, "What are you talking about? Enough! Get out!" The guards were ordered to take me back to my cell. My mother, wife and sister held onto me and wouldn't let me go, as the guards dragged me away.

My mother would rather have died than leave me in the hands of evil men, but they tore me from her like a pack of wolves attacking a defenceless sheep. Even in front of my family they beat me and ripped me away, pushing my elderly mother to the floor. They all wept bitterly, not knowing if they would ever see me again.

With a loud clang they slammed the iron prison gate. Even through the gate I could hear my mother crying out, "Son, remember your mother's words. You must stay alive! Stay alive for God!" I shouted back, "Mother, preach the gospel! Ask the churches to fast and pray for me!"

The guard slapped my face and took me back to my cell.

*   *   *

DELING: Everyone said my husband was going to be executed, but deep down I felt confident it was not the Lord's time for him to die. This may sound strange, but I didn't feel stressed and wasn't depressed at all because I never accepted that he would be put to death.

Actually, I believe it would have been far better for Yun to be killed than to spend his whole life in prison. If they shot him in the head at least it would be over in an instant and he'd be united with the Lord forever.

My husband was in prison and had fasted more than 70 days without food or water. The authorities were afraid he was going to die so they invited us to visit the prison, located in the centre of Nanyang City.

I was more than six months' pregnant and my pregnancy was showing already. I was excited to tell Yun that he was going to be a father. There had been absolutely no communication between us since he was arrested, so he didn't even know I had conceived.

It was April so the warmth of summer was already on the way. We arrived at the prison early in the morning. I rode on the back of a bicycle ridden by Yun's oldest sister. We met the other visitors outside the prison entrance. They had also come by bicycle. There were a total of eight of us.

We were told to wait in a room until he was brought to see us.

After some time a tiny figure was carried in. He was unconscious because he had been tortured just before we arrived. He looked like a little child. His ears had shrivelled to the size of raisins.

When we first saw him, none of us recognized him as Yun. We thought it was some kind of trick by the authorities. I declared, "This is not my husband!" Yun's sister protested, "There must be some mistake. This is not my brother!"

Only after Yun's mother saw his birthmark did she know it was truly her son. He was so little that he didn't even look like a human being. His whole body was covered with bruises, torture marks, dried blood and dirt. Most of his hair had been torn out. His face was gaunt. His eyes appeared larger than normal, and his mouth hung open, displaying yellow teeth. He was wearing filthy torn rags.

It was just unbelievable. I was in a state of shock. Indeed, I think we all were. My head started to feel light and I almost fainted.

Yun came to and spoke for the first time in many months. His voice was just a faint whisper that only his mother was close enough to hear. When we found out that it really was Yun we all cried. It was such an emotional time. He exclaimed, "Brothers and sisters, don't weep for me! Weep for the souls of men. Now, let us eat the body of our Lord and drink his blood."

A sister ran to a shop outside the prison to buy some crackers and juice so we could have the Lord's Supper. Yun told us he was going to be united with the Lord and so we should share the Lord's Supper together for the last time before he died.

We all wept and wailed loudly. It was just so unbelievable.

When we all left the prison, we were so overcome with emotion we sat down in a circle on the street in front of the entrance. We cried out to the Lord, "Father, God of justice and mercy, please forgive our nation. Have pity on us and on those who persecute your children. May they receive your salvation!"

There were many people passing us by on the street. When they heard us wailing, a crowd gathered and demanded to know what the matter was. Many people wept as we told them what we'd seen that day.

CHAPTER TWELVE

GOD GIVES ME A SON AND MANY BROTHERS

"But thanks be to God, who always leads us in triumphal procession in Christ and through us spreads everywhere the fragrance of the knowledge of him. For we are to God the aroma of Christ among those who are being saved and those who are perishing." 2 Corinthians 2:14–15.

After I was carried back to my cell, the guard kicked me and shouted, "How dare you speak and eat today after you have been quiet for so long? I will skin you alive! You wait and see!" He slammed the iron door shut as he left the cell.

The cell leader insulted me, "You are a fake! You pretended to be dying every day. I'm alive and well in prison even though I've killed and raped women. You came to the prison because you believe in Jesus and you're dying like a sick dog."

One of the other prisoners was a Muslim. He snarled at me, "How dare you preach Jesus against our nation's laws? You deserve to die. The heavenly law will judge pigs like you!"

All the prisoners knew I was very weak and needed to be carried everywhere I went. They hadn't heard me say one word for many weeks, but when I heard these insults the Holy Spirit came upon me. I stood to my feet, much to their amazement, and proclaimed in a loud voice: "Fellow prisoners, I have a message from my Lord. Please listen carefully!"

Everyone was astonished that I could stand and speak with such power and authority. I was just a bag of bones. They had been placing bets on when I would die, but now I was standing before them speaking with a loud voice!

I told them, "Friends, God sent me here especially for your sake. The day I entered this cell I told you I'm a pastor who believes in Jesus. The first night I sang to you and shared Jesus' salvation with you all. You have all closely watched me and you know I haven't taken a single grain of rice or one drop of water for 74 days. I ask you, over several thousand years of history, who has ever seen anyone do this for 74 days and live? Don't you realize this miracle is a demonstration of God's mighty power and his protection over me?

"Now my Lord has allowed me to stand before you to let you know that Jesus is the true and living God. How dare you continue in your sin, doing evil things! Friends, when the judgment day comes how do you plan to escape hell? Only Jesus can forgive you!

"This day the Lord has mercy on you and offers you an opportunity to repent and receive forgiveness of your sins. All of you should kneel down before Jesus Christ, confess your sins, and ask God to forgive you. How else will you escape the punishment of hell?"

After I spoke it was as though a bomb dropped on the men! They couldn't help themselves. The cell leader was the first to come and fall on his knees. He cried out, "Yun, what must I do to be saved?"

The other prisoners also knelt down, including the Muslim. They cried out in a loud voice, "What must we do to be saved? How can we be forgiven by God?" Every one of those sin-hardened men received the Lord Jesus Christ, repenting of their sins with many tears.

They also felt guilty for the way they had treated me. I forgave them in the same way that Joseph forgave his brothers. I encouraged them by saying, *"You intended to harm me, but God intended it for good to accomplish what is now being done, the saving of many lives."* Genesis 50:20.

Because we didn't have much water available, I used a few drops to baptize each one of them.

A prison guard in the hallway outside our cell heard the commotion and rushed to the door. He stood rooted to the floor for several minutes without saying a word, totally amazed at what he witnessed.

The entire atmosphere in the cell was drastically transformed. These sin-hardened men now had new tender hearts. Their language and behaviour totally changed. Previously hatred and selfishness reigned in cell number two. Now, joy and peace reigned.

For days the men walked around with tears in their eyes, amazed at how the Lord had poured out his mercy on them. When they were allowed into the yard they took every opportunity to share the gospel with prisoners from the other cells. In this way the gospel was preached throughout the prison and many repented and believed in the Lord!

By God's grace he now gave me a new job: to disciple the new believers in the prison!

*   *   *

At that time Brother Fu was about to be released from the prison. I wrote a message on a piece of toilet paper and asked him to deliver it to Deling. I challenged her, "What is happening to you is the way of the cross. Were you serious when you committed your life to him? Will you remain faithful to the Lord?" I wrote her a poem:

Our bodies are growing older and weaker
Our friends and relatives are fewer in number
The road we're travelling on is getting harder
But you should fully obey the will of the Lord
For you are his beloved child.

After our marriage Deling and I thought about having a baby, but at the time my name and photo was plastered everywhere by the police so we didn't get the chance to spend much time together. On one occasion before I was arrested I secretly sneaked home and during that visit my wife conceived.

Soon afterwards I was imprisoned.

One night in my cell I received a clear dream from the Lord. I saw my wife happily holding a baby boy. She came to me and gently asked, "What should we name our child?"

In my dream I took the baby from her arms and immediately a Scripture came to my mind, when Abraham named Isaac. In the dream I told my wife, "His name shall be Isaac." She smiled, and happily took the baby away.

When I woke up I couldn't fall asleep again. I kept thinking about what I had just seen.

The next morning, 19 April 1984, my family came to the prison to deliver the good news. A guard spoke to me frankly, "Yun, your wife has given birth to a baby boy. In a few days your family will hold a celebratory feast. Here is a pen and paper. Your wife wants you to name your son."

I immediately recalled the dream of the previous night. I thanked the guard and wrote, "His name shall be called Isaac." Then I penned the following words to my baby boy:

To my dear son Isaac,

When you were born your father was in prison because of the name of Jesus Christ. My son, I don't know if I will live to see you or not. People wish their children success. But your daddy only wishes you to follow and love the Lord Jesus. Isaac, always trust and obey the Lord and you shall grow up to be a man of God.

Your daddy.

The prison guard examined the note and said, "There is nothing written here relating to his case," so he took the pen and paper away and gave the message to my family.

*   *   *

DELING: A short time after our dramatic visit to Yun in prison, I gave birth to our son.

This was truly a miracle in itself. The midwife who helped me deliver Isaac said it was the first time she'd ever seen a woman give birth without pain. I'm not lying to say that I felt no pain whatsoever. It was a gracious gift of the Lord.

A few days before I gave birth I was told to go to the hospital and have an abortion. The government family planning office told me, "Your husband will never get out of prison. Do yourself a favour and don't let this child come into the world." They ordered me to return a few days later and they would give me an abortion.

I was terrified. Of course there was no way I would allow an abortion, but if I didn't go back to the clinic they would search for me and forcibly abort my baby.

I shared my burden with my mother and with the Christian brothers and sisters. They prayed earnestly, asking God to help me in my predicament. The Lord answered their prayers! Suddenly I gave birth, two months' early, before the government had the chance to conduct an abortion on me! When the family planning office came to see why I hadn't come to the clinic on the appointed day, there I was, sitting in a chair holding my precious baby! There was nothing they could do about it!

A note was sent to the prison notifying Yun of the birth. He wrote back, "His name shall be called Isaac." The Lord had shown him in a dream what to name our baby boy.

This time was very difficult. We faced severe poverty. The police came to our home and confiscated everything of value: pots, pans, furniture, even our clothing. Yun's mother and I had no choice but to work in the fields, otherwise we would have starved. She was already over 60 years old but was fit and strong.

Just one week after I'd given birth to Isaac, some loving brothers and sisters travelled more than 100 kilometres to help my mother-in-law and me to work in the fields. In our area only a few old ladies worked outside. It was a job for the young and the strong. But when these helpers visited my home they saw Yun's mother working in the fields every day, struggling under the load.

These friends gathered the wheat and tied it together for us, then left it on the side of the fields rather than bringing it to our storehouse. After they left a storm developed, so Yun's mother rushed outside to bring in the wheat before the rain arrived.

As it thundered, the large wooden cart Yun's mother was putting the wheat into toppled over and pinned her to the ground. One of her arms and one of her legs were stuck under the weight of the heavy load. She was trapped in a muddy ditch for a long time, soaked by the driving rain. I was inside with my newborn baby and had no idea what had happened.

Yun's mother suffered a broken arm and a badly injured thigh.

It was a complete disaster. I could hardly take any more. My husband was in prison, most of my friends and relatives had forsaken me, I was struggling with a newborn baby, and now Yun's mother was badly injured.

One day I became dizzy and fainted in the field out of sheer exhaustion. After a long time I came to and started to weep as I realized my own family had disowned me, and my sister-in-law and neighbours had insulted me. I looked up into the sky and began to sing Psalm 123, "I lift up my eyes to you, to you whose throne is in heaven . . . our eyes look to the Lord our God, till he shows us his mercy. Have mercy on us, O Lord, have mercy on us, for we have endured much contempt. We have endured much ridicule from the proud, much contempt from the arrogant."

*   *   *

YUN: During this season of persecution nine co-workers from our church and I had been thrown into prison. Many Christian families had their homes searched and were fined large amounts of money for having Bibles or other Christian material.

Many believers were frightened, but the Holy Spirit soothed their fears and gave new direction to the church. A fresh breeze of revival swept through. Prayer meetings lasted all night and many sleeping souls were awakened. Signs and wonders were commonplace. Many brought sick people to the house churches and they were healed. Those with mental illnesses and the demon-possessed received complete deliverance and healing in Jesus' name.

The Christians still in prison found their witness was empowered because of the many fervent prayers for us. Consequently, countless prisoners came to know the Lord.

Many government officials and Communist Party members received Jesus at that time. Some even started to witness boldly for the Lord.

There is one village called "Iron Buddhist Temple" – about 10 kilometres from my home. Sister Zhi lived in that village.

Her husband, a wealthy man, was not a believer. In fact, he worshipped idols and wouldn't listen to the advice of his wife to forsake false gods and worship Jesus. Their son suffered from a terminal illness that no doctor could treat.

This wealthy man, who had relatives in high government positions, asked the believers to come to his house and hold a prayer meeting for his son. Dozens of Christians attended. The same night, Brother Fong rode a bicycle to that village to tell the believers news from his visit to me in prison.

The Christians were deeply touched by what they heard about my fast and suffering. They all cried out in prayer for me and forgot to pray for the sick boy!

Sister Zhi's husband complained, "Tonight I invited you to come and pray for my son. Who is this Yun? He didn't eat anything for 74 days and he's still alive? How is that possible? Is he a god?" He commanded everyone, "Stop crying for this Yun! Please now pray for my son in the name of this Jesus whom Yun trusts. If this Jesus helps my son, then I'll use my contacts with the government to help him get out of prison."

For his glory, God listened to everyone's prayer. The boy was immediately healed that night. The whole family received Jesus. Sister Zhi's husband mobilized the whole village to hear the gospel and the majority of villagers committed their lives to God. Later, after I was released from prison, I would visit that village and hear this story from the people's own mouths.

One day Sister Zhi told her husband, "I've heard Yun's wife has given birth today. Why don't you visit his family, but make sure you take a gift. This is the child of Yun, whose God healed our son and saved your soul."

That day he brought many gifts to my family. When he first saw my mother he said, "Old lady, you don't know me, but I bring you gifts of thankfulness. None of you know me, but let me tell you a story . . ." Deling had been resting in her room. When she heard this man speak she got up and came to listen.

He carefully explained what had happened, how the Lord had graciously healed his son and saved most of the families in their village.

They all thanked God together. My family pleaded with him to visit his relatives in the government and arrange to deliver news of my son's birth to me.

Zhi's husband had a cousin who worked as an armed guard in the prison. He was one of the guards who had used electric batons to torture me and throw me into the human waste.

This newly converted brother went to his cousin and said, "Yun is my relative (he meant, relative in the Lord). The Jesus Yun believes in is the true and living God. Take good care of him and treat him well."

The guard felt ashamed for what he'd done to me. The fact that I'd fasted for 74 days without food or water was well known throughout the whole prison and also among every officer in the local Public Security Bureau.

From that time on things got easier for me in prison. The persecution stopped and I was even promoted to be the cell leader.

The birth of Isaac brought hope and joy to my family, and brought sunshine to our lives in the midst of a very dark year.

CHAPTER THIRTEEN

A PRECIOUS SOUL FROM THE LORD

"Mercy triumphs over judgment!" James 2:13.

Every day I taught the new believers in our cell. Righteousness and truth flourished. The men grew daily in grace and knowledge. Some of them testified that when the Holy Spirit convicted them and they repented of their sins, their lives and evil deeds flashed before them as if on a movie screen.

One morning the director of the prison called me to his office. He courteously offered me a cup of tea and asked me to sit on a soft chair. He said, "Yun, I know you believe in Jesus. Today I've decided to give you a special assignment."

I thought he was going to ask me to report on other prisoners, but the director continued, "In cell number nine is a murderer named Huang. Every day he tries to kill himself. He is crazy and tries to bite the other prisoners. We've decided to send him to your cell. From now until the day he is executed we want you to watch over him and make sure he doesn't harm himself or the other prisoners. If you don't remain alert, and he kills himself, we will hold you fully accountable."

When I heard this news I immediately felt Huang was a precious soul the Lord had given us to rescue.

I broke the news to my cell mates and everyone was terrified. They didn't want to receive him. One said, "He is not a man, but a devil." After everyone had voiced their protests I waited for a moment and calmly said, "Brothers, before we believed in Jesus we were just like him. We too were like demons. But Jesus rescued us all when our souls were about to die. We need to have mercy on this man and treat him as if he was Jesus himself."

My cell mates realized my words were true, and everyone changed their attitude. They waited for Huang to arrive like people waiting for a long lost friend.

When Huang was brought into our cell the next morning, I thought he was like the man possessed by a legion of demons, in the fifth chapter of the Gospel of Mark. He was handcuffed behind his back and had chains manacled around his ankles. He spoke filthy words and kept trying to mutilate his body by cutting himself with his ankle chains. He was ferocious and full of hatred, and just 22 years old.

Huang couldn't use his arms or legs, but if another prisoner would get too close to him he would try to bite his ear or nose off. Even though he was tightly bound, Huang jumped up and down until his white anklebones were visible through the skin.

In cell number nine the prisoners had treated him like an animal, kicking and punching him. They'd refused to feed him for days. Instead, they mocked him by deliberately pouring his food over him. His clothes were covered with food stains.

One day, out of sheer desperation and pain, Huang waited until nobody was watching and rammed his head into the wall as hard as he could, in a bid to kill himself. He survived, but left a dent in the wall.

The moment Huang entered our cell he knew something was different. All of us showed him love and sympathy. We welcomed him with open arms, placing his possessions in neat order next to his bed.

For many days he had not washed because of his chains, so he smelled terribly. Because of the love of God in our hearts, we loved Huang. The cell mates pointed to me and told him, "This is Yun. He is our leader and a Christian pastor." I told him, "Brother Huang, we've all been criminals. Do not fear. We will take care of you."

I encouraged him to sit down and be calm. I asked everyone to give Huang some of their precious drinking water. We filled a basin and I carried it to Huang's side. I tore off part of my shirt and dipped it in the water. Then I gently cleaned the dirt and dried blood from his face and mouth.

After drying his face I tore off part of my blanket and cleaned the cuts formed by his handcuffs and foot chains. I used a little toothpaste to disinfect his raw wounds, then carefully bandaged them.

Huang didn't say a word. He just sat there with his eyes wide open and stared at everyone. I knew the Lord was already touching his heart.

At lunchtime we each gave some of our rice to our new cell mate. Then we all said the Lord's prayer and began to eat. I used a spoon to feed Huang.

After lunch we all softly sang a song I had taught them, based on Matthew 6:25–34,

Our Heavenly Father is great in mercy
He feeds and clothes us every day
We will worship and humbly learn from him
For our Lord clothes the grass of the field.

Do not worry what we shall eat today
Or what we shall drink tomorrow
Surely our Heavenly Father will sustain us.

Look at the little sparrow, flying to and fro
Look at the lilies in the field, they do not labour or spin
Yet the Lord dresses them in all their splendour
Are we not much more valuable than these?

Brother, change your heart and follow Christ
For this world is not your home.

Then I spoke about the words of Jesus from Matthew chapter six, comparing the difference between our earthly fathers and the Heavenly Father, and emphasizing the value of a human life.

Dinner that evening happened to be the time for our weekly *mantou*. All the brothers looked at me. I knew they were so hungry. I told them, "Today we've already shared our rice and water with our new friend Huang, so we can eat our own *mantou* tonight, but I hope you'll share some of your soup with him tomorrow."

I fed Huang first and then started to eat my own meal.

When I took the first bite of my *mantou* I felt like crying. A tender voice welled up inside me, saying, "I died for you on the cross. How can you show me that you love me? When I am hungry, thirsty, and in prison, if you do these things to the least of my brethren, you do them unto me."

Immediately I knew God wanted me to sacrifice what was left of my *mantou* and give it to Huang. I bowed down and wept. I said, "Lord, I'm also starving. I feel so hungry."

A Scripture from the Bible came to mind, *"Who shall separate us from the love of Christ? Shall trouble or hardship or persecution or famine or nakedness or danger or sword?" Romans 8:35.*

I wrapped the rest of my *mantou* in a handkerchief and placed it inside my clothes, saving it for Huang. Immediately peace and joy returned to me.

The next morning's breakfast consisted of watery noodle soup, containing just a few strands of noodles. We all shared with Huang, but he wasn't happy even with his larger portion so he shouted to the guard, "I'm going to die! Why don't you give me a good sized meal? Are you trying to starve me before you execute me?"

Right then the Lord told me, "Hurry, take the *mantou* from your shirt and feed him." With my back turned towards Huang I broke the bread and placed the pieces of *mantou* in his soup bowl. Immediately Huang's stony heart broke. He dropped off his chair, knelt down on the floor, and wept. He said, "Older brother, why do you love me like this? Why didn't you eat your bread last night? I am a murderer, hated by all men. Even my own parents, my brother and sister, and my fiancé have disowned me. Why do you love me so much? I cannot repay your kindness now, but after I die and become a ghost I'll come back to your cell and serve you for the good deeds you've done."

I knew this was the time the Lord wanted me to share the gospel with him. I told Huang, "It's because Jesus loves you that we are treating you nicely. If we didn't believe in him we would have treated you the same way as the men in cell nine. You should thank God for his Son, Jesus Christ."

Immediately Huang said, "Lord, I thank you for loving a sinner like me." This hardened criminal tearfully accepted the love of Jesus into his heart. He was released from his burden of sin.

All the other prisoners were so happy. They realized that only the love of God can give true hope to those bound by sin.

After Huang received God's salvation the atmosphere in the cell greatly improved. Everyone began to sing together. Huang was so eager to learn all he could. I taught him about Jesus: his life, teachings, suffering, his resurrection and the Second Coming.

I warned Huang, "Suicide is a sin." When he heard this he fell down and wept, confessing his sin. He asked me to lift up his shirt collar, where he had hidden a small razor blade, intending to use it to kill himself when he got a chance.

Completely broken, Huang shared his story with me. His father was the wealthy manager of a large company and a Communist Party member. After high school, Huang was assigned to a job as a technician in a power plant.

When he was twenty years old Huang was engaged to be married. His fiancée loved him very much, but he was drawn into a local gang. He was quickly led astray. Every day he drank heavily. They looted stores, murdered innocent people and raped women.

One of the gang members was arrested and interrogated. He told the PSB that Huang was also involved. They arrested him. Because of the intervention of his father, the judge was lenient and Huang received a sentence of only three years, even though he was found guilty of murder. On 1 May 1983, Huang's father paid a large bribe to get him released early from the prison labour camp.

Although he was now "free", Huang's life was aimless. He felt there was no reason to live and was deeply depressed. He hooked up with some bad company again. One night he and a friend went out to drink. They said, "Life is so hopeless and insignificant. If we cannot live together, let's die together."

The two intoxicated friends made a suicide pact. They decided to steal two bags of dynamite, with eight kilograms of explosives in each bag, from the storehouse at the power plant where Huang used to work.

They decided to fight each other until one died, and then the survivor would carry the dead man's body to a large power transformer, where the dynamite would be detonated. The two comrades would die together.

The two started to fight, using metal truncheons. Huang's shoulder was hurt but he struck the other man's head, killing him instantly. His friend's skull split open and his brain spilled out. When he saw this, Huang was terrified and ran away. He didn't go back to retrieve the dynamite.

Huang knew the authorities would hunt for him so he decided to travel all over China and enjoy the pleasures of a sinful life. When he finished, he planned to return home to see his family one last time, before killing himself.

Huang purchased a sharp knife and robbed shops to finance his journey. He travelled around and raped many young innocent girls. He visited several famous Buddhist temples to worship idols, hoping to find peace in his heart. His foray into sin and lust did not satisfy him and only made his condition worse.

After his travels, he boarded a train taking him home to see his family one last time. He purchased two bottles of sleeping pills in order to take an overdose. His train stopped before his destination, so he jumped off. He didn't want to return home before dark so he hid in some bushes.

The police saw him and arrested him. In his bag they found the knife he had used to murder and also his suicide letter, which contained a confession to many of the crimes he had committed.

This time there was no way Huang's father could help him. The final straw that broke Huang's heart was when his father sent a shirt to the prison for him. On the back of the shirt was written, "I'm unable to see you now, but I will see you at the execution!"

Now Huang had fully repented and become a new creation in Christ. He loved to sing a song I'd taught him,

I love Jesus, I love Jesus
Every day of my life I love Jesus
When days are sunny I love him
When the storm clouds gather I love him
Every day along my way
Yes, I love Jesus.

Because of his change of heart, we renamed him Huang Enguang ("Grace and Light" Huang).

Even though he knew he would soon die, Huang asked many questions about how he could live out his remaining days to bring the most glory to Jesus.

Usually, if we made too much noise, the guards would punish us cruelly. They made us stick our heads through a small hole at the bottom of the cell door, just large enough for a man to put his head through. The guards would kick us or use their rifle butts to beat our heads. Therefore we always worshipped and prayed very quietly, ensuring there were no guards outside our door. Huang worshipped Jesus so loudly that often the guards came and told him to be quiet, but because of his impending execution they didn't punish him.

Because Brother Huang had nothing to lose, he sang at the top of his voice all the time. Cell number two became a praise and worship centre! Many of the prisoners in other cells were touched by the words they heard.

Huang asked me to carve a cross into the wall of our cell. The cement was very hard, but we all worked together to bless our brother. Huang told us if the guards noticed the cross he would take full responsibility. Whenever we were allowed out into the yard we searched for broken glass or old nails that we could use to scratch marks on the wall.

I etched a large cross into the wall. We also drew a picture of the world and wrote the words, "For God so loved the world" horizontally beneath the cross. Huang also asked us to etch out a picture of a grave below the cross, with a gravestone displaying his new name, to show that he belonged to Jesus.

When we had finished, Huang wept and shouted for joy. We continued our drawings until all four walls of the cell were covered with numerous Bible verses, such as "The prodigal has returned," "In tribulation trust in the Lord," and *"For all have sinned and fall short of the glory of God, and are justified freely by his grace through the redemption that came by Christ Jesus." Romans 3:23–24.*

Strangely, even though the guards saw our "work of art" they never said a word about it. The cross and Bible verses remain in that cell to this day. Hundreds of prisoners have read the words and many have repented and placed their trust in Jesus.

Using the tiny pins from our prison badges as needles, we carefully pulled threads from our towels one at a time. Each man embroidered a small cross on the upper left side of his prison uniform. A red cross was made for Huang's shirt. The new believers were so inspired! They gained much strength and encouragement now that they bore the cross on their chests.

On the evening of 16 August we baptized Brother Huang. Each prisoner received a daily ration of just one cup of water from the kitchen, but each man sacrificially gave half of his daily ration so we would have enough water to pour over

Huang's head in baptism. This was the best baptism we could do under our circumstances!

After his baptism he asked, "Can Jesus also save my family? Can my mother, father, brothers, sisters and my ex-fiancé believe and be with me in heaven?"

I told him what the Bible promises, *"Believe in the Lord Jesus, and you will be saved – you and your household." Acts 16:31.* Huang prayed throughout the night for his entire family to know God's salvation through Jesus Christ.

Huang's execution date was fast approaching. He desperately wanted to write a letter to his family. This was impossible, however, because his hands were tightly handcuffed behind his back.

After his conversion Huang had become gentle, and the whole prison noticed the difference. I pleaded with the authorities, assuring them Huang was no longer a threat, and that he wouldn't try to commit suicide. The guards gave him larger and looser handcuffs, but they refused to remove the cuffs altogether because it was prison policy to keep death-row prisoners bound at all times.

With his new loose handcuffs, Huang asked the guards to bring him a pen and two sheets of paper. He sat on the floor, with the paper placed beside him. By moving his hands to the side he was able to write, but after a few words his pen ran out of ink. In desperation, he leaned down and bit the forefinger on his right hand. It started to flow with blood. Huang continued to write a letter to his parents using his own blood as ink. He wrote,

Dear Papa and Mama,
I cannot see you any more, but I know you love me. Your son has dishonoured you. Please don't feel sad after I die. I want to tell you some tremendous news. I will not die, for I've received

eternal life! I met a merciful man in prison, the respected Brother Yun. He rescued my life and helped me believe in Jesus. He loved me, cared for me, and fed me every day.

Papa and Mama, I'm on my way to the kingdom of God. I will pray for you all. You must believe in Jesus! Please allow my Brother Yun to share the gospel with you. When he visits you, he will tell you the rest of my story. May you receive eternal life! See you in the kingdom of God,
Your son Huang Enguang.

I arranged for Huang's letter to be smuggled out of prison and delivered to his parents.

Huang was baptized on 16th August, wrote the letter to his parents on the 17th, and was due to be executed on the 18th.

On the last day of Huang's life the atmosphere in the prison was very tense. A double guard was placed on duty. Every five minutes the guards checked on the prisoners, shining a light into our faces to make sure everything was under control. We all knew this only occurred when a prisoner was to be executed the next day.

On the evening of 17 August, the Lord led me to wash Huang's feet, in accordance with Jesus' command. Huang was very calm and smiled to the other prisoners. He told them, "We shall all meet again in the kingdom of heaven."

The next morning we had an early breakfast. At 8 a.m. the guards came in with a list of names. They shouted three names, "Yun, Huang, Hong, come out!" Unexpectedly, Brother Hong and I were being sent to our own public trial that very same morning! The guards bound us tightly from head to foot.

Before they took Huang to the execution yard, he threw himself into my arms. He cried out, "I'll see you in heaven!"

In the yard, a guard kicked Huang's legs out from under him so that he was kneeling on the ground. He released the leg chains and handcuffs. They placed a hat on his head that said, "Condemned Criminal".

That was the last I saw of dear, precious Brother Huang in this life. They took him to a place where they shot him in the back of the head.

I heard the shot that sent Huang into the arms of Jesus.

I was both sad and full of joy at the same time. I thanked God he'd given me a chance to see my brother go to the kingdom of God. *"Precious in the sight of the Lord is the death of his saints." Psalm 116:15.*

*   *   *

Nine prisoners from the men's and women's prisons in Nanyang were to face public humiliation and trial that day. I was one of them. We were driven around the town, while our crimes were read out on a loudspeaker. I was so full of joy at the chance of being paraded in front of people for the sake of Jesus Christ! My heart was bursting with gladness.

On the way to the trial I couldn't contain myself. I'd just seen Brother Huang promoted to glory and eternity was so real to me. I sang out to God in a loud voice. The captain threatened me with his electric baton. "Shut up Yun! How dare you sing! If you continue to sing I'll skin you alive!"

All nine prisoners were chained together like animals and bundled into the back of an open truck. As the truck circled the streets a heavy rain shower suddenly came and drenched us to the bone. It was like refreshment from heaven to me. I cried aloud, "Lord, I thirst after your rains of grace! Abundantly pour out your showers of grace upon your servant!"

I kept on singing loudly. Many people, huddled under umbrellas, stared at us in total amazement. Because we were all locals, many of the other prisoners bowed their heads in shame, not wanting to be recognized by their friends and relatives.

There was one young woman, aged about twenty, in the back of the truck with me. Her name was Xiaowei. She was in prison because she had fought with her neighbours and had torn their clothes. The neighbours knew some government officials, so they got the police to imprison Xiaowei and her mother on trumped-up charges. Xiaowei was a Christian, but her walk with God had not been strong.

Xiaowei was weeping as I sang. She asked me, "Why are you so joyful during such a time as this?"

I told her, "How can I not be happy? This day I've been counted worthy to suffer for the name of Jesus!"

Xiaowei's face turned red. I continued to sing aloud,

Though the whole world hates me, and friends forsake me
Though my fleshly temple be destroyed by slander, persecution,
*   and beatings*
I will give my life and spill my blood to please my Heavenly
*   Father*
That wearing the crown of life I will enter the kingdom of God.

Xiaowei couldn't contain her tears and pulled a handkerchief from her pocket. I told her, "Xiaowei, the Holy Spirit is grieved for you. The prodigal's return is more precious than gold. Return, your Heavenly Father is waiting for you!"

With many tears she repented and cried out, "O Lord, have mercy on me, a sinner! Please forgive my sins." I prayed for her and thanked God for his mercy. She received peace and joy into her heart. Xiaowei then stood on tiptoe and wiped the tears from my eyes with her handkerchief.

The truck continued on in the direction of my home village. Xiaowei turned to me and said, "I heard there is a bold servant of God named Yun who lived in that village. Do you know what happened to him?"

I chuckled and asked, "Would you like to meet that man?"

She replied, "I heard his testimony from others in my church. How could I meet him?"

I said, "Yun is the man talking with you now."

Xiaowei again broke down in tears and thanked God we'd been given a chance to meet. She held onto me as our truck continued its journey through the streets.

All of the prisoners on the truck were totally soaked to the skin. Even the police – holding their machine guns under their raincoats – trembled from the cold wind and driving rain. Because of their discomfort the soldiers paid little attention to us, and none of the public came out to attend our trials. The meeting was cancelled. The whole day was a failure for the authorities.

Our chains and ropes were loosened back at the police station. All the police officers had a big meal. We were allowed to eat the leftovers when they were finished.

The officers gave Xiaowei special treatment because she was a lady. They gave her a *mantou*. She came to me and whispered, "Brother Yun, I want to give you my *mantou*. Please accept it."

I didn't want to take it because I knew she was so hungry. She saw I wouldn't accept her gift and she started to cry. I remembered the words of the Lord, *"It is more blessed to give than to receive." Acts 20:35*. I therefore accepted her loving gift with a thankful heart. I broke it and gave the larger portion back to Xiaowei.

We ate together, thanking the Lord for the rich fellowship we had enjoyed that day.

CHAPTER FOURTEEN

FUTURE HOPE

The time my family visited me at the end of my 74-day fast was the first time I saw them while in prison.

Much later I was allowed to see some of them again. They shared how God's kingdom was growing rapidly and a great harvest was being reaped throughout China. Even though the police were listening to every word, they didn't understand what my wife and friends were saying. I was greatly encouraged and strengthened by their visit.

The Public Security Bureau were still trying to gather evidence for my trial. They travelled to other cities and counties trying to piece together a case against me.

One morning at 8 a.m. the prison gates were opened. I was taken out for my trial. The presiding judge was a short man in his thirties. He had dark eyes full of disdain and disgust.

Assisting him was a tall man about 50 years old. He was crowned with white hair and looked very wise. His face seemed quite kind, but he was actually a very sly and tricky man. He told me, "Yun, our government has been very generous to you. Because of your physical condition we gave you a few months to rest and recover. Now you're stronger, and you've had plenty of time to think about what to say.

This is your opportunity. You must lower your head and confess your crimes!"

The judge started to question me, "Which counties have you been to and on how many occasions? What are the names of the people you visited? Who are your leaders? What kind of anti-government propaganda have you spread? What words have you used to stir up your followers against our religious policy? Have you taught against the Three-Self Church, telling your followers to avoid it because it is a harlot?"

I answered, "I don't know what you're talking about."

The judge furiously banged his fist on the bench. He shouted, "Let's see how you defend yourself. Comrade, bring the tape recorder!" A tape player was brought forward and placed on the bench.

The "play" button was pushed and it immediately started to broadcast a message I'd preached years earlier. The sound of believers weeping could be heard in the background. On the tape I said, "Brethren, don't be deceived by the harlot. Remain faithful to Jesus . . . Be like Phinehas who took a spear in his hand and honoured the name of the Lord (see Numbers 25:6–18). Be faithful and don't betray the Lord like Judas. Rise up and be willing to be a martyr! Proclaim the truth!"

On the tape I heard some brothers and sisters praying. I also heard the voices of dear Brother Xu, Brother Ying, and Brother Yu. I was so encouraged to hear their voices again and to hear my co-workers praying.

On the tape I sang aloud,

Be bold and courageous, be bold and courageous
For the Lord is with you, be bold and courageous
Though there are tens of thousands of demons

Though there are tens of thousands of enemies
Trust in the Saviour, don't be afraid
Be bold and courageous.

My closing prayer was what angered the PSB most. I prayed, "Lord, please drive away the dark clouds over our nation! Bind the power of the evil spirits that control our rulers. Lord Jesus, change the policies of our government. Release all the brothers and sisters who are in prison! Let our nation be governed according to your will. Lord, have mercy on China! Raise up leaders of your church in this generation who will take a stand for righteousness and truth like Daniel and Esther. Help us to listen to your voice and not to the voices of men!"

Then many believers said in unison, "Amen!"

With a click the tape stopped. I opened my eyes and saw the judge had a smug smirk across his face. He said, "Yun, you've heard your own words and prayers. You've also heard Xu's voice. Surely you cannot deny that you oppose our government? You said our nation's leaders are demons, and the Three-Self Church is a harlot. You've been caught red-handed! Now tell me the truth, apart from Xu and yourself, who are the other two people praying on the tape?"

I was so strengthened by hearing my brothers and sisters pray and sing that I wanted to listen to the tape one more time. I waited a moment and said, "I couldn't clearly tell who was speaking. The voices were unclear. Can you play it again so I can be sure?"

The judge fell into a furious rage. His eyes bulged as he banged the bench and pointed at me, "What are you talking about? The proof is here for all to see. You cannot deny it! The evidence has been piled up before you like a mountain.

I order you to kneel down before me and repeat the prayer you said on the tape!"

Several guards with batons came and beat my legs to make me kneel down. They screamed, "Kneel down! Kneel down!"

At that moment the power of the Lord filled me. A voice spoke to my heart, "Don't be afraid! Be strong in the Lord. Even if ten thousand enemies surround you, rest in Jesus. Be bold and courageous in the Lord!"

As the guards continued to beat and kick me I suddenly shouted at the judge in a loud voice, "By what authority do you order a servant of God to kneel down before you? You have no right! Your questions are unreasonable. Now, in the name of Jesus Christ of Nazareth I command all of you to kneel down! I will lay my hands on you and ask the Lord to forgive your sins. Kneel down, all of you! Kneel down! Kneel down!"

The judge, court officials, and the guards were stupefied. They stared at me for a few minutes in a daze. Then they snapped back to reality. The judge banged the bench and screamed, "How dare you, you counter-revolutionary criminal! This is treason! How dare you command the judge of the Public Security Bureau to kneel down before you? Are you inhuman?"

In my heart I wanted to say, "I am a heavenly man. In Jesus I am as strong as a diamond. You cannot break me."

The older officer stood up and calmly said, "Alright. Because Yun has preached so many sermons, he can't remember the occasion he spoke on this particular tape. Yun, you can now return to your cell to think about it. When we call for you next time you must clearly answer all of our questions. We have much more evidence against you than this tape. Your situation is hopeless. You'll do well to think and answer clearly."

I realized then that they planned to struggle against me for a long time. I thought about the words of the Apostle Paul, *"He has delivered us from such a deadly peril, and he will deliver us. On him we have set our hope that he will continue to deliver us."* 2 *Corinthians 1:10.*

Those local judges tried everything they knew to get me to confess my "crimes", but they failed. They had used the most barbarous tortures their minds could invent, but had not been able to make me say a single incriminating word. Therefore they turned my case over to the higher Prefecture People's Court. A pre-trial hearing was arranged. When I entered the room I discovered the judge was one of my cousins!

The Lord showed me this was a trick from the devil. My cousin said, "We have much evidence against you. It's clear you've opposed and insulted our government. You have stated our actions are shrouded in darkness and controlled by demons. Not only have you attacked our religious policies, but you've written many materials to stir believers up against the Three-Self Church and our nation.

"The evidence we have is already enough to sentence you to life in prison or give you the death penalty. Tell me, do these materials belong to you or not? Today I offer you an opportunity to atone for your crimes. Tell me what criminal activities your partners and co-workers have committed and I'll be lenient on you."

Before he finished his words the Holy Spirit spoke to my heart, "Yun, you are a Levite belonging to me. You should separate yourself from your relatives because you belong to me."

I immediately answered, "Although we are cousins, you work for the Communist Party and I serve Jesus Christ. I insist on practising my beliefs. What you've said about me is true, but I know nothing about the activities of any other people."

My cousin didn't know what to say to me and was silent for a moment. Then he said, "Yun, accept my advice or you'll regret it. During your trial you cannot act like this before the sentencing judge! You need to change your attitude or you'll be in even deeper trouble."

I was returned to my cell.

After a time my case was brought before the Prefecture People's Court. I was bound and taken to the court in a motor-tricycle, with armed guards on either side of me. My cell mates were praying earnestly for me. I felt great joy in my heart.

This was the first time I'd been in such a large courtroom. At the front of the room was a very tall stand with many empty seats. I didn't know where I was meant to sit, so I just sat down on a large round chair. When the judge entered he was furious and said, "How dare you, you crazy criminal? How dare you sit down in the judge's seat? Get down immediately!"

I didn't feel embarrassed at all. I answered him, "It's not my fault. Nobody told me where I should sit." In my heart I knew that one day I would sit with my Lord on his throne to judge the nations, and even to judge angels.

The trial began. I was told the head judge and all the top officials of the prefecture were present for my case. They sat in the high seats behind the bench. Another 40 to 50 official guests attended in the gallery. There were people from the United Front Department, the Public Security Bureau, the Religious Affairs Bureau, and the Three-Self Patriotic Church.

All the "evidence" against me – Bibles, spiritual books, tapes, and my notebooks – were placed on a long table. A personal letter written to me by Brother Xu was also there, appointing me to lead the ministry in southern Henan Province, and in the whole of Hubei Province.

The judge asked, "Yun, do all of these dirty things belong to you?"

I stood up and replied, "These are not dirty things. These are holy things sanctified to the Almighty God."

The judge didn't understand what I meant. He asked, "Whatever you say these are, they all belong to you, don't they?"

I felt no fear at all. I replied, "Let me have a look at some of these items so I can be sure."

A guard handed me my Bible. I opened it and looked at the inside of the front cover. It had a written inscription from Brother Xu: *"Blessed are those who hunger and thirst for right-eousness, for they will be filled." Matthew 5:6.* Brother Xu had signed and dated the page when he gave this Bible to me. My own name and signature were written on the page as well.

I told the judge, "This is my study Bible."

Then they handed me the daily devotional book, *Streams in the Desert*, for inspection. When I saw it, it was like seeing an old friend again after a long absence. I held it close to my heart, opened it, and found the Scripture for that day was John 19:11, *"Jesus answered, 'You would have no power over me if it were not given to you from above. Therefore the one who handed me over to you is guilty of a greater sin.'"*

I knew this was God's promise for me that very moment. I knew I must submit to the will of the Lord and be willing to go down the path he'd determined for me. I fearlessly pointed at everything on the table and declared, "Judge, I don't have to look at all these things. I acknowledge they're all mine."

Everyone was pleased with my good attitude. The judge

said, "I will play a tape recording for you. Listen carefully." After listening for a few minutes I said, "The voice on these tapes is mine."

The judge then pressed me to give information about other co-workers and leaders. I replied as respectfully as I could, "Your honour, I know nothing about these other people."

Before the court took a 30-minute recess they said they would announce my sentence when they returned. The PSB had told me I would either receive life imprisonment or the death sentence. I thought I would get a minimum of eight years in prison because the co-workers under my leadership had already received five- to eight-year sentences.

The officials shuffled back into the courtroom and took their seats. I was amazed when the judge announced, "Yun, we find you guilty as charged. We sentence you to four years imprisonment with hard labour!"

Only four years! I couldn't believe it! I was full of joy because God had given me hope for future ministry throughout China. The Lord had more work for me to do!

I longed to see my dear wife, and play with my precious little son. Now I had hope for a future. One day I could again pray with the brothers and sisters in our church. Now I could start to allow myself to dream. The rest of my life would not be wholly spent inside a prison cell.

As I was driven back to the prison I had a feeling of over-whelming joy and thankfulness for the Lord's mercy. When I shared the news with the brothers in my cell they lifted their hands and worshipped the Lord.

A few days after my sentence in October 1984, one cold morning before dawn, I was relocated from the Nanyang Prison to the Xinyang Prison Labour Camp, where it had been determined I would serve out the rest of my sentence.

*   *   *

DELING: Yun's four years in prison were the most stressful times I've ever had. Through prayer I received some release from the Lord. Some brothers and sisters helped to relieve some of the pressure.

In those days my relationship with the Lord deteriorated. Before the birth of Isaac I had a very close walk with the Lord. Every day I read his Word, worshipped Jesus and was full of God's joy. But after Isaac was born I went through a very dark time and my faith weakened. I was continually exhausted and hardly knew how I would get through each day.

When Isaac was about two years old, in the summertime, a pivotal experience took place in my life. Often during the summer months it was so hot that we took our beds outside and slept in the open air under a big tree. In my exhausted condition the devil had convinced me I didn't need to pray any more, that I could just pray to the Lord in my dreams while I slept!

Yun's mother had gone to a meeting that night. Isaac and I were just falling asleep when I saw a dark demonic figure standing at the foot of my bed. I was terrified.

I started to pray loudly and fervently. I shouted, "In the name of Jesus I fight against you, Satan. I stand against all your lies. You have deceived me into thinking I can pray in my sleep. I bind you in Jesus' name!"

I felt a demonic presence brush past me as I prayed these words. A tiny bell was attached to the end of my leather belt, which was hanging on the end of the bed. The bell started ringing by itself. I understood immediately that the devil wanted to distract me by this ringing, so I ignored it and continued praying. Soon the demonic presence left and a deep peace came upon us.

Many of our neighbours were also sleeping outside their homes, so many people heard me shouting and wondered what was happening to me.

Yun's mother was walking home at that same time. When she was still about one mile from our village she heard what she thought was dozens of Christians praying loudly, so she ran home to join the prayer meeting. When she arrived she was amazed to find it was only me who had been praying!

This was a turning point and my spiritual life improved from that day on.

God helped us greatly while my husband was in prison. There are two special miracles that I'd like to share with you from this time.

With only Yun's mother and me left to run the farm, things were desperate! We had no clue what we were doing. We decided to plant sweet potatoes, but didn't know how to do it. I found out later that we should have planted the roots about two feet apart. I had planted them just a few inches apart!

All summer long our neighbours who heard about my foolishness mocked us and made fun of us! The news spread rapidly and I was the butt of many jokes.

Then in autumn, all our neighbours started cursing because they had very poor yields from their harvest. Their sweet potatoes were only the size of tennis balls.

When we pulled up our sweet potatoes, we found they were almost the size of basketballs! It was a great miracle and everyone knew God had taken care of us.

Our neighbours respected us more from that moment on and they didn't view my husband as a cursed criminal any more, but as a man who'd been unjustly incarcerated. Our neighbours saw "the distinction between the righteous and the wicked, between those who serve God and those who do not." Malachi 3:18.

The second miracle took place when Isaac was three. We had to exchange a portion of whatever crops we produced because we owned no animals or fertiliser. Therefore it was imperative we had a good harvest, or we would not be able to buy food to eat or the other items we needed to survive.

This time I didn't know how to plant wheat seeds. I placed them so close together that they carpeted the soil!

Just a week before the wheat harvest, a severe hailstorm struck. Ice the size of tennis balls fell from the sky. I rushed outside when the hail started and could already see that some of our neighbours' wheat fields had been completely flattened by the storm. Yun's mother and I fell to our knees and cried out, "God, have mercy on us!"

A great miracle happened. Our field was the only one protected by the Lord. All our wheat was standing upright, untouched by the hail. Everyone else's fields in the whole area had been obliterated.

People came out of their homes after the storm subsided and saw how the Lord Jesus Christ had protected us. It was another powerful testimony to them.

While we enjoyed thick, healthy wheat that year, our neighbours had no harvest and were forced to use what was left of their crops as food for their animals.

Looking back, despite the hard times, the Lord was faithful to us!

CHAPTER FIFTEEN

A GRAVEYARD COVERED WITH THORNS

I was sent to the Xinyang Prison Labour Camp. Xinyang is in the southern part of Henan Province, near the border with Hubei. The area is home to numerous tea plantations. The weather there is bleak, with little sunshine throughout the year. Many days are marked with heavy fog and drizzle. The depressingly damp conditions are a haven for swarms of mosquitoes and numerous poisonous snakes.

There were more than 5,000 criminals in our prison camp, separated into four different work units. I was assigned to work in the irrigated rice fields and fish farms. In my work unit alone there were more than 1,000 prisoners.

Every morning we had to endure political brainwashing and military-type physical training. Our days lasted from sunrise to after sunset – 14 hours of work, seven days per week.

We dug fishponds by hand, and laboured continually in the irrigated rice fields alongside snakes and leeches. On only my second day we were forced to carry heavy basket loads of dirt and rocks on our backs. All day we had to climb with our loads up a ladder and throw the dirt on a nearby slope. I felt so weak. The small portions of food we were provided with were not enough to sustain us. Many times I fainted and fell off the ladder, back down into the pit.

All the time we were watched and harassed by armed guards. If we slackened off, they would beat us with their rifle butts. It was a miserable existence.

When we returned to our rooms every evening, many of us had badly swollen legs and shoulders from the hard labour. On many occasions I didn't even have the strength to climb up to my bunk, so I just slept on the floor at the foot of the bed.

My strength had evaporated and I could bear it no longer. I didn't know how I would survive another day.

To make matters worse, Xinyang is almost 300 kilometres from my home, so it was very difficult for my family to visit. During the first few months I not only felt physically weak but also I'd become spiritually weak.

I felt discouraged because I couldn't see my family. I wondered what my young boy looked like. Even though I'd been tortured mercilessly in the Nanyang prison, at least I knew my family and loved ones were not far away. Now I was tested in a different kind of way – a backbreaking form of slow torture. Not long after I arrived I penned a poem to describe this place,

> In spring, summer, autumn and winter
> Snow follows the rain
> Constant heavy fogs and a few clear days.
>
> Poisonous snakes, mosquitoes, and leeches abound
> As do leather whips, ropes, and electric batons
> This place is like a graveyard covered with thorns.
>
> He who enters with one devil will leave with seven devils
> For chains can never change a man's heart
> If one wants to reform his life he must repent and be born
>   again
> All things become new and daily he will praise the Lord!

At the end of 1984, before the Lunar New Year celebration, we were all ordered to write an annual report and outline our plans for the coming year.

I didn't know what to write. As I thought about it, a verse came to my mind, *"Remember the height from which you have fallen! Repent and do the things you did at first. If you do not repent, I will come to you and remove your lampstand from its place."Revelation 2:5.*

I penned a poem, admitting that my own devotional life with the Lord had been weak during the second half of the year. Because I was so exhausted I'd started to live only for food and sleep.

For my plans for the coming year I wrote that I had repented and the Lord had forgiven me. I vowed that each day, at 5 a.m. and 9 p.m., I would pray and meditate on the Word of God.

From that day on, I had a daily devotional time with my Lord. He exchanged my weakness for his strength and I was able to bear the workload much better.

One day the prison warden came to me and said, "I've read your court papers. You were labelled a counter-revolutionary and an enemy of the state, but I know you're really just a Christian pastor who wants people to believe in Jesus. I don't know why our government sends people like you to our prison camp."

I couldn't help but cry. Deep down I felt indignation for all the injustices I'd suffered. Suddenly the Lord told me, "Don't feel sorry for yourself. This is my will for you. You should walk in it."

Thank God he knew my weakness and limitations. The warden had watched me closely for a long time, looking to see if I would try to escape. When he saw I wouldn't, he re-assigned me from the fishpond to work in the fields. I had to carry buckets of human excrement to the vegetable garden for fertilisation. This job was easier than carrying the dirt and rocks.

I was also assigned to wash clothes and help some of the illiterate inmates write letters to their families. The Lord's favour rested on me. Many of the prisoners knew I was a sincere Christian and they started to respect me.

A guard came one day and told me, "In the vegetable garden work unit there is a 70-year-old Catholic priest. Have you met him? He is a good Christian."

This man had also been labelled a counter-revolutionary. He'd received a ten-year sentence because he refused to submit to the government-controlled Catholic Patriotic Association. He was already serving the final year of his sentence.

When I first met Father Yu, he already knew I was a Christian. Because I wasn't a Catholic he was very cool towards me and would not even greet me. I prayed for him and looked for ways to serve him. At lunchtime I put milk powder into his cup and gave him some of my food.

Later he realized that even though I wasn't a Catholic, I was a true believer in Jesus. He had heard about my suffering and how I'd fasted for 74 days.

Little by little he changed his attitude toward me. Father Yu showed me his notebook containing his personal spiritual devotions. He didn't want to get into any trouble by sharing his faith with the other prisoners, so he was very cautious. To avoid trouble he didn't want his fellow Catholics to bring him a Bible, so for all those years he had survived without the Word of God.

My family was able to visit me a few times. They smuggled parts of the Bible in with their food and gifts. On one occasion my wife brought me a specially baked loaf of bread.

This truly was a precious gift – she had hidden parts of the Bible inside the bread! On another occasion she concealed some pages inside a packet of instant noodles.

I shared my Bible with the priest and our friendship bloomed. He was well educated and could read and speak Latin, Hebrew, English and ancient Chinese.

After Yu left the prison camp he visited my home. Our co-workers lovingly gave many Bibles to the Catholic believers, and later they enjoyed good fellowship. After his release, Father Yu was promoted and became a bishop of the underground Catholic Church. He really loves the Lord.

The Lord was opening many doors for the witness of the gospel. In the camp there was one prisoner named Shi Zhou Ba. When he was a little eight-year-old boy he was sent to a large Buddhist monastery. After training he became a monk.

Shi was an expert calligrapher and also a kung fu master. One day as he walked through the market a pickpocket stole his money. He turned around and, using his kung fu skills, struck the thief. The thief fell down dead.

Aware of Shi's fighting abilities, several armed PSB officers came and surrounded him, beating him mercilessly. Shi fought back and injured some of the officers. The police finally subdued him by breaking his arm with a gun barrel. They beat him so severely that he was barely alive. Ultimately he ended up at the Xinyang Prison Labour Camp.

In the prison there were many men who asked Shi to teach Buddhist doctrine. Some young men even tried to worship him and asked him to teach them kung fu.

I had a deep burden to share the gospel with him. One evening we met together. I shared with him and that night Shi Zhou Ba accepted Jesus and was born again, repenting of his sins. He took his Buddhist books, amulets and charms and asked me to destroy them.

Many prisoners came from broken families. I shared the gospel with them and some dedicated their lives to follow Jesus. We baptized these new converts in the fishpond. Two of the new believers, Brother Xi and Brother Sun, became strong Christians. After he was released from prison Brother Xi pastored a church.

On Christmas Day, 1985, Brother Shen and Brother An came to visit me on behalf of the house churches. Christmas was especially difficult for believers in prison. We were forced to do hard labour and longed to celebrate the birth of our Lord Jesus with our brothers and sisters.

When the two brothers arrived at the prison I was working in the field, carrying excrement. The authorities told them to go away, but they had come a long distance to see me so they waited outside the gate.

When I heard about my visitors I rushed to the prison office. Normally prisoners were not allowed to meet visitors outside the reception room, but because I had a good reputation I visited the chief warden and told him, "Two relatives from my home town have come to visit me! They're being made to wait outside, but they need to use the toilet facilities. Will you please allow them to come inside the prison yard and use the toilet? If you let me walk with them, we could have a short visit."

Incredibly, the chief warden gave his permission!

As we walked we chatted freely and they reported to me everything that was happening. 1985 had been a powerful year for the house churches all over China. Great revival had spread the gospel far and wide and thousands of souls were being added to the church every day. To this day, the Chinese Christians look back on 1985 as a key year of breakthrough. I was so encouraged by what I heard that I started to cry tears of joy.

The three of us entered the toilet block and we worshipped together to celebrate Christmas. I knelt down on the dirty floor and prayed, "Lord, we only have this dirty toilet to worship you in. But you understand because you left the glory of heaven and were born in a dirty manger. You were willing to walk the path of obedience and suffering. We worship you today!"

My two visitors also knelt down next to me, and hand-in-hand we prayed to the Lord and encouraged each other.

At that moment one of the prisoners, a man named Yong, came in and saw us. He was a bad man with a violent temper. Because he continually reported on the other prisoners he'd been promoted to the position of group leader. Yong shouted, "Yun, how dare you bring outsiders into the camp to conduct superstitious activities! I'm going to report you right now to the wardens!"

The Holy Spirit filled me and I commanded him, "In the name of Jesus, how dare you speak against the Living God? Now, I command you to kneel down and repent of your sins. Receive the Lord and perhaps he will forgive you!"

Immediately, as if he had been struck by lightning, Yong knelt down and the three of us laid hands on his head and prayed for him. I learned that if we obey God miracles will happen, no matter what circumstances we find ourselves in.

After Yong received the Lord he became a good friend of mine. His heart longed for the Word of the Lord. Because he had been such a troublemaker he had many enemies among the other prisoners. To get back at him, many prisoners made false accusations against him after he became a Christian.

One day during our lunch break Yong lay down on his bed and secretly read my Bible, which I had carefully hidden in our cell. Yong was discovered. The guards took my Bible away. Yong lost his temper and started to fight them. He almost bit off the finger of one of the guards. They finally overpowered him and took him away.

Two brothers rushed to me and told me what had happened. I said, "Let's pray and ask God to help Yong." I visited the guards to try to help the situation, but they were so angry they wouldn't listen to me.

At that moment I saw one of the prison wardens. I ran to the gate and spoke with him, "Captain Wong, it was my Bible that Yong was reading. I know this is a serious matter, but can you please help me get my Bible back?" Wong was one of the wardens who had treated me kindly. He suffered from a terrible throat infection that made him cough day and night.

Captain Wong went into the office and shouted at Yong, "Who do you think you are to fight us? I will deal with you severely! But first, hand Yun's Bible to me."

A few days later, when the situation had calmed down, Captain Wong asked me to come to his office. He leaned forward and told me, "Yun, I've been reading your Bible but I don't understand it."

I knew this was a God-given opportunity. I told him, "If you want to understand the Bible it's very simple. First you need to accept Jesus into your heart. Trust him and he will help you understand every teaching in this book. Captain Wong, this Bible will not only tell you how you can receive salvation, but Jesus will also heal you of your throat infection."

I saw the Holy Spirit was touching him. I closed his office door and said, "Captain Wong, please kneel down. Jesus is coming to bless you."

He knelt down and prayed, "Jesus, I believe you are God. Please heal me."

I laid my hands on him and he repented and received the Lord. God set him free from his affliction and he was gradually restored to full health. From that moment Brother Wong became a disciple of Jesus. God promoted him and gave him a position with more authority, but he always remembered me. He transferred me from carrying excrement to working in the blacksmith's shop. I was also made a water-carrier for the guards.

My new assignment meant I had more time to read the Bible and pray. When my family visited me, we were allowed to meet together in the blacksmith's shop.

I was also assigned to shepherd a flock of sheep in the field, and to feed the fish in the ponds. I learned some lessons from this. I learned we should never beat the sheep, but must feed them if we want them to follow. While feeding the fish I took the opportunity to share the gospel with the prisoners who worked near the pond. Some of them believed in Jesus.

Time marched on in the prison camp. Days became weeks, weeks turned into months. The year of 1986 passed, then 1987. All the time prisoners were hearing the gospel and many believed. I was constantly busy discipling new believers. It was a pleasure to see them grow in the grace of God and share the gospel with others.

Finally, 1988 rolled around. It was only about three months before my release. I was excited and dreamed of the moment I would be in the arms of my wife Deling. My son Isaac was now four years old, but I didn't know him. I had missed his first steps and his first words. I hoped he would like me, but how could such a young boy understand what had happened to his daddy?

One night, without warning, the prison received an order from the central government. Every political prisoner was required to assemble. It was announced that the whole incident involved me and that I was in deep trouble.

The government had gone to my home and confiscated Bibles that had been printed overseas, as well as letters we had received from overseas Chinese pastors. One of the letters written to me by Brother Xu caused great alarm among the PSB.

Brother Xu's letter said, "The American Billy Graham is coming to China. He is meeting our President and Prime Minister. I want to meet with him and share your case. Perhaps he will help you to be released early. So please write down exactly how you've been treated in prison, and all your experiences."

This letter had been secretly delivered to me and I had responded immediately. But before my response was delivered to Brother Xu, the PSB had discovered both his letter and my response.

In part of my letter to Brother Xu I had written, "Through suffering I have learned much. I am not angry that I've been imprisoned, because God is the true judge. He will make all things right. The prison camp I'm in is like a huge graveyard. The prisoners are suffering terribly. We are chained and handcuffed, and we endure backbreaking work from sunrise to sunset.

"I was arrested because I love God and I desire to reach the souls of all men. Although the cross I have to bear is heavy, the grace of the Lord is sufficient. My heart is full of joy and I sing new songs to my Lord. Hallelujah! Glory to my God and King!"

When they found these letters, the police immediately drove to my prison camp. They arrived at midnight and started to question all the other prisoners in my cell about me. I was tied to the iron flagpole in the centre of the prison yard.

I was bundled into a van and taken to another place, pushed through several different iron gates and locked in a tiny dark cell with an iron door. The cell was more like a box. It was just four feet high, four feet long and three feet wide. It was so small that I couldn't stand up and I couldn't stretch out. Both of my hands were handcuffed behind my back.

The cell had not been used for a long time so it had a terrible stench of mildew. I felt dizzy and nauseated. The floor was always damp, which made me feel incredibly cold, especially at night. When I remember that room I don't think of it as my cell, but rather as my refrigerated coffin!

Above the iron door was a tiny window protected by three iron bars. This was the only place that light entered.

The next morning I crawled to the window and looked out. I saw birds chirping and flying around from branch to branch. I felt despondent and began to sing a new song. I was like a bird that desired to be free, but now I was locked away in a cage. I was away from the beautiful mountains, forests and trees. I longed to be like a bird flying free.

I'd been just a few months from freedom but now it looked as if I was in even more trouble. I asked the Lord, "When will I be free again? When can I witness to people and share your wonderful story?"

I lifted my hands up as far as I could and cried, "Lord, I'm willing to obey your will. Oh God, please tell me, where is this place? Where am I? Why am I here?"

The Word of the Lord came to me from Revelation 1:9, *"I, John, your brother and companion in the suffering and kingdom and patient endurance that are ours in Jesus, was on the island of Patmos because of the word of God and the testimony of Jesus."*

Suddenly the dark clouds over my heart disappeared.

In that tiny dark cell my heart overflowed with joy. I said, "Lord, thank you. Even when I was sixteen years old you put an intense desire inside me to memorize your Word and bind it up in my heart. I thank you for your precious Bible. Now, O Lord, I ask you one thing. Please give me a Bible again in this place, so I can recite your Words."

Suddenly I heard someone open the gate, then my iron door. Two officers pulled me out and took me to the interrogation room. When I arrived, the chief of the PSB, provincial leaders, and the director of the prison labour camp were waiting for me. They all wore grim expressions on their faces. I tried to find a chair to sit down. The PSB chief sternly said, "Kneel down, you deadly criminal! Do you realize what great crimes you've committed?"

He didn't know that I'd become used to this kind of threat and intimidation for several years. Therefore I didn't kneel down, but replied, "Since the day I was arrested I've obeyed every prison rule. I've submitted myself to the leaders, have done my work without complaining, and have helped my fellow prisoners. I was twice voted the best prisoner and have done nothing wrong in the prison camp."

The officer's face changed. He shouted, "Shut up, you trickster! We have your file. Four years ago you pretended to be crazy. Then you staged a hunger strike against our government. When we sentenced you we thought your attitude had improved so we only gave you four years. But after arriving in the prison camp you've gone from bad to worse and have continued your religious activities. We're afraid if we keep you locked up you'll take over the entire prison.

"Firstly, you've had contact with foreigners, and have received superstitious literature from overseas. Now, months before a religious delegation from America has arrived in China, you knew they were coming! Moreover, you were notified of this by Xu Yongze, who is the most wanted criminal in all of China.

"Secondly, you always oppose our government and our religious policies. You attack our Three-Self Patriotic Church and call it a harlot. During the past four years there is no indication that you've changed your ways or that you're sorry for your many crimes.

"Thirdly, we've taken care of you in prison like loving parents, but you had the audacity to write a poem stating our camp is like a big graveyard, a place of thorns! Our government has tried everything to try to make you useful and productive to our country, but you've resisted all our efforts."

The more he spoke the angrier he became. He shouted, "Today we're going to give you the most serious lesson you've ever had! Perhaps you will wake up and mend your ways."

Several guards were called in and told, "Take Yun away and entertain him properly!"

I was taken to a torture room. They handcuffed me and used electric batons, whips and sticks to beat and torture me. My flesh was ripped open and wounds covered my body. Before I lapsed into unconsciousness, the word of the Lord came to me, "This is your calling. You should patiently endure because of the Word of God and the testimony of Jesus."

After I regained consciousness I lay still on the ground like a dead man. The guards took me and threw me back into the tiny cell. My hands and feet were manacled with chains.

That same night the Lord gave me a vivid dream. In it, my handcuffs suddenly snapped and I was free! In the dream I was reading a study Bible. I preached to some of the brothers I'd been in prison with and encouraged them to testify for the Lord. The Catholic Father Yu came to me joyfully and repeated, "Jesus is victorious over all! Jesus is victorious over all!" I told him, "When I was first locked in this tiny dark cell I prayed God would give me a Bible to study." Then in my dream we both gave thanks to the Lord in heaven.

When I awoke from my dream I found that the handcuffs were still on my hands, but the Holy Spirit told me, "Relax your hands." As soon as I did, the handcuffs fell off! I prayed to the Lord according to what I'd seen in the dream. I said, "Lord Jesus, I love you. Thank you for allowing me to sing. Please give me a Bible."

At around 8 a.m. the next morning a remarkable thing happened. The prison director opened the iron gate and came to my cell. He called out my name, "Yun, although you've committed many crimes, we still respect your faith. Yesterday we had a meeting and decided to give you a Bible. Come, take it!"

Quickly I placed the handcuffs back over my hands. I reached out for the Bible and thanked the director. He told me, "Yun, please study your Bible well and repent of your crimes so you can be a useful man." He locked the door and left.

I knelt down and wept, thanking the Lord for this great gift. I could scarcely believe my dream had come true! No prisoner was ever allowed to have a Bible or any Christian literature, yet, strangely, God provided a Bible for me!

Through this incident the Lord showed me that regardless of men's evil plans for me, he had not forgotten me and was in control of my life. There is no government or human power that can prevent the Almighty God from carrying out his will! I was reminded of the time, when I was just 16 years old, when God had miraculously provided my first Bible. Here I was, now 30 years old, all alone in a tiny, dark, dingy cell, but God's provision and power had not diminished!

My hands were trembling. I slowly opened my Bible to the last page, *"He who testifies to these things says, 'Yes, I am coming soon.' Amen. Come, Lord Jesus. The grace of the Lord Jesus be with God's people. Amen." Revelation 22:20–21.*

For the next three months I remained in isolation in this tiny cell. There was just a little bit of light that came through the window, but it was enough for me to read. In the first ten days I read through the entire Bible. I used this time to memorize a total of 55 chapters of the Bible, from Hebrews to Revelation.

God helped me understand his Word and to love him more dearly. This was a precious time of communion with Jesus. He showed me glimpses of the future of the Chinese church, and how we shall take the gospel throughout the unreached world and back to Jerusalem before the Second Coming of the Lord.

One month before my four-year sentence was completed I had a wonderful dream. I saw an old woman with grey hair. She was carrying moonlight in her hands. She walked towards me smiling. Then I realized it was my own dear mother. I ran forward and leaped into her arms. She looked at me with loving eyes and said, "My child, don't be afraid."

I woke up and my spirit was full of joy. I thought it was a pity it had only been a dream, but I prayed the dream would come true and I would see my mother again.

Three days later, around 11 a.m., a guard entered my cell and took me to the head office. When I entered the room, my mother rushed toward me! She held me and wept. She saw I was handcuffed, pencil-thin, and my skin was yellow because of a lack of exposure to sunlight. She couldn't hold back her tears. I said, "Mama, please be comforted. This is all for Jesus' sake."

My mother stopped me and said, "Your mama knows.

Your wife and your family think of you day and night, longing for you to return home. My child, remember your mama's words, 'Listen to the words from above and obey the voice of God. Don't be afraid.'"

She caressed my hands and felt my tight handcuffs. Her heart was broken. The guard who was watching us spoke, "Hurry up! Speak quickly! You're not allowed to have visitors, but we know your mother has come a long way to see you. Hurry and finish before we get caught!"

My mama said, "Son, I came here and searched for you for three days. Nobody knew where you were. But last night the angel of the Lord spoke to me in a dream. He said, 'Don't be afraid. You shall meet your son.' This morning this guard saw me standing in front of the prison gate. He is a believer. He knew I was looking for you. He told me, 'Your son is locked inside a tiny cell in solitary confinement.' Today this kind-hearted man let us meet each other." My mama turned to the guard and said, "God will surely bless you for your act of kindness."

I asked the guard if I could write a letter to my wife and son. He gave me a pen and paper and took the handcuff off my right hand. My hand trembled as I wrote to my beloved family, exhorting them to remain faithful to the Lord and preach the gospel to the lost.

As I returned to my cell I turned and looked into my mother's loving eyes. She lifted her hand and waved to me.

*   *   *

Brother Xu was aware the authorities had intercepted his letter to me, but he decided to go ahead and attempt to visit Billy Graham during his trip to Beijing anyway. He determined it was worth the risk to share the truth of what was really happening in China. Xu was concerned that God's Church in China was being represented by the Three-Self Patriotic Movement, and not by the house churches.

The American preacher was scheduled to meet Three-Self Church leaders on 17 April 1988. Through a mutual friend, Brother Xu arranged to meet Graham later that same day.

The meeting never took place.

Ministry of State Security plain-clothed officers arrested Brother Xu as he visited a park at about 4 p.m. on 16 April. Because of our letters, the authorities were aware of his intentions and had launched a massive security operation designed to stop him before he had the chance to meet Billy Graham.

As news of Xu's arrest spread around the world, one foreign Christian writer quipped, "With regard to the nature and impact of his work, Xu may rightly be regarded as the 'Billy Graham of China', so it is somewhat ironic that he should be arrested while attempting to see Billy Graham."

Brother Xu spent three years in prison for his courageous attempt, being finally released in 1991. He was held, without ever being charged, in a prison in Zhenping County in Henan Province.

CHAPTER SIXTEEN

GOD POURS OUT HIS AWESOME POWER

"For you, O God, tested us; you refined us like silver. You brought us into prison and laid burdens on our backs. You let men ride over our heads; we went through fire and water, but you brought us to a place of abundance. . . . Come and listen, all you who fear God; let me tell you what he has done for me." Psalm 66:10–12,16.

Before my four years were completed, I fell into deeper trouble and now found myself crammed into a tiny cell. I thought I was surely going to be sentenced to death.

One morning the guard came and took me to an open interrogation session that had been scheduled to last all day. I had just finished a time of prayer with the Lord, and had been worshipping him with all my heart.

When the guard saw the joy on my face he asked, "What kind of nice dream did you have last night that made you so happy?" I continued to sing.

The guard interrupted me, "Don't be too happy. Today you'll have to deal with your grim predicament. You won't be singing by the end of the day."

He checked my handcuffs and pushed me towards the interrogation room. There were already eight officials seated, waiting for me. On a desk was a collection of different tools of torture. God had already taken all the fear from my heart so I inspected these instruments closely without feeling any anguish at all.

I sat down in a chair.

A judge said, "This is your last opportunity, Yun. I have the power to sentence you to another fifteen or twenty years if you refuse to co-operate and admit your crimes."

I looked at him and said nothing.

The deputy leader of the county PSB spoke, "Yun, according to our file you've had a lot of contact with the criminal Xu Yongze. You've interacted with foreigners to plot against our government. These facts are enough to sentence you to death if we choose. But now we want you to clearly acknowledge the fact that you've committed these crimes. Tell us who Xu's main leaders are. If you tell us their names we'll be lenient on you. Otherwise you'll deeply regret it."

Suddenly I was angry inside. I stood and lifted up my bound hands. In a loud voice I declared, "Don't say anything more! I'm fully prepared for the death sentence! I will not answer you. Do whatever you want to me!"

Then I sat down again.

In the depths of my heart I said, "Lord Jesus, even if they kill me I'll still love you."

Everyone in the room was astonished. An experienced judge from the provincial government said, "Alright Yun, we know you're a sincere Christian. But our government is willing to help you. We do not intend to kill you, so don't get so agitated. Just listen to the questions we have for you. Go back to your cell today. We'll call you in a few days and you can tell us your answers."

When I was alone again on the damp floor I sang a song,

Oh Lord, I don't know what tomorrow holds
But I would rather die for you
Because I know you have chosen me
And have called me to obey and love you.

A few mornings later, around 9 a.m., the chief warden personally came to get me. I was surprised when he said, "Yun, pack up your things and prepare to leave this cell."

I asked, "Why?"

He replied, "We're sending you back to your original county prison. There you'll face another trial."

I was driven all the way back to Nanyang in a police car. My blanket, clothing, Bible, and everything else I owned in the world came with me. I was handcuffed and made to sit in the back seat with armed guards on either side.

It was late afternoon when we arrived in Nanyang. It had been almost four years since I'd been in my home town. Instead of taking me to the prison they drove me into a large yard. I noticed a sign, "Prefecture Public Security Bureau."

The guards released my handcuffs and allowed me to wash my hands and face. They took me into a luxurious meeting room. A dozen people were already waiting for me. The chief of the PSB, the director of the Religious Affairs Bureau, local Communist Party representatives, and some Three-Self Church leaders were present.

The PSB chief said, "Yun, we think you already know how serious your situation is, so we don't need to repeat the charges again. According to our law we should give you a longer sentence, but we think you're too stubborn to change your behaviour. After discussion between our various departments, we've decided to let you go home."

The Holy Spirit reminded me of his Word, *"You would have*

no power over me if it were not given to you from above." John 19:11.

The officials continued, "We have several conditions you must agree to before we will release you . . .

1. For two years you'll be stripped of all political rights. There is no way you can avoid the disgrace of having been a political prisoner.
2. For two years you'll be placed under close police surveillance.
3. You must report to the PSB every month and tell them what you've done that month.
4. You're not allowed to travel outside your village. You cannot go anywhere to preach. If someone comes to your house to meet you, you must report it to the local authorities. If you don't, we'll punish you severely.
5. You must join a Three-Self Patriotic Church that is recognized and endorsed by our government."

After these five points were read out I was asked to sign a paper agreeing to these conditions.

I politely answered them, "Dear honourable leaders, there is one condition I cannot obey. It is number five. I will not, and cannot, join the Three-Self Church. It is a national political organization. I'm deprived of all political rights, therefore I must also be disqualified from joining the Three-Self Church."

They felt there was some reason in what I was saying. They didn't know how to reply, so they gave me a serious warning, "Yun, we know you are like a dog that cannot stop eating people's garbage. We know it's not easy for you to change your ways. No matter how clever you think you are, if you continue to stir up your followers against our nation's religious policy you will suffer the consequences for the rest of your life."

I found out they'd already purchased a bus ticket for me to go back to my home village. It was the last bus that night. They sent a car to take me to the station. My heart was bursting with joy and thankfulness.

It was 25 January 1988 – four years to the day since I'd been driven back to Nanyang in the police van, painfully handcuffed to a steel rail and splattered with my own blood. And it was also four years to the day since I began my 74-day fast.

I was finally released from prison!

Just before midnight I was let off near my village. I walked along the dark, icy path toward my home. I was excited and nervous at the same time. I knew my family had suffered much during my absence.

I hurriedly followed the narrow pathway, past a row of houses with smoke rising from their chimneys, the fires inside protecting their homes from the chilly winter air.

I saw my home. I paused, taking in the moment. It was like a dream.

I had experienced so much in those four years, but God had been faithful. I'd suffered some horrible tortures, but God had been faithful. I'd been dragged in front of judges and courts, but God had been faithful. I'd been hungry, thirsty, and had fainted from exhaustion, but God had been faithful.

Through it all, God was always faithful and loving to me. He had never left me nor forsaken me. His grace was always sufficient and he provided for my every need.

I didn't suffer for Jesus in prison. No! I was with Jesus and I experienced his very real presence, joy, and peace every day. It's not those in prison for the sake of the gospel who suffer. The person who suffers is he who never experiences God's intimate presence.

In a way, even though I was now free, I found it difficult to leave the prison. Inside, the spiritual fellowship with my fellow Christians had been very deep and sweet. The bonds we made were very strong. We served one another in love, and shared our whole lives with each other. In the outside world people are busy and have many things to do. Most of our relationships are little more than skin-deep.

My family wasn't expecting me. They knew approximately when I was meant to be released, but had received no news from the authorities. I found the front door of my house was locked. I knocked, and my precious wife Deling, with a completely astonished expression, opened the door and welcomed me inside. My little boy Isaac was already asleep. Deling woke him up and together they stared at me with their eyes wide open, trying to believe it really was me, and not a dream or vision.

Isaac was four years old, but we'd never seen each other before. He clung to his mother and asked, "Who is he? He's not my father! Who is he?" This cut my heart, but over the next few days my son warmed to me and came a little closer.

We all knelt down and thanked God for bringing us back together again. Then Deling and I hugged, laughed and cried throughout the night, as we shared stories of the struggles we'd endured and of God's goodness to us.

My mother was away when I came home. She had travelled to Nanyang, hoping to find out when I would be released. The authorities ignored her and wouldn't answer any of her questions. On the second evening after my release she came home, discouraged and with a broken heart. You can imagine the unspeakable joy when she saw I was already home!

One night, three days after my release, I received a strange dream but I instantly knew it was from the Lord.

In my dream a crowd of Christians were chasing me. I was carrying a bright light the size of an egg. People were trying to get the light off me, so I attempted to hide it, but it kept shining through my clothes. No matter what I did, people kept chasing after me.

I woke up and my shirt was drenched with sweat. I woke my wife and told her, "We need to pray. I've had a scary dream." When I told her the details, Deling said, "The Lord is telling us it is too difficult to hide you from the believers. When they find out you're here they'll come to see you. Then the authorities will arrest them. This is the reason they let you out of prison. They are using you like a light to attract moths. When the believers come the authorities will pounce on them."

The dream started to come true. Two weeks after I arrived home a large PSB and People's Congress meeting took place. In that meeting they declared that China had complete freedom of religion. They criticized the house churches. They announced I was under the strict surveillance of the local government and notified the delegates of the five points they had imposed on me before my release. They tried to embarrass me during the meeting.

One day several important co-workers came to my home before dawn. They took me to a special leadership meeting. My heart was burning with the Holy Spirit. We all prayed for revival. Many young people were there weeping before the Lord. We all re-dedicated our lives to the Lord's purpose.

The fire of the Holy Spirit burned in my home county, Nanyang. Many miracles and thousands of conversions took place in a short period of time. The fire then spread to other places.

I was being watched closely so I couldn't go wherever I wanted. I had to ask permission if I wanted to leave my village. Every month I had to visit the local Public Security Bureau and make a report of my activities. To me this was a thorn in my flesh.

One day I prayed, "Lord, you told Peter we should obey God and not man, so from now on I will not report to the government. I will only obey you."

The Lord immediately spoke to my heart, *"Submit your-selves for the Lord's sake to every authority instituted among men . . . For it is God's will that by doing good you should silence the ignorant talk of foolish men." 1 Peter 2:13,15.*

Therefore for the first two years I did everything required of me and made a monthly report to the PSB. I took every opportunity to share God's Word with the officers. During my reports I never told them where I'd been to preach the gospel. My reports consisted of the revelation the Lord had given me that month from his Word.

In March 1988, we heard that Bibles were available in southern China, in the city of Guangzhou. Foreign Christians had carried these Bibles across the border from Hong Kong. I was also told about an American pastor based in Hong Kong, who loved China with all his heart. He could speak and preach in fluent Chinese.

When my wife heard about this American pastor, she encouraged me to go to Guangzhou to visit him, and to collect some Bibles for our church. She told me not to worry about our local authorities. She would make an excuse for why I'd left our village.

I took the 30-hour train journey to Guangzhou and met the American brother. He shared how he loved China and was willing to sacrifice his life for the Chinese people. My heart was stirred. This was the very first contact I had with

Western believers. They started to bring in many bags of Bibles, which were greatly needed by the house churches.

From this time on we started to receive a small number of foreigners into our midst. We enjoyed their company and were thankful for the Bibles and materials they provided, but sometimes we struggled to host them. For example, at that time we always rose at 5 a.m. for our daily prayer meetings. After prayer and breakfast we would work diligently for the Lord until midnight.

The house church believers loved to hear long messages from God's Word. Many Chinese preachers could speak powerfully, without pausing, for several hours at a time. Then, after a meal break, they would continue for another several hours. This pattern continued day after day. We found that some of our foreign visitors could only speak for 45 minutes before they ran out of things to say! So we asked that only those who were able to teach for at least two hours at a time should come to us.

1989 was a very pivotal year for the house churches. We started to unite to reach the harvest. On 4th June, the Tiananmen Square massacre changed many people's hearts. It discredited Communism in the eyes of millions of people and was the trigger point for them to seek after spiritual truth.

In 1989 the Holy Spirit's power exploded all across China in many different ways. Fewer people wanted to join the Communist Party, while more people wanted to join the Christian church.

Between 1978–89 most believers were elderly farmers, but from 1989 many educated students and government workers started to follow Christ. Even a number of experienced Communists turned away from empty Marxist ideology and decided to accept Jesus.

Even in my own village the gospel greatly prospered. Several Communist Party members withdrew their Party memberships, believed in Jesus, were baptized, and started to preach the gospel! Many sinners found salvation and the sick were healed. The power of the gospel became the subject of conversation among the villagers. Everyone seemed to be gripped by the awesome power and reality of God. Even the neighbours who had mocked my wife during the years I was in prison repented and became strong believers. They were deeply sorry for the way they had persecuted my family.

On the night of my arrest in 1983, I had shouted, "I am a heavenly man! My home is Gospel village." This was now true! By the grace of God our village truly became a gospel village.

The authorities knew many people were being saved and great miracles were taking place at this time, but they decided to stay in their police stations instead of persecuting the house churches. They were afraid to touch us because they knew a mighty power was in operation. They knew it would be foolish and dangerous to oppose God's people.

Our co-workers had never received any seminary training, but they were truly filled with the Holy Spirit. Every time they preached the gospel people were amazed at their teaching and the name of Jesus spread. *"When they . . . realized that they were unschooled, ordinary men, they were astonished and they took note that these men had been with Jesus." Acts 4:13.*

All Christian leaders were so busy we didn't even have time to eat properly or even meet with our own families. Everywhere there was a Macedonian call to come and preach the gospel. It was an amazing season when we just tried to keep up with God and tried to bring in the harvest while it was still day time.

On one occasion I was invited to lead special meetings in Wenzhou, Zhejiang Province. Great miracles took place. The blind could see, the deaf could hear, and the lame walked. People who desperately needed the Lord surrounded us. They even touched my clothes hoping to receive healing from the Lord. Finally, it took six or seven strong co-workers to carry me away from the crowd and out of the meeting.

In Anhui Province more than two thousand people gathered for a meeting. Four people, who were considered demon-possessed by everyone who knew them, were brought to the front of the meeting while I was speaking. For years nobody had been able to control them. Doctors and specialists had tried to cure them, but they only grew worse.

One of these men was a terrible scourge to the church. He frequently tried to murder the pastor and demanded that the pastor bow down and worship the demons inside him. He was considered dangerous so the police handcuffed him during his worst spells. The believers had been praying for this man for some time, but he was no better.

When we prayed for these four afflicted people in Jesus' name, three were instantly set free. The man with the murderous spirit, however, put up a great struggle. We continued to pray fervently for his deliverance until four o'clock in the morning, but he just continued to curse and shout out threats. He especially wanted to kill me. The powers of darkness inside that man taunted me by saying, "You say you have power over demons, but you can't cast me out! This is my home and I'm not going anywhere!"

For hours we used every technique we could think of. We prayed many different kinds of prayers, but nothing worked. Finally, out of sheer frustration, we all gave up. We sat down and said, "Lord, we can't do anything."

Suddenly, while we were all sitting down in defeat, the Spirit of God came upon us and the demon-possessed man started shaking uncontrollably. We jumped to our feet and laid hands on the man. Immediately the demons left him.

We learned a lesson that morning. When we arrive at the end of our own strength it is not defeat, but the start of tapping into God's boundless resources. It is when we are weak that we are strong in God.

During this time people's hunger for God was incredibly intense. Unless you've ever been in such a situation it's difficult to explain what it's like. In some areas the power of God was poured out with such intensity that people came under the conviction of the Holy Spirit while walking to the meeting place. They would kneel down on the road and repent of their sins.

The needs were so great we didn't know what to do next. Brother Zhang Rongliang and his co-workers asked, "What shall we do? Every place has invited us to lead salvation and healing meetings. We've become like candles burning from both ends."

One day I heard a clear voice say, "Go to the wilderness and pray. You must pray and then preach. Pray first and then preach."

At that time many leaders received a burden to start training new converts. We had focused on evangelism but now we decided not only to win souls but also to nurture them and see them grow as disciples of the Lord.

In April 1989 we started intense training programmes. Many of these Bible schools took place inside caves that were cut into the side of hills.

When God starts to move, the best we can hope to do is go along for the ride. All man-made plans and strategies become futile and worthless, and are swept away like an umbrella in a mighty hurricane.

*   *   *

A short time after my release from prison I kept my promise to the late Brother Huang, and I paid a visit to his parents. It was three-and-a-half years since Huang's conversion and execution. They still had their son's "blood letter".

I told them, "Although your son's body is dead, his spirit is alive and he is with Jesus in heaven. His words to you in this blood letter are also alive. Today I've come to tell you about your son's last request. He said you must believe in Jesus!"

Both of Huang's parents were Communist Party members and people of high social rank. I could see the Holy Spirit was touching their hearts, but they knew it would cost them greatly if they were to become Christians.

After talking with them for some hours they stuffed a roll of cash into my pocket and thanked me for coming. I pulled the money out and put it on the tea tray.

I told them, "I don't want your money. I want your souls! Now in the holy name of Jesus Christ of Nazareth I command you to kneel down and accept Jesus as your Saviour!"

Huang's parents immediately dropped to their knees, and tearfully confessed their sins before the Lord.

To this day they have closely followed the Lord.

CHAPTER SEVENTEEN

SECOND TIME IN PRISON

"But while Joseph was there in the prison, the Lord was with him; he showed him kindness and granted him favour in the eyes of the prison warder. So the warder put Joseph in charge of all those held in the prison, and he was made responsible for all that was done there. The warder paid no attention to anything under Joseph's care, because the Lord was with Joseph and gave him success in whatever he did." Genesis 39:20–23.

From the time of my release from prison in January 1988 until the middle of 1991, churches all across China invited us to preach the gospel. The Lord used me to share his Word in many far-flung areas, and many sinners came to Christ. From morning to night we were too busy to eat properly. We woke early in the morning to spend time with the Lord, and then worked hard all day preaching, teaching, and travelling, before collapsing into bed around midnight. Before the sun rose the next morning we would be awake, preparing to repeat the whole process again.

On the rare occasions we were at home we had to work hard in the fields, catching up with many jobs that had been neglected during our absence.

At the beginning of 1991 the Lord warned me from

Revelation 2:3–5, *"You have persevered and have endured hard-ships for my name, and have not grown weary. Yet I hold this against you: You have forsaken your first love. Remember the height from which you have fallen! Repent and do the things you did at first. If you do not repent, I will come to you and remove your lampstand from its place."*

I was burned out in the ministry.

In May 1991 a season of strong persecution again came upon the house churches. One night as I lay down in bed my wife suddenly awoke from a dream. Her heart was pounding and she was frightened by what she had seen. She exclaimed, "We must grab our Bibles and leave now!"

I calmed her down and asked her to tell me her dream. Deling said, "It was windy and rainy outside and I felt so lonely in my heart. I was pushing a bicycle along a muddy path. Two bags of your favourite Christian books were on the bicycle, making it almost impossible to progress up the hill.

"I struggled with all my energy, but I was getting nowhere. When I became exhausted and ready to faint I came to a small road. I pushed the bags of books onto the sidewalk and rested.

"Yun, the Lord has showed me that if you do not obey his leading you will be taken to a place you don't want to go. God is warning us. Let's leave now while it's still dark, so we can flee from those who want to harm us!"

I told my wife, "Look, the time for the wheat harvest is almost upon us. Let's wait a few days, then we'll go."

I felt my logic was sound, and I tried to make Deling see my point of view, but she told me, "If you won't listen to me you will surely find trouble. You've become so stubborn in your heart and you always try to be a hero. You no longer listen to other people's advice. You need to repent and pray that God will purify your heart."

At that time the Holy Spirit even spoke to me from Matthew 2:13, *"Get up . . . take the child and his mother and escape."* He told me to leave right away, but I didn't listen to his warning.

Because I'd been operating in my own strength for months, I was physically, emotionally and spiritually exhausted. My spiritual eyesight had grown dim and my hearing dull. Pride had sprung up in my heart like a choking weed. Instead of obeying God's voice, I reasoned with human logic and based my decisions on my own wisdom.

My co-workers had warned me not to stay at home, but I didn't heed their advice. I wasn't waiting upon the Lord with a pure heart. This was the root of my failure. I was tired, overworked and backslidden in my heart.

Ministry had become an idol. Working for God had taken the place of loving God. I hid my condition from those who prayed for me and carried on in my own strength, until God decided to intervene in his mercy and love.

I was still getting up every morning at five o'clock and praying with other church leaders, and I was still reading my Bible every day, but I was doing these things out of obligation and habit, and not from a willing heart flowing from my relationship with Jesus.

Earlier in the year the central government had announced plans to arrest all house church leaders who refused to join the Three-Self Patriotic Movement. A law was passed that made all house church gatherings illegal. This allowed the authorities to prosecute us to the full extent of the law.

Four days after Deling's dream, plain-clothed PSB officers ambushed me outside my home. They bound and arrested me. Every three or four days they had been coming to my home looking for me, but I'd missed them as I was always coming from, or going to, a meeting somewhere.

Because of disobedience and disrespect for the Lord, my wife, and my co-workers, I went to prison for a second time. The Lord saw I was exhausted in the ministry, so he graciously allowed me to rest in him behind bars for a while and learn about inner spiritual life.

If you are a servant of the Lord, let me encourage you to please, please, humbly watch that you don't slip into the same error I did. The Lord God jealously desires us for himself. He is the lover of our souls. If we ever put anything before our relationship with Jesus – even our work for Jesus – then we will be ensnared. If you are burned out, stop! Rest! Your lamp needs a constant infilling of the Lord's oil or your light will be snuffed out. Remember that *"In repentance and rest is your salvation, in quietness and trust is your strength, but you would have none of it. . . . Yet the Lord longs to be gracious to you; he rises to show you compassion. For the Lord is a God of justice. Blessed are all who wait for him!" Isaiah 30:15,18.*

At my trial I was charged with "seriously disturbing the social order". The judge sternly warned me, "Today we are sending you to the Da'an Prison Labour Camp. We've heard that you can turn the world upside down. We know you preach Christianity everywhere and within a few days you convince people to follow your teachings. If you do this in Da'an, we'll be forced to teach you a lesson you'll never forget."

My co-worker Brother Chuan and I were sentenced to three years each. Guards handcuffed us and made us sit between two other criminals. We were put into a vehicle and sent to the detention centre, to be held for several months before being officially sent on to the prison camp.

I had already realized my sin and pride had caused me to fall into this situation. After arriving in the detention centre I repented with many tears and threw myself on the

Lord's grace and mercy. He forgave me and increased my faith.

When I entered the prison the Holy Spirit spoke the following Scripture to my heart, *"Who is going to harm you if you are eager to do good? But even if you should suffer for what is right, you are blessed. Do not fear what they fear; do not be frightened. But in your hearts set apart Christ as Lord. Always be prepared to give an answer to everyone who asks you to give the reason for the hope that you have. But do this with gentleness and respect, keeping a clear conscience, so that those who speak maliciously against your good behaviour in Christ may be ashamed of their slander." 1 Peter 3:13–16.*

All new prisoners, at least for the first few days, are "welcomed" to prison with severe beatings and torture. This is especially true of those who've been in prison before. It isn't the guards who do most of these beatings, but the prison cell leaders. It is a way for these brutal men to exert their authority and show newcomers who is boss. The guards stand aside and do nothing to prevent it.

I was prepared to receive a beating, but one of the prison officers heard that a Christian pastor had been admitted. He planned to rescue me from being beaten, so he came and asked, "Are you the one who believes in Jesus?"

I replied, "Yes! Do you also believe in Jesus?"

"All my family believes, but not I," he responded.

I told him, "You're the head of your family. Why don't you also personally believe in him?"

He smiled but refused to answer my question, saying, "I'll talk to you about this at a later time. But now, tell me what I can do for you."

My heart was filled with thanksgiving. I told the kind officer, "If possible, please loosen my handcuffs. They've already cut into my wrists."

He then asked, "Would you like me to pass a message to your family? I'm willing to help you." Within two days my family and some co-workers were allowed to visit me, through God's blessing and the help of that officer. I thanked God. This was a very different welcome to prison than my first experience in 1984!

In October 1991, five months after my arrest, the PSB sent a special team of armed guards to take me and several other prisoners from the detention centre to the Da'an labour camp, which is located in Ruyang County in the north-west part of Henan Province.

When we arrived, the chief guard said, "This is the big trouble-maker, the counter-revolutionary leader Yun." Prison officers gathered around me and asked, "Do you know Xu Yongze, the head of the counter-revolutionaries? Do you know the pastor called Faithful Hen?"

I replied, "Those men believe in Jesus!"

The officers brought out my file and said, "Don't try to trick us. We know you are a partner in crime with those men."

The first few days in the labour camp I wasn't allowed to speak with anybody, and nobody was allowed to say a word to me. The other prisoners thought I must be a very bad person, perhaps a murderer or rapist. I was beaten severely.

The men in that place badly needed the gospel. The camp contained many ill and malnourished prisoners. Some were so sick they just lay down all day, hoping to die.

During the first few months the guards watched me closely, but I never discussed politics. The Lord allowed me to see the other men through his eyes of compassion. I prayed for the sick and shared the gospel with my fellow prisoners whenever I had the opportunity.

I was able to do this by making the guards think I was a

skilled masseur. While I massaged the sick prisoners I secretly shared the gospel and prayed for them. In this way many received the Lord Jesus with tears in their eyes and were healed from their infirmities. Soon every prisoner and guard knew I was a believer in Jesus and that his power to save and heal was available to them.

One day I was sharing the gospel with a group of prisoners. The joy of the Lord was in my heart. Several guards commented, "Look, this criminal is even happier than we are, and we are free! Let's ask him to sing a song for us." I sang my favourite hymn, "Let the world know I have a Saviour. His name is Jesus."

Each time the prisoners returned to their cells they taught their cell mates the songs I'd taught them and the words they'd heard me speak. These men were desperate to grasp any spiritual light they could, because of their hard daily lives and hopeless situations. They felt they had no future hope or joy, so they cherished the Word of God like a priceless pearl.

One day the prison director got a sore neck, so he asked me to massage it for him. I spoke to him, and soon he realized I wasn't the kind of person my file indicated. He told me, "You don't act like the person the PSB warned us about. We've watched you closely for months. All the guards and prisoners have a good impression of you, so we've decided to let you become the leader of your cell. You're responsible for the morale and behaviour of the other prisoners, and for making sure they do their work properly."

The prison leaders' attitude towards me changed for the better. They transferred me into the front office of the labour camp and gave me a variety of tasks. Some of my jobs included organizing the educational programmes for the prisoners, and selecting and broadcasting music over the prison loudspeakers. I became the prison librarian, and I even helped edit the reports sent to the government to show how the criminals' lives were changing for the better.

I'd hardly ever attended high school. My father's sickness meant I had had to stay at home and work, but now the Lord had promoted me. I was working in four different departments: management, education, administration, and sanitation! There were some university graduates among the other prisoners, but the Lord placed his favour on me and caused me to be promoted.

My first two prison terms were very different experiences, yet they seemed to fit together as God's plan for my life. The whole experience was like a much-needed Bible seminary for me. I learned more of God's character and he taught me how to be a living witness for him. I wasn't persecuted or tortured as I had been during my first imprisonment.

My first four years had been like Joseph when he was thrown into prison, slandered, and persecuted. But my second term was like Joseph when God exalted him and placed him in a position of influence and authority. I learned the true meaning of the Scripture, *"No one from the east or the west or from the desert can exalt a man. But it is God who judges; he brings one down, he exalts another." Psalm 75:6–7.*

Let me clarify, however, that I wasn't totally free to do whatever I pleased! My co-workers were not allowed to see me. Only people with official written permission from the authorities were allowed to visit the prison camp. Many of my fellow believers were being hunted by the PSB at the time so they couldn't risk applying to visit me.

I received very little news from the outside world. I wasn't allowed to send or receive letters. Despite these restrictions the Lord did a wonderful thing to help me!

Along the outside of the prison wall was a line of small

shops. These shops had tiny windows in the wall that allowed prisoners to buy food and other small items from them.

One day I noticed one storeowner had a Three-Self Church hymnbook on the counter behind her. I asked, "Oh, can I please see that book?" She sternly replied, "You don't need to see my book. It's none of your business." She hid it below the counter.

This woman was a believer who attended a Three-Self Church. She thought all prisoners were bad people, so didn't believe I could possibly find her hymnbook of any interest.

I said, "I noticed that book is a hymnbook. I'd love to have a look at it because there are many songs in it I can sing."

She scoffed, "There are no good men in here. What's the use?"

I assured her, "Auntie, I'm a real Christian! I'm in this prison for the sake of the gospel and the testimony of Jesus. Please let me sing a hymn for you from the book. Please?"

She felt embarrassed for the way she'd spoken to me. She opened the book to a certain hymn I knew. With tears in my eyes I sang:

Praise God without ceasing
Give thanks to my Saviour for now and evermore.

Look! The Son of God was crucified
Nailed to Calvary's cross for you and me.

God's love is over our family and our friends
Sinners, receive God's grace today!
Devil, be gone from our presence.

Look! The Son of God was crucified
Nailed to Calvary's cross for you and me.

The old sister wept tears of joy. She put her hand through the window and gripped my arm tightly. She said, "May the Lord comfort your heart! Take the book and keep it."

Two days later I returned to the shop. She told me when she'd arrived home the Lord said to her, *"I tell you the truth, whatever you did for one of the least of these brothers of mine, you did for me." Matthew 25:40.*

She didn't know what she could do to bless me, so she cooked some dishes and asked another sister to secretly bring the delicious food to me, to bless me in Jesus' name.

She asked me to come to her store window from time to time so I could share God's Word with her and her friends. They entered into a deeper fellowship with the Lord.

This dear sister offered to become the messenger for letters to be passed between my family, my co-workers, and me.

God used her to bring great comfort to me, through the blessed little window in the wall.

CHAPTER EIGHTEEN

A PAINFUL FAMILY VISIT

One day I was working in the prison camp radio broadcast room, playing gospel songs over the loudspeaker.

Suddenly I heard someone in the courtyard below call my name. The prison's director of education, and a lady who was the director of the medical clinic, were looking up at me. I thought I was in trouble for playing Christian music. They ordered me to come downstairs immediately, so I ran down the stairway.

The education director told the doctor, "Yun is a good man. He never disobeys my command. See how he ran here as fast as he could?"

I asked him, "Sir, what can I do for you?" The director replied, "Let me introduce you to the head doctor of the clinic. She needs your help."

The doctor told me, "I've heard from the other prisoners and guards that you are a gifted masseur. I want to know where you were trained."

I relaxed when I realized they weren't scolding me for playing Christian music. I replied, "I've never been trained as a masseur. I'm just a Christian who wants to help relieve people with pain in their bodies."

The doctor poured out her heart, "My father has suffered

a stroke because of a blood disease. Now half his body is paralyzed. We've taken him to numerous doctors in many cities. One specialist advised us to use long term massage therapy to ease his pain.

"Your reputation as a masseur reached my ears. I've applied to your superior for permission so you can leave the prison and come to my home to massage my father. Would you please come and try? You can eat with us and we'll treat you like a member of our family. If my father recovers, I promise I'll get you released early so you can be reunited with your family."

Before she finished speaking the Holy Spirit told me, "It is time for you to glorify my name. You shall go." Immediately I told the doctor, "Yes, I will come. I also give you my word that I won't take advantage of this opportunity to escape. You don't have to worry."

I rushed back to my cell and shared the matter with Brother Chuan. He prayed for me and said, "Thank God, his grace is sufficient for you." I returned to the doctor and she took me to her parents' home.

It was a lovely house with soft chairs and bowls full of fresh fruit. The doctor asked me to sit down and eat but I said, "Thank you, but I'm fasting and praying for your father. I hope you don't mind. I'm praying he will receive a great blessing from the Lord." The doctor's mother was moved to tears when she heard my words.

The doctor had to return to the hospital. I leaned forward and assured her, "Go in peace. I won't try to escape. I need time to get to know your father a little and then I will massage him."

I told the dear old man how Jesus had borne his sin and sickness on the cross. I urged him, "Now, you have to open your mouth and invite Jesus Christ into your heart. Trust in him and you shall receive healing. I urged him not to delay, because, *"Now is the time of God's favour, now is the day of salvation."* 2 Corinthians 6:2.

I laid hands on the man and his wife, and comforted them with words of joy and hope. They tearfully renounced their sins and invited Jesus to be the Lord of their lives. Although the man did not immediately feel any better, I knew God had captured his heart and would soon heal his body.

I returned to the prison camp after dark and told Brother Chuan what had happened. We prayed together again.

Later that same night the doctor returned home from the medical clinic. Her father told her, "The man you brought to our house today, Doctor Yun, is a good person. He really loves God. Tomorrow morning you must invite him to join us for breakfast."

Neither of the doctor's parents realized I was a prisoner. They thought I was a doctor from the hospital!

The next morning before dawn, the old man suddenly felt someone strike him on his neck and back. For the first time in months he could easily move his head. He exclaimed, "It feels as if a rope around me has snapped!" He stood to his feet and freely moved his neck and back. The man's wife jumped around the room in gladness. The whole family came together and thanked God for his goodness to them.

That morning the doctor came to the prison and told me what had happened. She invited me to join them for breakfast, because her father wanted to testify about what God had done for him.

The old man's health recovered and soon he was able to walk up and down the stairs. This was remarkable for a man who'd been paralyzed by a stroke! He witnessed to all his old friends and sought forgiveness from people he'd wronged in the past.

The name of Jesus was being spread inside and outside the prison camp. We took every opportunity to lead people to the feet of Jesus. Brother Chuan and I became the unofficial pastors of the prison.

Because of the bold witness of the old man who'd been healed from a stroke, the news spread as far as the secretary of the Prison Labour Camp Political Committee. When the doctor reported to him what had happened, he said, "If this is true then we should send Yun to the Luoyang Massage School to give him advanced training. Then when he returns he can help many people."

Because I had no money, the prison even decided to pay my expenses so I could attend the school! On three mornings I was driven in a police car from the labour camp to Luoyang City – a distance of about seventy kilometres. Prison guards were assigned to watch me and make sure I didn't escape. I learned everything I could about the art of massage from the doctor. At the end of each day I was driven back to the labour camp, along with a stack of books I had been given to study.

Soon I was promoted to work in the medical clinic alongside the doctor! I massaged hundreds of people and always shared the gospel with them, even with some high-ranking Communist Party cadres!

Many of my patients invited me to their homes because they wanted me to share the gospel with their families and friends. People were hungry to know Jesus because of the emptiness of their hearts.

*   *   *

The first time I was imprisoned my wife was pregnant with Isaac. The second time I was incarcerated, my little daughter Yilin was only seven months old.

One day in March 1992, Deling and our two children came to the prison to visit me.

It was already after dark when they arrived. When Isaac saw me he shouted and tried to squeeze his body through the iron bars to hug me. The guards pulled him away. Isaac cried and screamed hysterically, "Mama, why won't this man let me see my daddy?"

I broke down and sobbed. Every time my family visited me the guards humiliated and insulted them. Later Deling told me, "If it wasn't for the love of Jesus I would never have gone back to that place again."

My family was only allowed to see me for 30 minutes each visit. We had so many words to share, but because of the close surveillance of the guards we couldn't say much.

At times it hardly felt as if dear Deling and I were really husband and wife. We'd been separated for so long because of the gospel. Our brief times together were often strained because of the pressure we were under. There was no opportunity for any romantic words or heart-felt emotion. We just exchanged messages to and from the church.

During one visit, my son and daughter ran to me before the guard could stop them. I held them in my arms and caressed them. They said, "Papa I love you." I told them, "I also love you very much."

The guard tore them out of my arms and said, "Yun, if you really loved your children you wouldn't be here in prison."

I noticed my son wore the same clothes every time he visited me – the same clothes he'd owned at the time I was arrested. Even though he was growing much bigger, he had to keep wearing the same shirt and trousers. His shoes had large holes in them. Deling, Isaac and Yilin were extremely thin. I realized they had no money at all and were struggling to survive.

I asked Isaac, "Do you miss your daddy?" He told me, "Mama said we don't have money to visit you, and we don't have money to buy new clothes or shoes. But we always pray for you at home."

I asked him repeatedly, "How is your school?" but Isaac looked down at the ground and refused to answer.

Finally he wiped the tears from his eyes and said, "Daddy, I want to go to school, but you aren't at home with us. The teacher doesn't like me. She told the other children, 'Isaac and his family stupidly believe in Jesus.' My classmates mock me and say, 'Your father is a dirty criminal who deserves to be in prison.'"

My heart was cut and I didn't know what to say. I tried to put on a brave face and told Isaac, "My child, your daddy dedicated you to the Lord when you were just a baby. Please study your Bible and pray more while you are young so you can better serve the Lord in the future. We should be happy when people attack us and say bad things about us, because it is for Jesus' sake."

Although I tried to comfort my family with encouraging words, when I saw the innocence of my dear wife and children I couldn't help myself. I knelt down, covered my face with my hands, and sobbed.

I've suffered many tortures and torments in my life. I've had electric batons placed inside my mouth. I've been kicked and beaten until I longed to die. I've fasted 74 days without food or water. But I tell you from my heart that the most difficult thing I've ever experienced was seeing the condition of my family when they came to visit me in those days. They were all skin and bones from lack of food, were dressed in rags, and I could see they were all struggling terribly. Deling put on a brave face but I knew she was in deep despair.

The paternal instincts inside me cried out to be a good

daddy to my precious children, and a good husband to my dear wife. But I could do nothing except pray for them. Often I blamed myself and felt great shame because I couldn't be the father and husband to my own family that I wanted to be.

Nothing I've experienced caused me such pain as those visits.

Although to this day I don't have any home or possessions to give my children, they love the Lord Jesus and they have a heart of compassion for others.

Once, while I was in prison, a house church leader visited my family. He asked my son, "Isaac, who loves you the most?" Little Isaac replied, "My Heavenly Father loves me the most. Jesus loves us all the most."

When I heard this I was very touched.

While still in prison I made a commitment to the Lord that I would not allow the families of any other imprisoned Christians in China to suffer similar deprivation. I've since done all I can to raise support for the families of imprisoned believers.

Some people may ask, "Why can't the local Christians take care of their own?"

Of course they do, as far as possible. But in some cases the demands have been on a scale too great to alleviate. For example, on one occasion in southern Henan 300 Christians were arrested from a single village, out of a total population of just one thousand people. Suddenly every family in that village was affected. The income earners were wiped out in one day. There just wasn't enough help to go around and everyone suffered together.

Many people pray for Christians who are suffering in prison, but we need to understand that often their families suffer even greater hardship. Usually the authorities come and confiscate everything of value from the prisoner's home, even pots and pans, clothing and furniture. Sometimes they even take away farm animals and seed.

In one raid on our home the authorities confiscated all our personal effects, including my precious black-and-white photographs of my father. To this day the only recollections I have of my father are those stored in my memory.

There are thousands of testimonies of Christians in China who have paid a great price for their faith. I'd like to share just one here.

Sister Yuen Meng'en came from one of the wealthiest families in Shanghai. She was a widow with two young children; a son aged eleven and a daughter, nine, when she was imprisoned in 1967. After a year in prison the PSB thought they would have "compassion" on her. The chief warden said, "This past year you've shown excellent conduct, so now we plan to reward you. All you have to do is write a confession of your crimes and you'll be free to go home and take care of your children. Surely your God would want you to take care of your own flesh and blood?"

The authorities arranged for her children to visit the prison. As soon as Sister Yuen saw them her heart was torn and tears of love welled up in her eyes.

The authorities asked her, "What do you want, your Jesus or your children? If you want Jesus you'll stay in this prison. If you want your children, you can go home." They gave her a pencil and a piece of paper and asked her to write down her choice.

When they read what she had written, they were amazed to find she had stated in large words, "Jesus cannot be replaced. Even my own children cannot replace Jesus." Sister Yuen chose to stay in prison. The warden shouted, "Listen, you kids! Your mother has rejected you! She doesn't love you!"

Sister Yuen was sentenced to a further 23 years in prison.

When she was released in 1981 her son was 34 years old, and worked in a government job in Tibet. Sister Yuen hadn't seen either of her children even once in all of those intervening years. Her son had been taken by the state and raised in atheistic schools, and had been told his own mother had disowned him. Many Christians had visited and shared the gospel with him, but he always responded by saying, "Your Jesus took my mother away from me, why should I believe in him?"

Sister Yuen travelled to Tibet to find her son. He rejected her, screamed that he had no mother, and pushed her from his home.

She has never seen her son again.

The path of following the Lord Jesus Christ is not an easy one. Along the way lies suffering and hardship, but nothing we experience will ever compare to the suffering Jesus endured for us on the cross.

I have a problem with the "prosperity" teaching prevalent today, which tells us if we follow the Lord we'll be safe and comfortable. This is completely contrary to Scripture as well as to our experiences in China. In addition to serving years in prison, I've been arrested about thirty different times for the sake of the gospel of Jesus Christ.

To follow God is a call not only to live for him, but to die for him also. *"If we live, we live to the Lord; and if we die, we die to the Lord. So, whether we live or die, we belong to the Lord."* Romans 14:8.

*   *   *

DELING: To be a servant of the Lord in China brings many difficulties. One of these difficulties has been that my husband and I have spent little time together.

I really struggled when Yun went to prison the second time. In a way, I even resented him a little because he always had wonderful stories of how God was blessing him and using him to win many people to the Lord. He was even given a pass, allowing him to leave the prison whenever he wanted!

I was stuck at home with two children and no husband. We barely had anything to eat. My son wasn't allowed to attend school and we had absolutely no money at all. The pressure on us was so great I nearly gave up.

Some government officials came to my house and told me we had violated the one-child policy. I was ordered to go to our local police station. I left the two children at home to be looked after by our relatives.

I was interrogated and fined ¥ 4000 for having a second child. Because we had no way of paying the fine the PSB came and destroyed the main door of our house as punishment. They also took Yun's mother away and locked her up without food. In China when someone breaks the law the whole family is held responsible. The Planned Birth Control Office forcibly gave me an operation to prevent me having any more children.

When I returned home I went through a very difficult time. I felt as if I'd been physically, emotionally and spiritually violated. I felt depressed and cried uncontrollably.

When he wasn't in prison, Yun was preaching and travelling all the time, often with Brother Xu. They were two empty pockets with nothing to give. Once he came home and gave me ¥ 5 (about 70 cents). That was all he had in the whole world.

Please don't misunderstand me; my husband isn't stingy. In fact, he's the most generous person I've ever met. He wasn't able to provide for us simply because he never had any money.

Sometimes it was very hard for me because of his generous heart. I had two small crosses that had been given to me as a sentimental gift. They were precious to me. But one day I couldn't find them and I discovered Yun had given them away to another believer. He sees no value in any worldly thing. He just likes to give away everything to bless others. His large heart has been a struggle for me to keep up with sometimes.

The things I admire most about my husband are his close relationship with God and his love for other people. He sees the best in others when nobody else believes in them any more.

CHAPTER NINETEEN
GOD'S OIL STATION

I was in the Da'an Prison Labour Camp for 19 months, in addition to the five months I had spent in the detention centre immediately after my arrest. I had been sentenced to three years, but was granted an early release after two years because of good behaviour. The two years had flown by.

Deling was informed of my release. Immediately she came to the prison camp to pick me up. After all the procedures were completed and we were about to leave the administration office, a phone call came in. I was ordered to have an interview with the Chairman of the Political Committee.

We were shocked and wondered what the sudden change meant. I thought something had happened in the church and I was in even more trouble. I told my wife to leave immediately and take my belongings with her, including notes I'd made during my devotional times over the past two years.

When I entered the office of the Chairman of the Political Committee, I saw several top PSB officials waiting for me. I was asked to sit down. The Chairman said, "Yun, the other day when I visited the Provincial Bureau I was specifically asked about your case. They wanted to know if you have changed your behaviour at all. I told them you've done very well the past two years, and you have been a model prisoner. They were glad to receive the news."

I replied, "I want to thank you and the whole prison administration for caring for me over the past two years."

The guard handed me the release paper and said, "Alright Yun, now you are free to go!"

I walked out of the prison on 25 May 1993. Deling was still waiting for me in front of the prison gates. All the way home on the bus my wife and I gave thanks for God's mercy.

When we arrived home the first thing we did was give thanks to the Lord with my mother. I understood the broken heart my mother had for me, and the thousand burdens she had carried during years of suffering. She prayed for me every day without ceasing. We sang a song together, then my beloved wife and I prayed together.

Our two children were fast asleep and we didn't want to wake them up. I walked into their room and gazed upon their beautiful faces. I was so happy that now I could sit them on my lap and stroke their faces, instead of seeing them through iron bars with a guard listening to our every word.

Outside in the fields it was harvest time, but in our hearts we wanted to reap an even greater eternal harvest for the Lord – a harvest of souls. In the comfort and joy of the Lord we lay down and rested.

The next day I faced a new challenge. The Lord told Deling and me to leave everything, climb a mountain near our village, and seek God for his direction in our lives.

My wife suggested that the training of young leaders was the most pressing need for the Chinese church. I agreed with her. But I knew there was so much work already waiting for me to join. Within days of my release one house church leader had already scheduled many meetings for me. Another brother invited me to travel with him to many different provinces, training and strengthening the churches. Yet another brother was starting a discipleship training school and he wanted me to come and help.

But I had learned a lesson from the error I made last time. I turned these offers down and waited with my wife to hear the word of the Lord for us.

After one week of fasting and prayer, I suddenly heard the Holy Spirit tell me these words, "Oil Station". When the Lord returns his followers must have oil burning in their lamps. He showed us that the oil of the Holy Spirit is the greatest need of this generation. We needed to train workers who were able to carry the presence of the Lord with them wherever they went.

The Lord Jesus made his will clear to us. There were many empty vessels in China, but not enough carriers of God's oil to fill them up. He didn't want us to get too busy again, but wanted us to help ignite the flames of many other servants of God, to faithfully serve the body of Christ.

We met with our church leaders and elders. They'd been praying the Lord would give me direction for the church.

I hadn't yet shared the vision of the Oil Station with the leaders when Brother Fu told me, "I pray for the church three to four hours every day, but I have so little knowledge about biblical truth. Because I can't read, I can remember only a few Scriptures. I know many pastors and their children have lost their first love for Jesus and have gone back to the world." Brother Fu wept as he continued, "Brother Yun, now you've returned to us. Can you gather our young generation together and teach them to follow the Lord?"

Sister Sheng added, "While you and Brother Chuan were in prison these past two years our church has been like orphans without any guidance. Only a few people have been attending our meetings. The preachers don't know what to teach. Some of our co-workers have been forced to leave the ministry and get jobs to pay the fines the police have imposed on them."

We all wept. I realized it was truly God's call for us to start an "Oil Station". Without good training the light of God in our midst would gradually be extinguished.

I stood up and shared the vision God had given me for an Oil Station. Most of our co-workers are simple men and women from farming backgrounds. They didn't understand. After a few minutes of silence Brother Fu said, "Oil Station! Are we going to open a business? Our whole church has just a little money between us. Now it is the harvest season. We must spend the money to help the needy families, orphans and widows. How can we possibly start an oil station? Could you please explain?"

I laughed and told them, "I want to start a Holy Spirit Oil Station!" They finally understood what I meant.

After prayer, thirty young believers were selected to receive two months' training at the first Oil Station. It was held inside a cave on top of a mountain.

Until that time our church had experienced God's great power in our midst, and had seen miracles and many people come to the Lord. But this was the first time we ever seriously implemented a training programme to send new workers into the harvest field. We called the Oil Station the "Prophet Samuel Training Centre".

During the school, each student was required to read through the entire New Testament and memorize a chapter a day. One month after the start of the class most of the students could quote the whole Gospel of Matthew by memory.

We all lived and ate together in the cave. Before this time there had been many different personality clashes, improper attitudes and jealousies among us. But now that we were all stuck together in the Oil Station, we learned to pray together and sincerely love one another.

Eighty per cent of the students didn't know how to pray in public at first, but after a few weeks everyone could pray and had a burden for lost souls.

Every morning we awoke at 4:30 a.m. and washed. At five o'clock we worshipped the Lord. We then prayed for all our co-workers in the field for the next few hours. At eight o'clock the first class of the day commenced. Every day we ate only two meals, at 10 a.m. and 5 p.m. We took turns at cooking and doing other chores. In the evening we all had homework to do.

This was a special time. Each day was unforgettable as God showered us with his blessing.

On 5 January 1994, it was my turn to give thanks during breakfast. I noticed the meal was only half the portion we usually had. My wife told me, "We have no more noodles or vegetables left." Deling and Sister Hannah proposed that we conclude the training that day and let the students return home to put their training into action.

I disagreed! I proposed we should continue being filled with God's Spirit, even if it meant we had empty stomachs. I said, "If we dismiss the class just because we have nothing to eat, then these soldiers will not be fully equipped when they go into battle. We need to pray in faith and wait upon the Lord to provide."

That evening, after most of the students were asleep, some of the leaders and I knelt down on the dirt floor of the cave and prayed. The Lord showed us that our priority should be to send workers to the poorest and most needy areas – where people had yet to hear the name of the Lord Jesus.

When we shared this with the students they all dedicated themselves to this task, committing their bodies as living sacrifices to the Lord's service. Not long after that evening, letters started coming to us from all over the country. Believers in the most unreached parts of China like Guizhou, Guangxi, Hunan, Tibet, Gansu, and Qinghai pleaded with us to come and help them.

These young workers, filled with God's oil, were welcomed and appreciated all over China. They became gospel warriors. On 16 January our church elders laid hands on the young workers and sent them out into the field. They scattered from our home base to all parts of China.

Our biggest challenge was that we had no money to support the new workers.

When I returned home at the end of training, there was a registered letter waiting for me from a brother, saying he urgently needed to contact me. We had no telephone in our village so I travelled into the nearest town to make a call from a shop. I was shocked to hear an American answer! He was so excited to hear from me!

His Chinese was not very good, but I understood that he wanted to come and see me. We planned to meet in Zhengzhou City the next evening, but somehow our communication broke down and I couldn't find him. I visited several hotels but he was not staying in any of them. I returned home discouraged.

I found out later that he had stayed in a small hotel and cried all day as he thought he had missed the opportunity to see me. He didn't give up however, and again he sent a message to my address. I once again made the long journey to Zhengzhou and this time we met!

After greeting each other he said, "The Lord clearly told me to contact you and give you this gift to support your workers." He handed me an envelope full of money.

This time I returned home with my heart bursting with

gladness. After I shared what had happened we were so happy that the Lord had provided for the needs of our workers. We all knelt down and thanked the Lord for his provision. Although this money would run out, this incident strengthened our faith to trust him for the future.

Many house churches in southern Henan and Anhui began to rise up for the Lord at that time. Zhang Rongliang's group started the "Gospel Month" movement. Between Christmas and the Lunar New Year, each church member was required to lead at least three people to Christ. The standard was higher for church leaders, who had to lead at least five people to the Lord during the same period.

In this way the gospel spread rapidly and the house churches experienced tremendous growth. After the first Gospel Month initiative, 13,000 new believers were baptized!

Those new Christians were then trained and challenged to participate in the next year's Gospel Month programme. At the conclusion, just two years after the initiative began, 123,000 people were baptized! The following year and the ensuing years saw spectacular growth again, but *it was so much that he stopped keeping records because it was beyond measure*". Genesis 41:49.

The Gospel Month continues to this day, and has contributed to the exponential growth experienced by house churches all across China. More and more workers desired to come and be trained at the Prophet Samuel Training Centre, resulting in teams of new workers being sent out.

Many of the workers from the early schools returned to the cave on the mountain and gave wonderful testimonies of how God had helped them in their ministries. This encouraged and strengthened us even more.

Also during this time Deling and I put our efforts into

uniting the Chinese house churches for mission. We travelled across China, training churches to send their workers out as pioneer evangelists and missionaries. We encouraged each place to start training centres. The vision for training spread quickly as they saw what tremendous growth it brought to the work of the kingdom of God. Soon hundreds of workers were being sent out.

On our travels we visited an old sister in Guangzhou, who had a special message for my ears alone. She warned me, "Yun, you should not only love the Lord, but from now on you should love and stay with your wife also."

This admonition cut deep. I admitted, "Since we married I've not been able to spend much time with my wife. I've been in prison or on the run for about ten years. From now on I will change my thinking. I'll put God first and my family second. We'll travel together into the harvest field, growing together as we minister for the Lord."

I believe my second imprisonment was a crossroads for my marriage. The Lord warned me that if I didn't repent and change my priorities, I would lose my family. I did change, and have never regretted it, even though many of the other house church leaders disagreed with my stance. Some believe the Lord's work should be made a priority before the family. I started to put my love for God first in my life, my love for my family second, and my love for ministry third.

Once, not long after my release from prison, I was invited to speak to a group of house church leaders. I spoke on the importance of putting our families above our ministry. As I shared from my heart, I saw tears welling up in the eyes of many of the leaders. They needed to hear such a message. When I finished they all clapped and continued to weep. I spoke from my own experiences, and also the testimonies of many brothers and sisters in China who've lost their fami-

This picture of my mother and wife was taken soon after my escape from prison in 1997. I never saw my mother's face again.

After my family fled China in 1999, I travelled to see them. This was my first trip to Myanmar, and the first time in two years I had seen Deling.

With my family in Myanmar (Burma), 2000.

Writing in my journal at the courthouse in Yangon, Myanmar, while waiting for sentencing.

*Finally we were together again! My family warmly welcomes me
back from prison, Frankfurt, September 2001.*

lies because they paid more attention to travelling and preaching than to their own flesh and blood.

I taught that the church should not give in to Pharaoh's trick, when he tried to convince Moses and Aaron to leave their women and children behind while the men went to worship the Lord (see Exodus 10:10–11). I encouraged the leaders to include their families in their ministry for the Lord, and even to take their spouses and children along with them if possible. I pointed out that even the apostles faced a similar dilemma, promoting Paul to ask, *"Don't we have the right to take a believing wife along with us, as do the other apostles and the Lord's brothers and Cephas?"* 1 Corinthians 9:5.

The leader of that house church network, however, disagreed with me. When I finished speaking he privately rebuked me, "Yun, I can't believe you've used your opportunity to teach such a message. Are you trying to destroy my leaders?"

Not surprisingly, many of the marriages and families of the leaders from that group are in complete disarray. Many appear to be "successful" in their ministries while their families are falling apart. For all the strengths possessed by China's house churches, this area is one of its weakest points.

Next, we received an invitation to visit picturesque Guilin City. After sharing our vision with the house church leaders there, I was introduced to a Scandinavian brother, who happened to be visiting Guilin at the same time. When he heard our vision he repeated, "Amen, amen, amen." He asked us, "What can we do to help?"

I told him, "You should co-operate with the vision of the house churches and invest your faith with us. Because you are a white man you stick out in China. But if you are willing to have the heart of a servant, to count the cost and not fear, I'll take you to train our co-workers in Henan. Besides, we desperately need you to help us with Bibles and other materials. We never have enough Bibles because our churches are growing so fast."

My new friend asked me how many Bibles were needed. Without thinking I replied, "Thirty or forty thousand would not be too much." He replied, "How about 100,000 Bibles right now? We have them available already." My co-workers and I discussed how to get these delivered safely to churches in many different parts of China.

He later told me, "The Lord has sent us to help you in the vision of unity among the house churches. We haven't come to China to dominate your work or control anything. We haven't come to impose our own agenda or to build beautiful church buildings. We submit ourselves to the vision God has given the house churches and we want to serve you in any way we can to see that happen."

Little did I know at the time how God would closely unite me in ministry with that Scandinavian brother for many years to come. The Lord has used him to be a blessing to both the Chinese church and my own family.

The Lord Jesus was beginning to bring us all into a place of influence where millions of believers could be equipped for ministry. Many overseas believers, both Chinese and Westerners, came to help train our workers, and send them out as warriors for the Lord. Some were moved by the Lord to help provide for the practical needs of the workers. We appreciated this, but we always remembered the help was from the Lord. We were careful never to look to man to provide our needs.

As we travelled around China we had only enough money for our train fares. We had no money for eating or anything else, but the Lord provided so that we always had just enough for each trip.

My family lived in a rickety old home, which was falling apart. We wore old clothes and my children had holes in their shoes. We always believed the best of our possessions, time, and money should go to training the workers so they could go to the poorest and most needy places. We all practised tithing. If we had only ten ducks, we would dedicate the biggest duck and its eggs to the Lord.

While I was in prison each man received just ¥2.50 (about 30 cents) per month, so we could buy small items like paper and toothpaste. But even then the believers set aside a tithe from our meagre income. We stored it up while in prison and gave it to the Lord when we were released.

One day, back at the Oil Station, we laid hands on a team that was being sent to Sichuan Province. Brother Wei asked the young men and women, "You have no money and you are going far from home. What is the one thing you are most afraid will happen to you?"

The new workers responded in one voice, "We are not afraid of going hungry or of being beaten. We are willing to die for the gospel! We are only afraid of going without God's presence. Please pray he will be with us every day."

These missionaries suffered much for the gospel. They had to get backbreaking jobs so they could eat and preach the gospel. Some fed pigs, some cut firewood, while others carried buckets of manure. Many people who saw the quality of their lives and the power of their witness believed in Jesus.

Not all of our meetings had glorious results however! Sometimes in the house churches in China not everything operates smoothly, and not everyone is glad to receive our teaching. On one such occasion we were in Shandong Province.

The key leader prepared a meeting for seven days. On the

afternoon of the sixth day, while Brother John was sharing, some of the Shandong believers started to find fault with our message. They quizzed John with some difficult questions about controversial verses in the book of Revelation. John replied, "I'm sorry, there are many hidden treasures in the Bible. Even the great Bible scholars are not sure about these verses."

One old man, an elder of a church, and two other men stood up and exclaimed, "You teachers from Henan need to shut up! You're so young and inexperienced. You are dirt-poor and know nothing. How can you teach us when you don't even know the meaning of these Scriptures?"

The three old men picked up their belongings and started to leave the meeting. They commanded their church members to leave with them. I immediately followed them into the courtyard and prayed in a loud voice, "O Lord, thank you for my honourable brothers. Please help them not to be so angry because we are so ignorant of the Scriptures."

Two of the disgruntled leaders laughed at me and called out, "Yun, take your soldiers back to where you belong. Roll up your flag and take it back to Henan."

I knew this incident was a disturbance from the devil. With sincere tears in my eyes I pleaded with them to return to the meeting so we could all pray and seek the Lord's will. Their hearts were touched, so they quietly returned to their seats. I asked everyone in the meeting to kneel down and seek the Lord. I commanded everyone to repent of his or her sins. The love of God was poured out on all of us. There was much wailing and many broken hearts. I stood up and con-fessed my own sins, followed by many of the other men and women present.

Those three elders came forward and knelt down in front of the people. They bowed their heads and said, "Brother

Yun, please forgive us for speaking such rude and insulting words." The whole congregation, when they saw the contrite hearts of the three elders, knelt down and prayed with many tears. The elders asked us to stay and teach for several more days in different places around Shandong.

*   *   *

Although we were travelling a lot and were very busy, our home life was also experiencing a lot of challenges. As I travelled around China I met many Christian families who were facing tremendous difficulties because of the one-child policy.

The government was trying to force many Christian mothers to abort their second pregnancies. Some sisters were forcibly sterilized to ensure they wouldn't get pregnant again. Families found with more than one child were fined huge amounts of money and had certain government privileges removed, such as health care and education benefits.

When I heard the stories of many pregnant Christian women my heart was torn. They didn't know what to do. I prayed and came up with an idea! I told them, "It's a terrible sin to have an abortion, so that is not an option. If you agree to have your baby secretly, I'll commit to take it and raise it in a Christian home."

This pleased these families and soon I felt like Abraham, a father of many!

There were terrible stories behind some of the babies we adopted. Two single Christian women from an area in Sichuan Province decided to join us in ministry. While they were travelling to Henan an evil gang kidnapped them and took them into a mountainous area about two hundred kilometres from Chongqing City.

These two beautiful young women were literally chained up and used as sex slaves for more than a year. Nobody knew what had happened to them. Finally they managed to escape and made their way home, inwardly destroyed from their ordeal.

I travelled to Sichuan and met with the girls and their families. One of them had become pregnant just before their escape. The girl's parents wanted to abort the baby, but I pleaded with them not to kill the child. They were reluctant, until I told them, "If your daughter gives birth I promise to take full responsibility for the baby."

A little girl was born, whom I named Yang Mu Ai ("The Shepherd's Love"). We took care of her for a while until we found a Christian family who agreed to raise her.

*　　*　　*

DELING: Because we had two children we were harassed and fined by the local government. Then, without a word of warning, Yun came home one day with a baby girl in his arms! He had been at a meeting where a church leader shared his burden. He already had two children and now his wife was pregnant with a third child.

The authorities came to their home and told them that because of the one-child policy, they either had to agree to abort the baby, or if they refused to undergo an abortion, the mother would be imprisoned until she gave birth, and then the baby would be taken away and murdered.

When Yun heard this, his loving heart bled. He told that brother, "Whatever you do, don't abort your baby. The Bible says 'Sons are a heritage from the Lord, children a reward from him.' Psalm 127:3. Take your wife into hiding and after the baby is born, I will take full responsibility for its welfare."

This is how Yun started to bring home new babies. In total we adopted ten or eleven children! I'm not even sure of the number because he didn't bring all of them home to show me. I kept hearing from others about more children that Yun had taken responsibility for.

Some children came from the families of pastors who'd been imprisoned and tortured. The family just couldn't bear any more burdens and were unable to raise another child. Another baby was given to us after a young Christian girl was tricked into taking a job in the city. She was raped and became pregnant.

Yun found Christian homes for them, although many of the families who took them in were so poor that we had to continue supporting them financially. We were also very poor but Yun had faith that God would provide, and he always did, somehow.

When my husband first started bringing all these babies home I was angry! I asked him, "What's wrong with me? If you so desperately want more children why don't you tell me?" But over time, and after hearing the stories behind each child, I gradually learned to have mercy and patience with my husband.

I grew to understand more of the compassionate heart of God. Because of my husband's merciful example, many churches started to take care of orphans and abandoned children.

CHAPTER TWENTY

THE ROAD TO UNITY

During the special time of training across China in 1992 and 1993 we enjoyed many wonderful and fruitful times with the Lord. When God is blessing us, the devil is always active, doing his best to try to stop the advance of the kingdom of God. Satan tried to extinguish the fire of the Lord through persecution and hardship, but God continually poured his oil into our lamps, making our flames grow higher and brighter!

At the start of 1994 God showed me that the different house church networks must be unified before he would truly pour out his power on China.

Throughout the 1970s there had been just one house church movement in China. There were no networks or organizations, just groups of passionate believers who came together to worship and study God's Word. The leaders all knew each other. God had brought them together during times of hardship. They learned to have fellowship and trust one another while shackled together in prison. After being released they worked together for the advancement of the gospel. In those early days we were truly unified. Suffering had broken down all denominational walls in the Chinese church.

When China's borders started to open up in the early 1980s, many foreign Christians wanted to know how they could help the church in China. The first thing they did was smuggle Bibles to us from Hong Kong. These gifts were greatly appreciated and so desperately needed!

Once I took a train with various house church leaders to the southern city of Guangzhou, to receive Bibles from our Western friends. After a day or two of fellowship we boarded the train again and headed home with our precious gifts. We were so happy and full of love for one another.

However, after a few years these same mission organizations started putting other books at the top of the bags of Bibles. These were books about one particular denomination's theology, or teaching that focused on certain aspects of God's Word.

This, I believe, was the start of disunity among many of China's house churches.

These booklets told us we must worship in a certain way, or that we must speak in tongues to be a true believer, or that only if we were baptized in Jesus' name (instead of in the name of the Father, Son and Holy Spirit) could we be saved. Other teachings focused on extreme faith, still others argued for or against the role of women in the church.

We read all these booklets and soon we were confused! The churches started to split into groups that believed one thing against groups that believed another. Instead of only speaking for Jesus, we also started speaking against other believers who didn't conform to our views.

After a while our foreign friends started giving even more things to us. They gave money, cameras, and other things they felt were necessary to help us serve the Lord more effectively. I clearly remember how this caused division among the leaders. In our evil hearts we asked, "Who got the most books?" or, "Why was that brother given more money than me?"

It was a real mess. Within a year or two, the house churches in China split into ten or twelve fragments. This was how so many different house church networks came into existence.

It was easy for a house church to split. Sometimes an outsider would come and spend time with a group of second or third-level leaders. They would hand out "support" money and their contact cards. Within a short time a new movement would be established. In their zeal to help, our foreign brothers were actually causing the house churches to split and be weakened. *"For I can testify about them that they are zealous for God, but their zeal is not based on knowledge." Romans 10:2.*

I'm not saying it was purely the fault of our foreign brothers! Our own hearts were in error and we easily succumbed to temptation. I'm also not saying we don't need or want help from Christians around the world. We do! We have tremendous needs and we pray that God will provide however he chooses, including through foreign Christians. But the motive in giving and receiving must be pure, and these gifts should only be given through the existing church leadership, so that younger leaders are not tempted to use these gifts to usurp the authority of the leaders above them.

The leaders could no longer walk together in unity before the Lord. We felt that to do so would be to compromise our new beliefs!

This situation gradually worsened for more than fifteen years, until some house church networks believed they were the only ones who held the truth, and despised other groups as cults that should be avoided at all costs. The leaders no longer spoke to or loved one another.

As we travelled around China we met with believers

from many different groups and networks, and noticed the spirit of denominationalism was rampant. The Lord gave me a burden to seek unity among the house churches, so I started to look for like-minded leaders who shared the same vision.

I met with Zhang Rongliang, the leader of one of the largest networks. Zhang was the brother I had sheltered with all night next to the freezing pond many years before, when a wave of persecution threatened to sweep us away. He was also the brother who gave me his scarf the night I was arrested and sent to prison in 1983.

When I told him my vision for unity, Zhang laughed, "That's impossible! The different groups you want to bring together are typical cults. We'll have nothing to do with them!"

I was so upset I wanted to punch him, but I knew Zhang had been deeply hurt by the other leaders. In years gone by Zhang had greatly respected Brother Xu, the leader of the Born Again house church network. One day Zhang heard Xu was conducting meetings in a village about twenty kilometres away.

Having not seen Xu for a few years, Zhang decided to ride his bicycle to talk with him. When Zhang arrived at the entrance to the village, Brother Xu's co-workers – who had been posted outside to watch for trouble – stopped Zhang and refused to let him enter. They didn't know who Zhang was. In their zeal they refused to go and check with Xu, and ordered Zhang to leave. The truth is that if Brother Xu had been told Zhang was outside, he would have come and hugged him dearly.

Because of many sorry incidents and misunderstandings like this, distrust and bitterness sprang up in the hearts of many house church leaders against one another.

I also travelled to the eastern cities of Shanghai and Wenzhou, where I met with some old men who were leaders of the church. They weren't able to accept my vision for unity. They said there was no way they'd ever work with the other groups.

I left greatly discouraged and deeply grieved. I felt like giving up. The vision for unity seemed impossible, but the Holy Spirit told me, "Don't cry. You're not my first choice to bring unity among my people. Several others were called but did not persevere in the vision."

I re-dedicated myself to the Lord and to the vision he had given me. God encouraged me from Matthew 19:26, *"With man this is impossible, but with God all things are possible."*

The first breakthrough came when I met with Brother Xu and his sister Deborah in 1994. I shared the vision for the Chinese church to take the gospel outside China as missionaries, but told them this would never happen as long as the house churches remained divided and full of hate for one another. The servant of God, Brother Xu, said to me, "From today we will live for the same vision. We will love each other like Jonathan and David."

Brother Xu and his group became the first to join the unity movement.

We arranged for Zhang Rongliang and the leaders of his Fangcheng Church to meet with us. This was a big step because of the tension that had existed between his group and Brother Xu's group for many years. The day before Zhang arrived we had a time of prayer. Brother Fan said, "Brother Xu, I believe the Lord has given me a word for you, but I'm not sure you can accept it."

He continued, "I feel that when Zhang Rongliang and his leaders arrive you shouldn't sit down with them and talk straight away. You shouldn't even pray with them at first.

When they arrive you should immediately get on your knees and wash their feet one by one."

Brother Xu, who leads millions of believers across China, immediately responded, "I accept this as a word from the Lord. I'll certainly wash their feet."

The next day Zhang Rongliang and his co-workers arrived. Everyone greeted each other and sat down for a meal. Then we all started to talk. For thirteen years there had been no contact between the two groups. Each side was sure they were correct and that the other group was, at best, believers who had strayed from the narrow path and had embraced dangerous beliefs.

The atmosphere deteriorated until it became like a business meeting, with everyone talking at once about different subjects. Many old wounds resurfaced and it became apparent the two groups were as far apart as they'd ever been. It looked as if Brother Xu had missed his chance to wash their feet.

Suddenly Zhang slapped his knee and announced, "All this talk is a waste of time. Let's pray and then we'll leave."

Brother Fan pushed Brother Xu in the back and instructed him, "Quick! Get some water and do what the Lord told you to do!"

Zhang was praying with his eyes closed when Xu knelt down in front of him and started gently to take his shoes and socks off. Zhang opened his eyes and was amazed. He couldn't believe the great Xu Yongze, leader of the largest house church movement in China, would ever kneel down and wash his feet! Zhang cried out and wrapped his arms around Brother Xu in a warm embrace.

Deborah Xu then brought out a bucket of warm water and started to wash the feet of Zhang's co-worker, Sister Ding. The two of them knelt down on the floor and hugged and wept.

Thirteen years of rumours, bitterness and jealousies were washed away. Everyone in the room sought the Lord's mercy and forgiveness. Many confessions of sin were made from one leader to another. It was a powerful time. Puddles of tears formed on the floor of that blessed place.

We sang together,

> *When the sun starts to set*
> *Our hearts long to go home*
> *For we are one family forever.*
>
> *We left the family when we were young*
> *And launched out on our own paths*
> *Each of us has suffered alone*
> *So now we can understand each other's pain.*
>
> *We should accept each other as brothers*
> *Walking down the gospel road*
> *All streams and rivers finally join the ocean*
> *For we are one family forever.*

These two house church networks committed to work together wherever possible from that day on. Our hearts had been totally conquered by God's love.

The Lord put a deep burden in the heart of Brother Xu to be reunited with other house church leaders as well. Together we visited many more leaders from other groups. All those leaders who wouldn't align themselves with the Three-Self Patriotic Movement were asked if they wanted to join the unity movement, which we called the "Sinim Fellowship". We believe the "Sinim" mentioned in Isaiah 49:12 (KJV) refers to China, *"Behold, these shall come from far; and, lo, these from the north and from the west; and these from the land of Sinim."*

We prayed with them and shared the vision for unity. Slowly the Lord granted us favour and these leaders began to see the importance of being united for the sake of the Lord.

Many leaders had never even met Brother Xu before, yet they had opposed him because of what they'd been told by others. When they heard from his own lips what he believed, and saw how his life and character displayed the gentleness and fruit of the Holy Spirit, they realized they'd been lied to. They embraced Brother Xu as a true man of God and a genuine believer in the Lord Jesus Christ. Many of the barriers fell down, and unity grew deeper and stronger. The leaders started preaching in each other's churches, singing each other's songs, and strategizing together in the work of the Lord.

By the start of 1996 many of the top leaders had agreed to unify, but the second- and third-level leaders, especially the younger brothers, still couldn't totally accept each other. They didn't want to give up their own methods.

I made a covenant with God for the sake of unity among the Chinese church. I told him, "Lord, from this day on I won't eat eggs or meat until the leaders genuinely accept each other." One day at a leaders' meeting one brother noticed I wasn't eating eggs or meat. He asked why. I told him, and immediately he stood up and made an announcement, "From this moment on I too refuse to eat eggs or meat until the house churches are unified."

In October 1996, five men were elected to be the first elders of the Sinim Fellowship. They were Brother Xu Yongze, who was voted the Chairman, Zhang Rongliang, Wang Xincai, Shen Yiping and myself. Each man represented a different house church network.

In November 1996, the leaders of the five networks met

together in Shanghai for our very first official Sinim meeting. God again moved in a fresh and powerful way, breaking down barriers. Some leaders confessed they had harboured ill feeling against the other groups for many years. They repented before God and asked forgiveness from those present.

Brother Xu stood up and said, "We don't want to follow our own pet doctrines any more. We want to learn from one another's strengths and change in whatever way the Lord wants, in order to make us stronger and closer to Jesus."

Although not all differences were ironed out, the leaders got to know each other for the first time, and saw how they had far more in common than they had reasons to remain separate. They also found their theological differences centred upon issues that weren't essential to the faith.

Each group clearly heard how God was moving in wonderful ways among the other groups represented in the meeting, and gave glory to God. We decided to speak in each other's churches, and to share Bibles and resources between us, so that one or two groups would not end up receiving the majority of help from overseas Christians while other groups got nothing.

On the second day, all the leaders took communion together. It was probably the first time in more than 50 years that the top leaders of China's church had taken the Lord's Supper in unity.

The unity movement continues to this day, although in 2002 the leaders decided to drop the title "Sinim" and just meet as brothers in Christ without an official name. Several more house church networks have joined. At a special meeting in January 2000, the leaders for the first time estimated the number of believers in their networks. The combined total was 58 million.

CHAPTER TWENTY-ONE

THIRD TIME IN PRISON – MY LOWEST POINT

In March 1997 eleven house church leaders gathered together in Zhengzhou City, the capital of Henan Province. We planned to meet on the second floor of an apartment building. An elderly American-Chinese sister was invited to attend, but it appears government agents followed her to the meeting.

We didn't know it, but Brother Xu and several of the other leaders had already been arrested and taken away before we even got to the apartment. Armed Public Security officers then hid in the apartment and waited for the rest of us to arrive.

It was a rainy, overcast evening. I telephoned the apartment to enquire if Brother Xu had arrived yet. A voice I didn't recognize answered and said, "Oh, please come up. Please come up!"

When we arrived we found the apartment door ajar. We walked in and were faced with an array of guns pointed right at us! The officers started to take our belts off and bind our hands behind our backs. The only thought in my mind was to escape. Before my hands had been bound, I backed up towards the window. In a flash I opened it, shouted "Run!" and jumped out, feet first.

241

I never expected the PSB would have about a dozen officers waiting below the window. I awkwardly crashed to the
ground and, because of the height of the fall, badly injured
my feet. The officers on the ground never imagined someone
would be bold enough to jump out of the window, so for a
brief moment I looked at them, and they looked at me, and
we both shouted in shock and surprise!

The officers rushed at me, held me down and viciously
kicked and beat me. They stamped on my legs and chest
with their heavy boots, and pulled my hair back and pistol-
whipped me. My bones crunched and snapped under their
savage blows and kicks. They then produced a dreaded electric baton and tortured me with electric shocks.

I was thrashed so severely that all I could do was curl up
and focus on Jesus, trying not to pay attention to the blows.
Finally, I lost consciousness.

The incident was so savage that it was a miracle I wasn't
killed. Later I was reminded of the words of the Psalmist: *"If
the Lord had not been on our side when men attacked us, when
their anger flared against us, they would have swallowed us alive;
the flood would have engulfed us, the torrent would have swept
over us, the raging waters would have swept us away. Praise be to
the Lord, who has not let us be torn by their teeth. We have escaped
like a bird out of the fowler's snare; the snare has been broken, and
we have escaped. Our help is in the name of the Lord, the Maker of
heaven and earth."* Psalm 124:2–8.

When I awoke I was in a holding cell at the Zhengzhou
City Public Security Bureau headquarters. Brother Xu and
the other leaders were with me. I was covered in mud from
the officers' boots, my ears were swollen from being beaten,
and I couldn't hear properly.

We learned the order to arrest us had come all the way
down from the central government in Beijing. They had

somehow learned that we were planning to unite. The house churches were already a thorn in the flesh of the atheistic Communist state, and to think about what could be accomplished if we were unified brought terror to the highest levels of the government. The order from Beijing forced the Henan provincial authorities to treat our case extremely seriously. Not understanding that God's kingdom is not a kingdom of this world, they feared our unity talks would result in the formation of a political opposition party that would threaten the stability of our country.

The authorities videotaped and photographed the arrest. News of the incident leaked out of China and became known around the world.

We were all tortured horrendously. We were handcuffed and tied together with rope, then beaten with sticks and batons. We expected to be taken out and executed at any time.

The authorities tried to gather evidence against me, so just three days after our arrest they travelled to my home town of Nanyang. When they arrived they found a large church meeting already in progress with about 120 believers present, including my wife Deling. They were all arrested. The main leaders from that meeting were identified and sent to prison, including Deling. Most of the other believers were ordered to pay fines and then released after being interrogated and beaten.

At my court hearing the judge said, "Yun, I'm sick of you. For many years you've opposed our government and turned our society upside down. You've escaped from custody on numerous occasions. This time you jumped out of the window and fractured your legs. Tell me Yun, if you have the opportunity to escape again, will you take it?"

I thought about it and answered truthfully, "Judge, that is

244 THE HEAVENLY MAN

a good question. I don't want to lie to you. If I have an oppor-
tunity, I will try to escape. I'm called to preach the Good
News all over China, and I must do all I can to obey the call
God has placed on my life."

The judge, court officials and guards were all furious at
my answer. The judge snarled, "How dare you, you delin-
quent! I'm going to break your legs permanently so you'll
never escape again!"

I was taken to an interrogation room where several guards
forced me to the floor and made me sit with my legs apart. I
begged them not to beat my fractured legs, but one sinister-
looking man hardened his heart and pulled out his baton. To
ensure I would never be able to escape, he struck my legs
between my knees and feet repeatedly. He destroyed my
legs until I could stand the pain no more. I lay on the ground
screaming like a wounded animal. Excruciating pain surged
through my body and mind. All I could do was try to focus
my thoughts on the Lord Jesus and his suffering on the cross.

I thought I was surely going to die but the Lord sustained me
because he wasn't finished with me. My legs below my knees
turned completely black and there was no feeling in them at all.
My entire body ached and was bruised from head to toe.

When my torturers carried me back to my cell, however, I
wanted to show them defiantly that they could never break
my spirit, so I laughed and told them, "I want to thank you
for the wonderful massage you gave me today. I feel much
better. Thank you!"

After my court hearing I was transferred, along with the
other brothers, to the Zhengzhou Number One Maximum
Security Prison. I was placed in solitary confinement. My cell
was near the duty officer's room, and shared a wall with
Brother Xu's cell. The guards thought I'd lost my mind and
gave me two nicknames, "crazy" and "cripple".

At the start, I was beaten and questioned non-stop from eight o'clock in the morning until the evening of the next day. The interrogators took shifts so that they could keep up the pressure on me and beat me throughout the night. I wasn't given any food or water the whole time.

Whenever the guards beat me I repeatedly shouted, "Jesus, save me! Help me, Lord Jesus!" This was the only way I knew to distance my thoughts from the punishment and pain being inflicted upon me.

After that initial experience, we were locked inside our cells except when we were taken for interrogation every second day. Despite my condition, they still regularly tortured me, hoping to break my spirit. Sometimes we were driven back and forth to the Dingshui Police Station for interrogation, at other times to the Zhengzhou Number Nine Public Security headquarters, so we could "taste two flavours" of torture. They especially beat us on our heads, hands and legs.

I had no Bible with me, so I meditated on God's Word from memory and prayed in tears for the churches. I shouted out Bible verses at the top of my voice, clinging to God's promises such as Psalm 27:1–3, *"The Lord is my light and my salvation – whom shall I fear? The Lord is the stronghold of my life – of whom shall I be afraid? When evil men advance against me to devour my flesh, when my enemies and my foes attack me, they will stumble and fall. Though an army besiege me, my heart will not fear; though war break out against me, even then will I be confident."*

I sang out loudly day and night. On one occasion the on-duty guard was mad at me. He asked, "Are you going to spend the rest of your life in here, you professional criminal?"

I replied, "No! When the Lord's time has arrived I'll be released immediately."

At least on the outside I acted courageously and boldly, but inwardly I was grieving and in great pain. During one interrogation the officers told me I would either be sentenced to life in prison, or, if my attitude improved, I might receive a ten- to fifteen-year sentence.

Faced with such a dim future, I grumbled and complained to the Lord, and even accused him, "O God, I just want to serve you and spread your gospel, but now I'm stuck here in this cell and cannot even walk. You're weak and failed to protect me!"

Because I couldn't walk, three different Christian prisoners, including Brother Xu, were given the job of carrying me between my cell, the torture room, and the toilet. I was in a separate cell from the other leaders so we eagerly longed for these brief moments of fellowship.

The torture room was three floors away from my cell, so that afforded us the longest opportunity to talk. Brother Xu didn't want to carry me to that room, but I told him not to worry, as they would just provide someone else to do the job if he didn't. Often the few precious minutes we had together strengthened me to endure the beatings and humiliations meted out inside that dark room.

Brother Xu is a softly spoken man. He didn't tell me what he was going through, but one day I saw him returning to his cell. He has a very powerful build and is a fast runner, but that day he could barely hobble along the corridor. I realized that he too was being tortured.

A young guard carried me around on certain occasions. He saw I was in great pain, and knew I'd received no medical treatment. This young man sympathetically told me, "I am seeing a man truly suffer for Jesus' name."

Surprised, I looked into his face. He continued, "After I graduated from the police academy I came to work here. I come from a Christian family but we're not strong believers like you. Why should anyone believe in Jesus and preach for him, if this is what you get in return?"

I told him, "You might not see any benefits in my life right now, but in the future I will receive a great blessing from Jesus because of these sufferings."

This young man continued reluctantly to beat me as his job required, but he always targeted the parts of my body that would result in the least damage to me.

A "false criminal" was placed in Brother Xu's cell. He pretended to be a Christian but it was obvious he was in the cell to spy and gather as much information as he could. He often acted sympathetically towards me in front of the other prisoners, and would ask Brother Xu, "Do you think Yun will try to escape?" Despite my crippled legs, the authorities were still afraid I would try to escape when I had the chance!

One day it was time for the prisoners to go to the toilet. The spy had fallen gravely ill. His face was pale and it looked as if death was knocking at his door. I told the guard, "I have some experience as a masseur. Please give me five minutes with that sick man and he'll feel better."

The guard had me carried into the cell. When I entered, Brother Xu looked at me with eyes of fire. He nodded his head and started to pray. I prayed for the sick man in the name of Jesus and laid my hands on his head. After a few moments he exclaimed, "I feel a hot breeze inside me!"

A few minutes later the guard returned. He asked, "How is the massage going?"

The sick man replied, "It's going well. I've almost recovered."

The Lord totally healed that man. To show his gratitude, he used some of his money and influence to give me good food. After this incident even some of the prison guards asked me to massage their bodies when they were in pain, so they started to treat me better.

Even though that man had been sent to spy on us, God used him to bless me greatly. He claimed to be a believer, and said his wife had managed to smuggle a Bible into the prison for him. More likely, the authorities had given him a Bible to help him appear a Christian, so he could win our confidence. Because he didn't have any interest in reading his Bible, I borrowed it and studied every evening and morning. I wrote down many Scriptures on small pieces of paper and passed them to the brothers to strengthen them by God's Word.

Some days later Brother Xu carved a picture on the toilet wall to teach the believers we should be faithful and not deny the Lord. I added the words, "Blood, Death, Testimony" under the picture.

Later, Brother Xu wrote a few Scriptures and some words of encouragement on a piece of toilet paper. He rolled it up and placed it inside a *mantou*, then threw it to me across the prison hall. He wrote, "From the beginning of the church until today, all who follow Jesus have had to take up their cross and pay a high price." Brother Xu also hinted to me that he thought I should try to escape if I had an opportunity.

As the weeks slowly passed, I became more and more depressed at my situation. It seemed as if the Lord had rejected me and left me to rot in prison forever. My legs were crippled and my spirit crushed. Each night I propped my lame legs up against the wall to try to lessen the pain.

My beloved wife Deling was in the women's prison, and I had no idea what had become of my two children.

It was the lowest point of my life.

*   *   *

DELING: Because of our abnormal lives, it has been extremely difficult at times for our children, but they've also experienced so much love from fellow Christians to help lessen their pain.

No boy of Isaac's age should ever have to deal with the kind of pressures he has faced. The most difficult time for him was in March and April 1997, when both his parents were in prison for the gospel. Isaac was just 13 years old.

When both parents are imprisoned in China the state tries to take control of the children and place them in a "protective environment". This means they brainwash them with atheistic teaching, and try to alienate them and cause them to hate their parents.

When both Yun and I were in prison, Christian friends moved Isaac and Yilin from our home village to Nanyang, where they attempted to go to school under assumed names. But the security police were searching for them so they were moved to Zhengzhou City, capital of Henan. But even there it was unsafe, so our children were sent to faraway Shandong Province, where a Christian family took care of them.

This was a very stressful time for Isaac and Yilin. In just a few months they had to change schools and move three or four times. Isaac had a lot of responsibility resting on his young shoulders. He had to look after his little sister, all the while trying to understand what had happened to his mother and father.

Later we were told that in Shandong, Isaac walked around looking down at the ground all the time, hoping to see some money that might have been dropped. The family who hosted them was very poor and could hardly afford to buy food.

After my release from prison I was secretly smuggled out of Henan and taken to see my children. When I first saw Isaac, he told me, "Mama, I have great burdens in my life now."

I asked, "Isaac, you are just a child. How can you carry heavy burdens at your age?"

My 13-year-old son replied, "Father is in prison again. How are we going to survive? I worry about the future."

CHAPTER TWENTY-TWO

A MIRACULOUS ESCAPE

"Now get up and stand on your feet." Acts 26:16.

It was at this lowest point of my life that I bitterly complained to the Lord.

I was 39 years old but saw no hope or future for me. I told the Lord, "When I was young you called me to preach your gospel in the west and south. How can I do that now? I'm sitting here in this prison with crushed legs and I'm resigned to rot in this place until the day I die. I'll never see my family again. You have cheated me!"

Rumours abounded as to what would happen to us. Even outside the prison, believers knew our arrest was extremely serious because the order had come from the central government.

And now, Brother Xu was suggesting to me that I should try to escape! I know Xu is a man of God who listens closely to God's voice, so I politely told him, "My legs are smashed and I am locked in my own cell with an iron door. I cannot even walk! How can I escape? Your legs are fine. Why don't you escape?"

On the evening of 4 May 1997, like every evening for the previous six weeks, I reached down and took hold of my limp legs. Pain raced through my body as I propped them up against the wall. I found this was the best way to minimize the agony. By diverting the blood flow away from my legs they became numb and I could sleep fitfully throughout the night.

The very next morning, in my depressed and hopeless condition, the Lord encouraged me with a promise from Hebrews 10:35, *"So do not throw away your confidence; it will be richly rewarded."* I awoke with these words in my mind.

As the prison slowly stirred to life, I started to read the Book of Jeremiah. The Lord related it to my injuries and my situation in a very powerful and personal way. It was as if the Holy Spirit was speaking to me directly through his Word: *"Let my eyes overflow with tears night and day without ceasing; for my virgin daughter – my people – has suffered a grievous wound, a crushing blow. . . . Have you rejected Judah completely? Do you despise Zion? Why have you afflicted us so that we cannot be healed? We hoped for peace but no good has come, for a time of healing but there is only terror. . . . For the sake of your name do not despise us; do not dishonour your glorious throne. Remember your covenant with us and do not break it."* Jeremiah 14:17,19,21.

I felt just like Jeremiah. I was overwhelmed and it seemed as if the Lord had abandoned me to rot in prison forever. I cried out to the Lord, echoing Jeremiah's words, "Oh God, why have you afflicted me so that I cannot be healed? I hoped for peace, but no good has come. Please Lord, do not despise me."

I continued reading, *"Alas, my mother, that you gave me birth, a man with whom the whole land strives and contends! I have neither lent nor borrowed, yet everyone curses me."* Jeremiah 15:10.

Once again the words seemed to leap off the paper and

into my spirit. It was a very holy time, as though God Almighty himself had descended into my cell and was dealing with me face to face.

I had so much grief stored up inside me, and it all started to gush out before the Lord. I sobbed, "Lord Jesus, just like Jeremiah said, everyone strives against me and curses me. I can't take any more. I've reached the end of myself."

I wept so hard that my eyes became swollen from all my tears.

My Lord comforted me like a loving father holding his little boy. He reassured me with the next verse, *"The Lord said, 'Surely I will deliver you for a good purpose: surely I will make your enemies plead with you in times of disaster and times of distress.'" Jeremiah 15:11.*

From my inmost being I cried out to the Lord from Jeremiah 15:16–18, *"When your words came, I ate them; they were my joy and my heart's delight, for I bear your name, O Lord God Almighty. I never sat in the company of revellers, never made merry with them; I sat alone because your hand was on me and you had filled me with indignation. Why is my pain unending and my wound grievous and incurable? Will you be to me like a deceptive brook, like a spring that fails?"*

Many times I asked him why I was in such pain. I could bear it no more. My heart was downcast and I was ready to give up.

God's Word came again to me with both a severe warning and a promise, *"Therefore this is what the Lord says: 'If you repent, I will restore you that you may serve me; if you utter worthy, not worthless, words, you will be my spokesman. Let this people turn to you, but you must not turn to them. I will make you a wall to this people, a fortified wall of bronze; they will fight against you but will not overcome you, for I am with you to rescue and save you,' declares the Lord. 'I will save you from the hands of the wicked and redeem you from the grasp of the cruel.'"* Jeremiah 15:19–21.

As soon as I read these verses, a powerful vision suddenly came to me even though I was wide awake.

I saw my wife Deling sitting beside me. She had just been released from prison and was preparing some medicine. She lovingly treated my wounds. I felt greatly encouraged and asked her, "Have you been released?"

She replied, "Why don't you open the iron door?"

Before I could answer she walked out of the room and the vision ended.

The Lord spoke to me, "This is the hour of your salvation."

Immediately I knew this was a vision from the Lord, and that I was meant to try to escape.

My solitary cell shared a wall with the cell containing Brother Xu and some of the other believers. We had a pre-arranged signal that if any of us were in trouble and needed urgent prayer we would knock twice on the wall.

Brother Xu heard my knock.

I called to the guard. He came to my door and asked me what I wanted. I told him, "I need to go to the toilet right now."

Because it was Brother Xu's job to carry me around, the guard opened his door and ordered him to carry me to the bathroom.

Whenever prisoners were allowed outside their cells, an iron gate in the corridor was locked, so there would be no chance of escape. A stairwell leading down to the floors below was on the other side of the gate. We were still completely closed in. The gate opened for people on the outside coming back in, but could not be opened from the inside.

Each floor of the prison was protected by an iron gate. Normally two guards were stationed on either side of every gate, so to make it to the prison courtyard I would have to go through three iron gates on three floors, and pass six armed guards.

Brother Xu came to my door. As soon as he saw me he commanded me, "You must escape!" He then went back to his own cell, and collected his toothbrush and towel so the guards would think he was about to use the bathroom.

When Brother Xu returned, he again solemnly ordered me, "Yun, you must escape!"

I was dressed only in my underwear, so as quickly as I could I pulled my trousers up. I had written Scriptures from the Gospel of John and 1 Peter on a long piece of toilet paper. I fashioned it into a belt of truth, fastening the Word of God around my waist. I prayed, "Lord, you have shown me that I must try to leave this prison. I will obey you now and will try to escape. But when the guards shoot me, please receive my soul into your heavenly dwelling."

It was now more than six weeks since my legs had been smashed. Even putting a little weight on them caused tremendous agony. But I believed God had told me in three different ways that I was to try to escape: through his Word, through the vision I'd received that morning, and through Brother Xu.

I have learned that when the Lord tells us to do something there is no time for discussion or rationale, regardless of the situation we face. When we are sure God has told us to act, as I was on this occasion, blind obedience is called for. Not to obey God implies that we are wiser than him, and that we know better how to run our lives than he does.

It was just before eight o'clock in the morning of 5 May 1997. To the natural mind, this time of day was the worst possible time to try to escape! There was normally so much activity throughout the prison, with all the guards at their posts.

I shuffled out of my cell and walked towards the locked iron gate in the hallway. My mind was solely focused on obeying God. I looked straight ahead and prayed beneath my breath with every step I took.

A guard who pushed a button when he wanted the gate to open and close sat at the top of the third-floor stairwell. It was impossible to see to the other side because the gate was made of iron and the small windows were covered with black cloth. At the exact moment I reached the gate, another servant of the Lord, Brother Musheng, was returning to his cell and the gate was opened for him. That morning he had been ordered to sweep the prison courtyard. As Musheng passed me I told him, "Wait! Don't close the gate." I walked through without even breaking my stride! The Lord's timing was perfect!

As we passed, Musheng asked in a whisper, "Are you leaving, Brother Yun? Are you not afraid to die?" Then, with an astonished look on his face, he returned to his cell.

There had been a guard accompanying Musheng back to his cell, but at the exact moment he opened the gate for Musheng, a telephone rang in an office down the hallway and the guard turned and ran to answer it.

I noticed a broom leaning against the wall in the stairwell. I picked it up and continued walking with it down the stairs to the second floor. An armed guard was positioned at his desk facing the second iron gate. That gate was sometimes left open. Because an on-duty guard was assigned to watch the gate day and night, it wasn't considered a risk to leave it unlocked. At that moment the Holy Spirit spoke to me, "Go now! The God of Peter is your God!"

Somehow the Lord seemed to blind that guard. He was staring directly at me, yet his eyes didn't acknowledge my presence at all. I expected him to say something, but he just looked through me as if I was invisible!

He didn't say a word.

I continued past him and didn't look back. I knew I could be shot in the back at any moment. I continued to silently ask the Lord to be ready to receive my spirit, thinking these moments were to be my last in this world.

I continued walking down the stairs, but nobody stopped me and none of the guards said a word to me!

When I arrived at the main iron gate leading out to the courtyard I discovered it was already open! This was strange, as it was usually the most secure gate of all. There were normally two guards stationed at the first-floor gate, one on the inside and one on the outside, but for some reason neither of the guards was present and the gate was open!

I discarded the broom I had carried with me from the third floor and walked out into the courtyard. The bright morning light made me wince. I walked past several guards in the yard but nobody said a word to me. I then strolled through the main gate of the prison, which for some strange reason was also standing ajar!

My heart was pounding! I was now standing on the street outside the Zhengzhou Number One Maximum Security Prison! I was told later nobody had ever escaped from that prison before.

Immediately a small yellow taxi-van pulled up next to me, and the driver – a man in his late 20s – opened the passenger door. He asked, "Where are you heading?"

I got in and replied, "I need to go to my office as quickly as possible, so please drive fast." I gave the driver the address of a Christian family I knew in Zhengzhou and we drove away from the prison. I told him that if we came to a traffic jam to drive around it, and not to stop for any reason.

All of these events seemed to happen in just a few moments. It was like a daydream. I was unsure if the whole thing had really happened or if I was dreaming. I don't know how the Lord did it or why all those iron gates, usually so tightly locked, were standing open for me. All I knew was I was sitting in a taxi and we were heading to the home of my friends.

When we arrived I asked the driver to wait while I went to borrow some money to pay the fare.

I climbed the stairs to the third-floor apartment and rang the doorbell twice. One of the daughters of the family looked through the security hole in the door and immediately recognized me. She excitedly said, "Oh Brother Yun, you have been released from the hospital (meaning, prison)!"

I told her, "Yes, I've left the hospital, but I didn't do so by the normal procedure. Can you please lend me some money so I can pay my taxi fare?"

She was so excited to see me that she forgot to open the door! Finally she returned and gave me the amount. I quickly ran downstairs to the waiting driver and paid him.

The precious Christian family warmly welcomed me inside their home. One of the daughters told me, "The whole church has been fasting and praying for you and your co-workers for more than a week. Yesterday the Holy Spirit told my mother, 'I will release Yun and the first place he will stop will be your home. He will stay for a short time and will pray with you.'

"My parents told us to expect your arrival and we have organized a secret place for you to hide. Nobody else knows about the place except us. My mother has already prepared some food and clothes for you. Come, change your clothes and we'll take you there."

After we prayed together, I was given a bicycle and one of

the family members rode on the back, directing me to my hiding place, wisely travelling down small alleyways to avoid the roadblocks being set up on the main streets because of my escape.

The moment I started to pedal the bicycle was the first time I realized the Lord had healed my feet and legs! My mind had been so focused on obeying the Lord and preparing to be shot that I never even noticed that God had healed me. I never felt any healing power. From the time my legs were smashed with a baton until the day I escaped, my legs had remained completely black and unusable. I couldn't even stand up, let alone walk. The most I could do was crawl a short distance by grabbing hold of the wall.

Brother Musheng told me later that when he passed me on the third floor I was walking normally, so it seems the Lord must have healed my legs while I was still in the prison cell. As I rode along on the bicycle I was reminded of God's Word, *"Make level paths for your feet, so that the lame may not be disabled, but rather healed." Hebrews 12:13.*

As soon as we arrived at the hiding place the heavens opened. Torrential rain blanketed the whole of Zhengzhou City and a howling wind rattled windows and blew bicycles over. It was a huge storm. Although it was still morning time, the sky turned black.

I entered the hiding place and was left alone. This dear family treated me like an angel from heaven. They placed a family member outside my door day and night to guard me.

Later, Christian friends told me they had seen a report on the television news on the evening of my escape. The Security Police, the Public Security Bureau and soldiers from the People's Liberation Army had been mobilized to find me. They searched every house in Zhengzhou from door to door. They set up roadblocks at all the major intersections and searched every vehicle. Officers were dispatched to every bus station, train station and to the airport.

I was told trained police sniffer-dogs were used in a bid to pick up my scent, but their efforts were all in vain. I was safe in the secret hiding place of the Lord. The storm had hampered the authorities and washed away all traces of me.

God reminded me how thirteen years earlier, during my 74-day fast in prison, he had given me a powerful vision of a series of iron gates opening, one after another.

Now, all these years later, his promise had come true. I marvelled at God's goodness and faithfulness to me. To this day I consider my escape from prison the most amazing experience of my life.

That night I slept like a content newborn baby in the arms of my Lord.

*   *   *

BROTHER XU: After Brother Yun tried to escape by jumping out of the window he broke his legs. They then beat him severely in the mud, smashing his legs further so he wouldn't be able to walk.

When I saw Yun's unconscious body being carried back to his cell, his whole face was covered in mud. They had beaten his head so he lost all hearing for a while.

After we'd been transferred to the Zhengzhou Prison I was given the job of carrying Yun to the bathroom and the prison interrogation room, because he was crippled and in terrible pain. In this way we were able to have brief moments of contact when we encouraged each other in the Lord and strengthened each other's faith. Even if we were unable to speak, just to look into each other's eyes gave us strength and fellowship. Yun and I go back a long way and have experienced much of God's grace together.

I told Yun the Lord wanted him to escape. The Lord surely led me to tell him this. I felt God wanted Yun to escape, but that he wanted me to stay.

One morning the Lord directly showed Yun it was time to escape. As he walked down the prison stairs towards the courtyard, another Christian brother was coming in. The security door was opened for him at exactly the same time Yun walked out!

That brother then ran to our cell and told everyone he had seen Yun walking out of the prison! The prisoners climbed up and looked out of the cell window into the courtyard. We watched as Yun walked out the front gate of the prison to freedom!

This act of God's mercy and power greatly encouraged us. We once again saw that nothing is impossible for God – absolutely nothing. He holds all our lives in his hands and not a thing will happen to one of God's children unless it is part of his plan and will for our lives.

I believe one reason why God chose to release Yun in such a manner was because the prison authorities had mocked the Lord and Yun when they smashed his legs. They said, "We'd like to see you escape now!" The Lord is always up to meeting a challenge!

Within a few minutes of Yun's escape the guards discovered he was missing and a huge manhunt was launched. A thorough investigation was held by the authorities to find out how a crippled prisoner in maximum-security solitary confinement could walk out of the prison and disappear!

Interestingly, the investigation concluded that Yun had received no human help from any of the prisoners or guards during his escape.

I testify that this is entirely true.

It was all the sovereign hand of our Almighty God.

*   *   *

BROTHER MUSHENG: I was privileged to witness Brother Yun escape from prison in 1997, by the hand of the Lord.

I had been called to work in the prison yard at seven o'clock that morning. As I walked back to my cell, escorted by a guard, we stopped to be let through an iron security gate. I couldn't believe it when I saw Yun walking out! We all knew that he was crippled, so to say I was surprised to see him walking is a great understatement! He walked right past me, but the guard with me didn't see him at all.

It wasn't until I returned to my cell that I realized I hadn't seen Yun walk since his legs were broken. I was one of three men who carried him around the prison. The guards even called him "the cripple". His legs were completely bruised from all the beatings he'd been given. He couldn't do anything for himself because of his sorry condition. We even had to wash his clothes for him.

It dawned on me that Yun was trying to escape. I immediately fell to my knees and begged God to save his life as I thought the guards had purposely let him out into the prison yard so they could shoot him. I climbed to the cell window and watched him cross the yard and disappear through the gate.

There were probably thirty prison guards in the yard at the time, but no one noticed Yun escape! He even walked right past several of them.

A short time later a great rainstorm came.

Back on the third floor of the prison, the guard noticed Yun was missing just a few minutes after his escape. He searched everywhere, calling out "Cripple, where are you?" To start with the guard was quite relaxed, but as the number of places Yun could have been hiding diminished he grew more and more anxious. After about five minutes he raised the alarm and the whole prison was in an uproar over Yun's escape.

The prison authorities interrogated us but we truthfully told them we hadn't helped Yun in any way. Two of the guards lost their jobs.

CHAPTER TWENTY-THREE

LEAVING THE BAMBOO CURTAIN

The morning after my prison escape I asked my friends to contact a house church leader in Zhengzhou, to let him know I had escaped, and to tell him I would visit his home that evening after dark.

The same morning at about 11 a.m., my wife received a vision from the Lord. Deling had been released from prison about two weeks before my escape and was hiding in a believer's home.

In her vision she saw I had been released. I was sitting in front of her and my face looked joyful and content. I asked my wife to assemble all the church elders and co-workers so we could have a meeting. She pointed her finger at me and said, "Don't you dare! Don't you have any fear? Are you not afraid to die?" I smiled at her and said nothing.

In response to her vision, Deling caught a bus to Zhengzhou. The first place she stopped was the home of the leader I was planning to visit that evening!

When my wife entered the old couple's house they asked her, "Are you aware that God's servant Brother Yun has escaped from prison?"

Deling stuttered, "Can you repeat what you said? Is it true? Has he really escaped?"

My wife slumped down in a chair and shared the vision she had received from the Lord earlier that morning. The brother laughed and exclaimed, "Ha! This proves that communication from the Lord is much faster than any telephone or computer!"

That evening when I arrived at the house I was amazed to see the face of my dear wife, and a number of co-workers who had assembled to see me.

The morning before God took me out of the prison he had shown me in a vision that my wife was free. She had then received a vision that I was free, and now, by the mighty hand of God, we were together! We hugged and sang together from Psalm 126:1–3,

> When the Lord brought back the captives to Zion,
>   we were like men who dreamed.
> Our mouths were filled with laughter,
>   our tongues with songs of joy.
> Then it was said among the nations,
>   "The Lord has done great things for them."
> The Lord has done great things for us,
>   and we are filled with joy.

Even though I was free, I longed to return to the prison to visit my co-workers and share with them what God had done. It's hard to explain how close the bonds are between Christian brothers in prison. I missed them and was concerned for their welfare.

*   *   *

DELING: About two weeks after my release from prison I was secretly staying in the home of two sisters. One day they went out and the Lord gave me a clear vision. I saw Yun was free and was preparing to go somewhere for a meeting! I asked him, "How did you escape? Why are you so busy?" He replied, "The Lord helped me come out. Now I must go and preach the gospel."

When the two sisters returned home I told them the Lord had shown me Yun was no longer in prison. At this time all the Christians were sure Yun would either be executed or imprisoned for life, so the two sisters didn't believe me. They said, "Oh, you must miss him very much!" and "We're sorry that you've suffered so much because of your husband's imprisonment."

They thought I was crazy! One was laughing at me and the other was concerned. She stared into my eyes to see if I'd lost my mind. I ignored them and caught a bus to Zhengzhou.

A few hours later I was told that Yun was free!

The whole incident of my husband's prison escape, and the way God told me about it in my vision, completely enlarged my understanding of God's greatness. For the first time I really knew that absolutely nothing is impossible for him!

*   *   *

YUN: The church leaders in Zhengzhou wanted us to leave the area and move as far away as we could, for they believed it was too dangerous for us to stay in the city.

The police were still searching everywhere for me. My escape was a major embarrassment for the government and especially for the prison authorities.

I was told later that the Public Security Bureau even sent undercover female officers to house church meetings in the city, pretending to be Christians. They said, "We are friends of Brother Yun and we heard how the Lord helped him escape. Do you know how he's doing?" They were hoping to elicit some information on my whereabouts.

Because both Deling and I had been arrested, our children had to be sent to another province to be cared for by a Christian couple. Arrangements were made for us to be reunited with our dear children.

One swelteringly hot summer's day, my family and I met with some house church leaders. My little daughter Yilin rushed into the room shouting and crying, "Mother, the police are coming! Father must escape right away!"

We ran onto the roof of the house and were preparing to jump when we were told the police officers had gone in a different direction and weren't looking for us. We were relieved, yet this incident reminded us of the pressure we were under.

At this time Deling started to share with me that she was praying God would open a door so we could have a more settled family life. She was deeply concerned at the impact such a stressful lifestyle was having on our children.

I wasn't in good health at this time. I felt great pain in my chest and couldn't breathe properly, so I went to a clinic and got an X-ray. The doctor grimly told me, "You have either tuberculosis or a tumour." He wanted to admit me to the hospital immediately. My wife also advised me, "It's God's will for you to rest."

At first I stubbornly refused to be admitted. I wanted to keep on meeting with Christians, but the house church leaders from my home town visited and told me, "You must stop working and spend some time waiting upon the Lord. The authorities are searching for you everywhere. Under no circumstance should you return home, both for your own sake and for the sake of the other believers."

For the first time since I preached the gospel as a 16-year-old boy in Henan, all the doors firmly closed to me. My escape from prison had become well known and the authorities were doing everything possible to hunt me down. Church leaders knew that if they invited me to speak and the PSB raided the meeting, they would all face severe penalties. It was just too great a risk for them to take, so they advised me to lie low and keep out of public ministry.

During my period of illness I really struggled. I didn't really want to rest in God alone. Instead, I wanted to rest in the *work* of God. I realized again that I was a labourer who worked without real peace from the Lord. I loved *doing* things for the Lord so much that it had become my security and my source of joy. God wanted to remove this idol from my life.

My illness also allowed me to spend more time with my wife and children. We prayed together and waited upon the Lord to tell us what steps to take.

One morning during prayer I was overcome by the Lord's presence. He spoke to me like a friend, "I will send you to a new place. You won't understand a single word of their language. There will be many strange faces before you, but you must obey my command: 'Go and awaken those people!'"

I shared these words with my wife and children. They didn't know what to say. I hid the promise inside my heart.

On another occasion I was meditating upon the Apostle Paul's life and ministry. The Lord spoke to me, "*Quick! Leave ... immediately, because they will not accept your testimony about me.*" Acts 22:18. He continued, "Yun, you must hurry up. Leave China. Do not delay! Your witness for me in China is complete. The people will not accept your ministry among them any more for they are too frightened."

The next day I received a telephone call from a dear friend. His words – spoken without any knowledge of what the Lord had told me – confirmed God's leading. He said, "Brother Yun, the Lord has shown me he is preparing a new ministry for you. It's the fulfilment of what he called you to do as a child: 'Go west and south and preach the gospel.'"

After that call I fully realized the Lord was leading my life in a drastically new direction.

I shared everything with my wife. Deling agreed from the bottom of her heart that the Lord wanted me to leave China and go to the west and south.

I had one major problem. I had no passport and had never travelled outside China in all my life. I couldn't apply for a passport because I had a criminal record. If I applied I would be immediately arrested.

We prayed and committed this need to the Lord.

A short time later I met with some Christian brothers. When I shared what the Lord was calling me to do, a businessman with a passport felt the Lord prompt him to give his passport to me. He said, "Brother Yun, here is my passport. Use it as the Lord leads you. Don't worry about me. If trouble comes to me later because of this, I will accept it."

When we looked at the passport we noticed another problem. The picture of this brother looked absolutely nothing like me! He was balding and wore glasses. I had shaggy hair and completely different features. This brother was also much older than me!

Believing the Lord had told me to preach his gospel among the nations of the world, a time was set for me to leave China and a ticket was purchased from Beijing to Frankfurt with Air China on 28 September 1997.

The day before my departure I taught all day at a house church Bible school that I had helped establish in the Beijing area. When I shared that God had commanded me to take his gospel to the nations of the world the students were deeply touched, and prayed fervently for me with many tears. I asked them to pray for me continuously from that evening until noon the next day, by which time my flight would have departed. These young men and women stayed up all night calling on the Lord in prayer, asking him to protect me and grant success. On many occasions since that day I've remembered the deep love those beautiful students had for the Lord and for me. Today they are serving God all across China in remote areas like Tibet and Inner Mongolia.

The night before the flight I was very nervous. I'd never been on a large aircraft before. I knew that if caught, I would be detained on the most serious charges and would surely – unless the Lord intervened – face the death penalty once the authorities realized I'd escaped from prison. I wanted to make sure I was acting according to God's will, and that we had his seal of approval. If anyone had expressed a reservation to me that evening I would probably have cancelled my plans. But not one of my co-workers or the students gave me anything except words of encouragement and confirmation.

Three co-workers and I also stayed up all night seeking the Lord's protection. By morning I felt exhausted from struggling all night, like Jacob when he wrestled with God. I kept thinking about what might happen to me, and what I would say if the airport officials questioned me. I was also concerned because it was just a few days before National Day on 1 October, so security in Beijing was tighter than usual.

During intense prayer at dawn, one of my co-workers said, "Servant of God, don't panic. I've received a word from the Lord for you." The message was from Genesis 27:20, *"Isaac asked his son, 'How did you find it so quickly, my son?' 'The Lord your God gave me success,' he replied."*

This verse greatly encouraged me and summarized what had happened to me. In response to the prayers of many, the Lord had put the whole thing together quickly. One day I was in prison with broken legs and no hope or future. Now, just a few months later, I was preparing to leave China for the first time in my life, even though I was a wanted "criminal" with no passport or identity card.

I replied by quoting the Apostle Paul, *"So keep up your courage . . . for I have faith in God that it will happen just as he told me." Acts 27:25.*

Before dawn the Lord gave me a strong word of warning, "When you enter the customs hall at the airport, say only what I instruct you to say" and with it came a Scripture, *"When words are many, sin is not absent, but he who holds his tongue is wise." Proverbs 10:19.*

Outside Beijing Airport I called Deling and the children and asked them to pray for me. Deling sounded very calm, because she had perfect peace that God was leading me to leave China.

Because I'd never been through airport procedures before, one brother showed me how to fill out the forms, where to check in, and where to pay my departure tax. I then walked into the customs area, remembering what the Lord had told me, "When you enter the customs hall at the airport, say only what I instruct you to say."

I waited in line for my documents to be checked. Finally I reached the front of the line. I handed over the passport and boarding pass. The officer looked at the picture and then at me, and started to laugh, "Ha! This photo isn't you! It looks nothing like you at all!" He then held the passport up for the officers in the other booths to see. They too laughed contemptuously.

This may sound difficult to believe, but I felt completely calm inside. I'd been nervous the previous night, but the Lord had made it clear that I was to leave China and now I was one hundred per cent confident I was in his will. A supernatural peace flooded my heart.

The officer then went into a side office, came back and again said, "It's not you!" He was determined to find out who I was. I stared with a look of intense fire directly into his eyes.

Several minutes passed and the line of passengers behind me began to grow impatient and chastised the officer for taking so long. Sensing their growing anger, he told me to stand to the side while he processed the other passengers.

When he had finished he told me, "It's obvious this passport doesn't belong to you. But even if I let you go, there's no way you will get permission to enter Germany. They'll place you on the next flight back!"

Incredibly, he stamped my passport and said, "Go!"

There was no human reason for the officer to do this. All I can say is that the Lord was in control of the situation, influencing the officer to do his will.

Next I progressed to the X-ray machine for the customs check. As I placed my carry-on bag on the scanner I noticed an officer speaking into his walkie-talkie while staring straight at me. I walked forward and collected my bag, and the officer didn't say a word. Again, by the hand of God, I was allowed to pass!

In the waiting area I called a brother on a public telephone to let him know I'd made it through. Within a few minutes I boarded the aircraft, the door was locked, and the Air China jet pulled away from the gate. Soon I was airborne! A torrent of joy and thanksgiving welled up inside me. As soon as the wheels lifted off the tarmac I couldn't help singing out loud,

Lord, you have chosen me from among the people
You have spread your wings of love over me
Your grace has saved so many lost souls
And taught us how to live in your light
Therefore I will praise you forever!

All the passengers in front of me turned around and stared at me, wondering who this madman was who'd been let onto the plane!

I left China for the first time in my life, that I might bring glory to the King of Kings before many peoples and nations.

During the long flight I thought back over my life and thanked God for his boundless grace. I know that I am the least part of the body of Christ in China. I am nothing. It's certainly not because of any special skills or abilities that God chose me to be his ambassador to the nations. It was only by his mysterious, undeserved grace.

About ten hours later my plane touched down in Frankfurt, Germany, and I proceeded to the immigration desk.

When I got to the front of the line the German officer looked at my passport. Immediately he raised his eyebrows and a stern look came across his face. He spoke to me but I couldn't understand, so I just stood there and smiled. He motioned for me to stand to the side.

Three other officers came to inspect my passport. They knew it wasn't mine. They shook their heads, and said in threatening voices, "No! No!"

At that moment a Scripture came into my mind, "The righteous are as bold as a lion." Proverbs 28:1. With the fire of God in my heart I stared at the main officer with a look of judgment in my eyes. The officer looked at me, stamped my passport, handed it back, and motioned for me to go!

It was only by the grace of God.

I was in Germany! As I sat in a vehicle taking me to a pastor's house, the Holy Spirit powerfully spoke these words to my heart, "In the same way that I brought you out of prison, and out of China, I will bring one hundred thousand of my children out of China to be my witnesses throughout Asia."

Two days later I phoned Deling and my children in China, and told them the Lord had safely delivered me to Germany. Deling's first question was, "When will you be back?" I told her I felt like Jesus when Joseph and Mary took him to Egypt as a baby. Only the Lord knew when I would be back. Deling and I made a solemn covenant before the Lord that if it looked as if I wouldn't be returning to China within two years then we would ask the Lord to miraculously bring my family out of China to be with me.

Two weeks after my arrival a Christian friend took me to a refugee detention centre in the city of Hamburg. The officers there were very surprised to hear my story and transferred me to another refugee centre in eastern Germany.

Because I didn't have any identification at all I couldn't prove who I was. Government officials came with a Chinese translator and asked me many questions about my past, my arrests, and how I had escaped from prison. I answered their questions absolutely truthfully, but they didn't believe me and their manner was very rude. The translator even told me to stop telling such fantastic lies, as it was harming my application! He said no Chinese person had been granted refugee status by the German government for more than two years.

By this time news had reached some German Christians that I had left China and was in their country. Some of these dear brothers had ministered with us in China before. They came to the refugee centre with copies of newspaper articles with my name on them, published after my arrest in March. The German brothers also showed photos of themselves with me in China, to prove they'd known me before I came to Germany. They signed statements and backed me up as much as they could. It seems the German Embassy in Beijing was also asked to investigate my claims. They soon discovered who I was.

At the detention centre I was given a full physical checkup. They saw my body still bore the scars from my tortures in China. I was told I either had tuberculosis or lung cancer, and that I would have to go to hospital to recover. I had lived with lung problems for more than ten years, ever since the guards had stamped on my chest in prison.

The detention centre was a very basic facility, but it was far better than prison in China! We were allowed to travel outside during the daytime, although we weren't allowed to travel a distance of more than fifty kilometres from the centre.

I spent 69 days in the hospital, and a further three months in the detention centre while my application for refugee status was being considered.

*   *   *

DELING: After Yun's miraculous prison escape, the whole country seemed to be searching for him. It was very tense. The church leaders told him he couldn't train workers or lead meetings because the risk was just too great for the believers. The PSB were close on his trail and everyone he had contact with was put in great danger.

For a month after Yun's escape we hid in Wuhan City in Hubei Province, but the people who were hiding us were so fearful they couldn't sleep at night.

We relocated to Shandong Province, but after staying there for a little while we discovered the host family also could not sleep. They were too worried about their safety and the consequences if Yun was caught in their home. We cried out to God, "Lord, how can we serve you? Everywhere we go people are on edge and are unable to sleep."

God seemed to be saying that Yun might possibly leave China and go to the West. We prayed about it for more than a month to find out if it was God's will. Finally the Lord confirmed to us that this was indeed his plan. We laid a fleece before the Lord, "Father, if it is your will for Yun to leave China, we pray you will help him leave without any problems whatsoever."

In Beijing, Yun miraculously boarded an aircraft and left China. We all knew this had been completely in God's will.

*   *   *

YUN: More than two years later, at a meeting in Finland, I shared the testimony of my prison escape and how the Lord enabled me to leave China.

Afterwards a Christian businessman came up and told my translator and me something remarkable, which made me realize how merciful God had been on the day I left Beijing.

The Finnish brother said, "I work for a certain telecommunications security company. Several years ago we won the contract to install state-of-the-art voice recognition software at various border points around China, including at Beijing Airport.

"Using hidden microphones, these programmes allow officials to quickly match the voice of suspicious passengers against a computerized database containing the voice patterns of wanted criminals. You can be certain your voice was in their database, because so many recordings have been made of you preaching.

"If you had opened your mouth that day in Beijing Airport and said anything, you would surely have been arrested on the spot."

I thanked the Lord for his wisdom and mercy, when he told me, "When you enter the customs hall at the airport, say only what I instruct you to say." He hadn't prompted me to say anything to the officials, so I didn't say a word.

It always pays to obey the Lord!

*   *   *

My dear Brother Xu had told me to escape while we were in prison in 1997, and now he remained behind bars while I was in the West.

God worked a great miracle for Brother Xu. Many people believed he would receive the death sentence, and in fact a few months after our arrest it was erroneously reported in newspapers around the world that he had been executed.

At the trial Brother Xu refused to defend himself or answer any charges, claiming that the "trial" was little more than an artificial act to legitimize a pre-arranged verdict. He was given a ten-year sentence. For an unknown reason it was later reduced to three years, and he was released in May 2000. We know this was nothing short of a great miracle and blessing from the Lord.

During his three years in prison, Brother Xu experienced much torture and affliction. The prison officials even hand-cuffed his wrists to each side of an iron gate in such a way that when the gate was pulled open he was stretched up off the ground in a crucifix position, causing his internal organs to be agonizingly stretched.

His torturers would then relax the gate, giving Xu a moment's relief, before again pulling the gate open. They repeated this process again and again, causing my dear brother to say later, "I came to know how Jesus must have felt on the cross."

In May 2000 I was in the United States on a speaking trip. I knew the day Brother Xu was to be released and wanted to surprise him. Security around Brother Xu in prison had been so tight that he had no idea what had happened to me after I escaped in 1997. For three years he didn't know if I had been killed, captured, or remained free.

Just minutes after he walked free I called Brother Xu on his co-worker's mobile phone. Xu's deep, rich voice answered. "Dear Brother Xu," I excitedly exclaimed, "This is your old cell mate Brother Yun! I'm calling you from America! God has taken me out of China by his mighty hand!"

Brother Xu, with overwhelming joy in his voice, shouted, "Hallelujah! God has sent you out of China so the Chinese and Western churches can co-operate for the gospel. You will be a witness of the Lord's mighty work in China!"

We shouted and talked excitedly, trying to catch up in a few minutes with the three missing years since we last saw each other's face.

In the early years I viewed Brother Xu as my father in the faith. I looked up to him as a great leader of China's church. I still look up to him of course, but in recent years I've come to view Brother Xu as my dear brother in the faith. Outside my own family, Brother Xu is my dearest friend and co-worker in the work of the gospel.

CHAPTER TWENTY-FOUR

BACK TO JERUSALEM

Although China is a long, long way from Jerusalem, it's one of history's remarkable facts that the Holy Land has been connected to China by road for more than two millennia.

Some old accounts even suggest the gospel may have first entered China down this road just a few decades after Jesus' death and resurrection. Seven centuries ago the famous explorer Marco Polo came to China along the same highway. This key trading route allowed herbs and spices, treasures, new religions, and invading armies to flow in and out of China. At the other end, Jerusalem acted as a hub from where products dispersed into Europe, North Africa, and the Middle East.

The European aristocracy was amazed when they first imported a most remarkable creature from China – the silkworm. It lent its name to this rugged route – popularly known as the Silk Road.

Today, the nations along the ancient Silk Road are the most unevangelized in the whole world. The three biggest religious strongholds that have refused to yield to the advance of the gospel – Islam, Buddhism, and Hinduism – have their heart here. More than 90% of the remaining unreached people groups in the world live along the Silk Road and in the nations surrounding China. Two billion of the earth's inhabitants live and die in this area, completely oblivious to the Good News that Jesus died for their sins and is the only way to heaven!

In the 1920s God first led a group called the "Jesus Family" to take the gospel on foot all the way from China to Jerusalem. They called the initiative "Back to Jerusalem". Other Chinese church groups received similar visions to start missionary movements that would impact many nations in Asia and the Middle East.

Founded in 1921 in Shandong Province by a Christian named Jing Dianying, the Jesus Family believed members should sell all their possessions and distribute their wealth among the other family members. The five-word slogan of the Jesus Family encapsulated their commitment to Christ and their pattern of frugal living: "Sacrifice, abandonment, poverty, suffering, death."

They targeted towns and villages, preaching the gospel as they walked from one place to another. Their example of communal living and the Jesus Family's deep Christian love amazed many onlookers. It attracted those searching for answers to life as well as those who were homeless, destitute and despised. Many blind people and beggars joined the Jesus Family and found eternal life in Christ.

As they continued to grow, the Jesus Family suffered terrible hardships. Often when this mobile community entered a new town the entire population came out to beat, scorn and humiliate them. The opposition didn't deter them, however, and when they preached the gospel there always seemed to be a few people who were willing to forsake all that they had to follow Jesus.

By the late 1940s there were some 20,000 Chinese believers enlisted in more than 100 different Jesus Family groups throughout China.

Several groups believed God had called them to take the gospel back to Jerusalem on foot, preaching and establishing the kingdom of God in all the territories along the way. After thousands of miles and many years of travel, a band of faithful preachers reached the border town of Kashgar in the Xinjiang Region of north-west China.

*   *   *

In the autumn of 1995 I was speaking at a house church gathering in central China. The Lord had given me a deep desire to be part of his plan to send many Chinese Christians as missionaries into Hindu, Buddhist and Muslim lands. I encouraged the believers to seek God for a worldwide vision. I challenged them not only to continue in their present ministries, but to expand their horizons to include the unreached nations surrounding China.

With tears in my eyes I sang a song I had learned from an old book about the Back to Jerusalem Movement:

Lift up your eyes toward the West
There are no labourers for the great harvest
My Lord's heart is grieving every day
He asks, "Who will go forth for me?"

With eyes filled with tears
And blood splattered across our chests
We lift up the banner of Christ
And will rescue the perishing sheep!

In these last days the battle is drawing near
And the trumpet is sounding aloud
Let's quickly put on the full armour of God
And break through Satan's snares!

Death is knocking at the door of many
And the world is overcome with sin
We must faithfully work as we march onward
Fighting even unto death!

With hope and faith we will march on
Dedicating our family and all that we have
As we take up our heavy crosses
We march on toward Jerusalem!

While I was singing, I noticed an old man in the congregation who was visibly moved. He was weeping and could hardly contain himself. I had no idea who he was, and thought my preaching must have been really powerful to cause such a response! The old brother, crowned with white hair and a white beard, slowly walked to the front of the room and asked to speak. A respectful hush fell over the audience.

He said, "I am Simon Zhao, a servant of the Lord. Forty-eight years ago my co-workers and I wrote the words you just sang. All my co-workers were martyred for the name of Jesus."

He continued, "I was one of the leaders of the Back to Jerusalem Band. We marched across China on foot, proclaiming the gospel in every town and village we passed through.

"Finally in 1950, after many years of hardship, we reached the border town of Kashgar in Xinjiang Province. We stopped for a while and applied for visas to enter the Soviet Union. We were nervous and excited at the same time at what lay ahead!

"Before we ever had a chance to leave China, the

282 THE HEAVENLY MAN

Communist armies under Chairman Mao took control of
Xinjiang. They immediately sealed the borders and implemented their strong-armed style of rule.

"All the leaders of our movement were arrested. Five of us
were sentenced to forty-five years in prison with
hard labour. All the other leaders died in prison long
ago. I'm the only one who survived. . . . For the sake of the
vision to take the gospel back to Jerusalem, I spent 31 years
in prison for the Lord."

We were all stunned. We sat there with our mouths wide
open and tears running down our cheeks, dripping onto the
floor.

I asked Simon Zhao, the man of God, "Uncle, will you
please tell us more?"

He continued, "When the Lord called us to this vision, I'd
been married just four months. My beautiful bride had just
found out she was pregnant! We were both arrested and
imprisoned. Life in the prison was difficult and my wife suffered a miscarriage."

He wiped away his tears before continuing, "At that time
the Communists killed many missionaries and their Chinese
converts. In the early months of my imprisonment in 1950 I
saw my beloved wife twice from afar, through the iron bars
on my window. Then I never saw her again. By the time I
was released many years later my precious bride was
already long dead."

We all wept loudly. We felt that we were standing on holy
ground in the presence of the Lord.

I asked Uncle Simon, "When you were released from
prison, did you still have this Back to Jerusalem vision in
your heart?"

He responded to my question by singing for us,

How many years have bitter winds blown?
How many times have the storm clouds gathered?
Through the icy rain we couldn't see God's altar
The altar of God where he accepts our sacrifices.

God's leaders are crying with broken hearts
Jehovah's sheep are scattered far and wide
Tears of sadness well up in the chilly wind
Where have you gone, Good Shepherd?
Where have you gone, soldiers of God?
Where have you gone?
Oh, where have you gone?

After Uncle Zhao rested for a while, I asked him again, "Uncle, do you still have this vision in your heart?"
He continued to sing,

Jerusalem is in my dreams
Jerusalem is in my tears
I looked for you and found you in the fire of the altar
I looked for you and found you in Jesus' nail-scarred hands.

We wandered through the valley of tears
We wandered towards our heavenly home
After walking through the valley of death for forty years
My tears dried up.

Jesus came to destroy the chains of death
He came to open the path to glory!
The early missionaries shed their blood and tears for us
Let's hurry to fulfil the promise of God!

He spoke in a faltering voice, "Every evening for decades in the labour camp I faced toward the west, in the direction of Jerusalem, and cried out to the Lord, 'Oh God, I'll never be able to reach Jerusalem on foot. Our vision has perished. Heavenly Father, I pray you will raise up a new generation of Christians in China who are willing to lay down their lives to take the gospel all the way back to where it started in Jerusalem.'"

I held his hand and assured him, "The vision God gave you has not died! We will carry on the vision!"

We brought comfort to the heart of Uncle Zhao. He stood up, blessed us with his holy hands, and encouraged us from Luke 24:46–48, *"This is what is written: The Christ will suffer and rise from the dead on the third day, and repentance and forgiveness of sins will be preached in his name to all nations, beginning at Jerusalem. You are witnesses of these things."*

He exhorted us, "You must recognize the way of the cross is the call to shed blood. You must take the gospel of Jesus Christ to the Muslim countries, then all the way back to Jerusalem. Turn your eyes to the west!"

That meeting was a pivotal point in my life. I felt as if God passed a flaming baton from this dear old man of God to the house churches, giving us the responsibility to complete the vision.

The Lord had already placed the Back to Jerusalem vision in my heart, but after meeting Simon Zhao it became the primary focus of my life. I came to understand clearly that the destiny for the house churches of China is to pull down the world's last remaining spiritual giants: the house of Buddha, the house of Mohammed, and the house of Hinduism, and to proclaim the glorious gospel to all nations before the Second Coming of our Lord Jesus Christ!

You need to understand that when we speak about "Back to Jerusalem" we're not saying that Jerusalem is the main goal. We are not planning to rush there for a big conference!

Jerusalem was the starting point for the gospel two thousand years ago, and we believe it will circle the whole world and return to its starting point. Our aim is not merely to evangelize the city of Jerusalem, but the thousands of unreached people groups, towns and villages located between China and Jerusalem.

The vision for Back to Jerusalem is now the primary goal of all the house church leaders in the Sinim Fellowship. This is not one project we have among many. This is the main thrust and focus of all our activities. We talk about it over breakfast, lunch and dinner. We pray unceasingly, asking God to raise up labourers and remove all obstacles. We dream about it in our sleep.

A few years ago the Sinim leaders prayed about their involvement in the Back to Jerusalem mission. We then came together and each house church network revealed the number of missionaries they were committed to train and send overseas. When we added the number of workers together it totalled 100,000. That means we intend to send 100,000 missionaries outside China in the coming years!

A closer examination of history reveals there were actually three main "silk roads" leaving China. The one starting in Xian and heading through Central Asia and the heart of the Islamic world is the best known one. The second major trading route went through Tibet, across the Himalayas to Bhutan and Nepal, then towards Pakistan, Afghanistan and Iran, connecting up with the main highway to Jerusalem. The third Silk Road went through south-west China, where the majority of unreached minority groups live today. It headed south into Vietnam and then westward into countries like Laos, Cambodia, Thailand, Myanmar (Burma) and India. This route went deep into the heart of today's Buddhist and Hindu worlds.

After we considered these facts the church leaders decided God was calling us to follow these three main directions with the gospel. The Holy Spirit had already called certain networks to focus on specific areas. For example, one network had many missionary families already working in Tibetan areas. It was natural for them to lead the thrust into the Tibetan Buddhist world. Another network for years had the burden to reach the minority groups in south-west China. Most of these tribes spill across borders into countries like Vietnam, Laos, Thailand and Myanmar (Burma). That network assumed the responsibility of taking the gospel "back to Jerusalem" via the southern route.

We are not ignorant of the fact that these nations don't welcome the gospel! We're well aware that countries like Afghanistan, Iran and Saudi Arabia will not take kindly to preachers in their land!

We also understand that in order to send missionaries they will need to be equipped, trained with language and cultural skills, and supported so they can fight for the Lord with maximum effectiveness. Today there are hundreds of Christians inside China learning foreign languages such as Arabic and English, in preparation for missionary service outside China.

We have also come to understand that the past thirty years of suffering, persecution and torture for the house churches in China were all part of God's training for us. The Lord has perfectly fitted us to go as missionaries to the Muslim, Buddhist and Hindu worlds.

Once I spoke in the West and a Christian told me, "I've been praying for years that the Communist government in China will collapse, so Christians can live in freedom." This is not what we pray! We never pray against our government or call down curses on them. Instead, we have learned that

God is in control of both our own lives and the government we live under. Isaiah prophesied about Jesus, *"The government will be on his shoulders." Isaiah 9:6.*

God has used China's government for his own purposes, moulding and shaping his children as he sees fit. Instead of focusing our prayers against any political system, we pray that regardless of what happens to us, we will be pleasing to God.

Don't pray for the persecution to stop! We shouldn't pray for a lighter load to carry, but a stronger back to endure! Then the world will see that God is with us, empowering us to live in a way that reflects his love and power.

This is true freedom!

There is little that any of the Muslim, Buddhist or Hindu countries can do to us that we haven't already experienced in China. The worst they can do is kill us, but all that means is that we will be promoted into the glorious presence of our Lord for all eternity!

The Back to Jerusalem missionary movement is not an army with guns or human weapons. It isn't a group of well-dressed, slick professionals. It's an army of broken-hearted Chinese men and women whom God has cleansed with a mighty fire, and who have already been through years of hardship and deprivation for the sake of the gospel. In worldly terms they have nothing and appear unimpressive, but in the spiritual realm they are mighty warriors for Jesus Christ! We thank God that he *"chose the foolish things of the world to shame the wise; God chose the weak things of the world to shame the strong. He chose the lowly things of this world and the despised things – and the things that are not – to nullify the things that are, so that no one may boast before him." 1 Corinthians 1:27–29.*

God is calling thousands of house church warriors to write

their testimonies with their own blood. We will walk across the borders of China, carrying the Word of God into the Muslim, Buddhist and Hindu worlds. Thousands will be willing to die for the Lord. They will see multitudes of souls saved, as well as awaken many sleeping churches in the West.

Hundreds of Western missionaries spilled their blood on Chinese soil in the past. Their example has inspired us to be willing also to die for the Lord wherever he leads us with his message. Many of our missionaries will be captured, tortured, and martyred for the sake of the gospel, but that will not stop us.

God has not only refined *us* in the fire of affliction for the past thirty years, he has also refined our methods. For example, we're totally committed to planting groups of local believers who meet in homes. We have no desire to build a single church building anywhere! This allows the gospel to spread rapidly, is harder for the authorities to detect, and allows us to channel all our resources directly into gospel ministry.

Some people have challenged the fact that we are sending missionaries outside China. They say we should stay in China and win our own country before we go out. To this illogical argument I respond with a simple question, "Then why does your country send missionaries? Is everyone in your country saved?"

If we stay in one place and refuse to advance until we've completely finished the job there, we'll never be able to impact the world with the gospel. Surely God's way is for us to be winning our home at the same time as we're sending new workers to the ends of the earth! Believe me, our vision to reach the world does not mean we'll stop or slow down our efforts to reach all of China with the gospel!

The two will take place hand-in-hand.

In fact, I believe the best way for the Chinese church to remain strong is to keep it motivated to reach out to the nations of the world. When believers focus on serving the Lord and reaching the lost, God blesses them and the church remains sharp. When we become self-centred and critical of each other, Satan has won already and the church will become a blunt, useless instrument.

We knew from the beginning that there is a high price to pay for this Back to Jerusalem mission. I'm not just talking about money! I'm talking about the many Chinese who will be martyred and suffer as this vision unfolds. Many will go on one-way tickets, realizing they'll never return to China to see their loved ones again.

We also realize Back to Jerusalem will cost a lot of money, but even though our churches are so poor, we have already collected tens of thousands of dollars to support our missionaries. Like the Macedonian church, many Chinese believers have given literally all they own, *"Out of the most severe trial, their overflowing joy and their extreme poverty welled up in rich generosity. For I testify that they gave as much as they were able, and even beyond their ability."* 2 Corinthians 8:2–3.

The Chinese church is willing to pay the price.

Since my escape from China in 1997, I've been responsible for the training and implementation of the Back to Jerusalem missionaries.

When the first batch of thirty-nine missionaries left China in March 2000, thirty-six of them were arrested. They didn't lose their vision however. They went back home, prayed, and found another way to get across the border.

Little more than a year later, the number of Chinese house church missionaries outside China already exceeded four hundred, serving in more than ten countries. The floodgates are beginning to open.

Each Back to Jerusalem missionary receives training in several main subjects. These include:

1. How to suffer and die for the Lord. We examine what the Bible says about suffering, and look at how the Lord's people have laid down their lives for the advance of the gospel throughout history.
2. How to witness for the Lord. We teach how to witness for the Lord under any circumstance, on trains or buses, or even in the back of a police van on our way to the execution ground.
3. How to escape for the Lord. We know that sometimes it is the Lord who sends us to prison to witness for him, but we also believe the devil sometimes wants us to go to prison to stop the ministry God has called us to do. We teach the missionaries special skills such as how to free themselves from handcuffs, and how to jump from second-storey windows without injuring themselves.

This is not a "normal" seminary or Bible College!

If you ever visit one of the places where we are training our Back to Jerusalem missionaries, you will see how serious we are to fulfil our destiny in God. You may see people with their hands handcuffed behind their backs, leaping from second-storey windows!

Nothing less is required if we are to break down the walls that separate Muslims, Hindus and Buddhists from knowing the sweet presence of Jesus.

*   *   *

When the elders of the Sinim Fellowship heard how God had miraculously allowed me to escape from China, they appointed me as their "Authorized Representative", to speak for the house churches around the world.

The elders of the Sinim Fellowship drafted the following letter for me:

To Brother Yun, our holy brother who is a close comrade of Christ the Lord and who is filled with the Spirit of the Power of God:

You are the "chariots and horsemen of Israel" of God! You carry the victorious message of the expansion of the kingdom of Christ in you!

Dear Brother, you are sent by God from the Sinim Elders' Committee of the Chinese house churches as our authorized representative overseas!

God has shown you, according to his guidance and Lordship, that life is the foundation, building up the church is the centre, and the training of workers is the point of breakthrough – the strategic place from where expansion can be carried out in all directions, radiating to every nation and people in the world, so that the ground that the sole of your foot walks on will become your inheritance!

March forward towards the Muslims, the Hindus and the Buddhists in Europe, America, Africa, Australasia and Asia!

We pray the Lord will give you wisdom and power from above, so that your message is filled with heavenly authority. Like the fire Samson tied to the foxes' tails, it will burn wherever you go.

May you accomplish the holy mission God has given you, to take the gospel back to Jerusalem, until the last holy disciple is added to the church and the bride is prepared to welcome the return of our Saviour Lord Jesus Christ, so that the kingdoms of the world become the possession of our King! Our holy goal is that he will be King forever and ever.

We are ready to work hard with servants of the Lord all ove the world, who are members of his body, serving one another with the spiritual gifts we have received, so that the holy mission of God can be fulfilled!

Dear Brother Yun, this is the conviction of all the servants of God in the Sinim Elders' Fellowship. May the Lord strengthen the task entrusted to you, lead you, and open the way ahead. We and all our co-workers are your solid shields. May the will of the Lord be done quickly, on earth as in heaven. Amen!

Your co-workers in Christ and Elders of the Sinim Fellowship.

CHAPTER TWENTY-FIVE

REFLECTING ON FOUR YEARS IN THE WEST

My first experience of a Western church was an interesting one! A Lutheran church was located near the refugee detention centre in Germany. On Sunday mornings I attended the service to be with other believers on the Lord's Day, and to try to pick up some German by mimicking the preacher's words.

After what I was used to in China, I found these church meetings strange indeed! I sat on the front pew of the huge, old building, right in front of a high platform that the minister, fully arrayed in ecclesiastical robes, climbed on to in order to preach. He always looked directly at me when he spoke. Despite the size of the sanctuary, the congregation consisted of just a handful of grey-haired old ladies.

The pastor and the old ladies seemed to like me. Although we couldn't communicate verbally, we smiled at each other. I had the impression the pastor thought it was cute that a poor, smiling Chinese man came and sat in his church every Sunday morning.

*　　*　　*

Some time later I was again sitting on the front row of a Western church, but a very different scene from the Lutheran church in Germany. I was about to speak in Times Square Church in New York City.

My eyes were as wide as saucers as I took in the amazing scene before me. A large multi-ethnic choir, arrayed in robes, swayed and sang to Jesus with all their hearts. Behind me several thousand New Yorkers declared the praises of God from the depths of their souls.

Of the hundreds of churches I've been honoured to preach in throughout the Western world, I would have to say Times Square Church is one of my favourites.

It has an atmosphere of grace and fire that sweeps visitors off their feet, and a spirit of truth and receptiveness that makes people's hearts supple and eager to hear God's Word.

When I'm at that big church, in the centre of New York, I can close my eyes and feel as if I'm back in China again.

*   *   *

About six months after my arrival in Frankfurt I was granted refugee status by the German government and was given a travel document. Some Western friends visited me. We prayed to discern God's purposes in bringing me out of China and how we could work together for the glory of God.

We also sought the Lord for wisdom about how to bring my wife and children to Germany, so we could start our new life together. In May 1999, Deling, Isaac and Yilin travelled through south-west China into the country of Myanmar (formerly called Burma), where they were to stay for what we expected to be a short time until the necessary paperwork was prepared to bring them to Germany.

The Lord opened doors for me to share in many churches in the West. I travelled with my faithful Scandinavian friend, who translated for me wherever I went. This is the same brother I met in Guilin City years before, when God bonded our hearts together to serve the Lord.

Over the next few years we travelled extensively in Europe, Asia, and North America, challenging God's people to pray for and to partner the Chinese house churches, so that together all of China will be reached, and we will see the kingdom of God established all the way back to Jerusalem.

I visited my family frequently in Myanmar, but getting them out of that country proved far more difficult and painstaking than we first imagined. Because of the delays my family settled into a room at a Bible school and my children started to attend a public school.

Before I travelled to the West I had absolutely no idea that so many churches were spiritually asleep. I presumed the Western church was strong and vibrant because it had brought the gospel to my country with such incredible faith and tenacity. Many missionaries had shown a powerful example to us by laying down their lives for the sake of Jesus.

On some occasions I've struggled while speaking in Western churches. There seems to be something missing that leaves me feeling terrible inside. Many meetings are cold and lack the fire and presence of God that we have in China.

In the West many Christians have an abundance of material possessions, yet they live in a backslidden state. They have silver and gold, but they don't rise up and walk in Jesus' name. In China we have no possessions to hold us down, so there's nothing preventing us from moving out for the Lord. The Chinese church is like Peter at the Beautiful Gate. When he saw the crippled beggar he said, *"Silver or gold I do not have, but what I have I give you. In the name of Jesus Christ of Nazareth, walk!" Acts 3:6.*

In a similar way, I pray that God might use the Chinese

church to help the Western church rise up and walk in the power of the Holy Spirit. It's almost impossible for the church in China to go to sleep in its present situation. There's always something to keep us on the run, and it's very difficult to sleep while you're running. If persecution stops, I fear we'll become complacent and fall asleep.

Many pastors in Europe and America have told me they want to see great revival. I'm frequently asked why China is experiencing revival but most places in the West are not. This is a big question to answer, but some reasons are very apparent to me.

When I'm in the West I see all the mighty church buildings and all the expensive equipment, plush carpets and state-of-the-art sound systems. I can assure the Western church with absolute certainty that you don't need any more church buildings. Church buildings will never bring the revival you seek. The pursuit of more possessions will never bring revival. Jesus truly stated, *"A man's life does not consist in the abundance of his possessions." Luke 12:15.*

The first thing needed for revival to return to your churches is the Word of the Lord. God's Word is missing. Sure, there are many preachers and thousands of tapes and videos of Bible teaching, but so little contains the sharp truth of God's Word. It's the truth that will set you free.

Not only is knowledge of God's Word missing, but obedience to that Word. There's not much action taking place.

When revival came to believers in China, the result was thousands of evangelists being sent out to all corners of the nation, carrying fire from the altar of God with them. When God moves in the West, it seems you want to stop and enjoy his presence and blessings too long, and build an altar to your experiences.

You can never really know the Scriptures until you're willing to be changed by them.

All genuine revivals of the Lord result in believers responding with action and soul winning. When God truly moves in your heart you cannot remain silent. There will be a fire in your bones, like Jeremiah, who said, *"His word is in my heart like a fire, a fire shut up in my bones. I am weary of holding it in; indeed, I cannot." Jeremiah 20:9.*

Furthermore, it's only when we step out in obedience and share the gospel with people that we come to know God's blessing in every area of our lives. That is why the Apostle Paul wrote to his co-worker Philemon, *"I pray that you may be active in sharing your faith, so that you will have a full understanding of every good thing we have in Christ." Philemon v.6.*

I've seen people in Western churches worshipping as if they're already in heaven. Then someone invariably brings a comforting message like, "My children, I love you. Don't be afraid, I'm with you." I'm not opposed to such words, but why is it that nobody seems to hear a Word from the Lord like, "My child, I want to send you to the slums of Asia or the darkness of Africa to be my messenger to people dying in their sin"?

Multitudes of church members in the West are satisfied with giving their minimum to God, not their maximum. I've watched men and women during offering time in church. They open their fat wallets and search for the smallest amount they can give. This type of attitude will never do! Jesus gave his whole life for us, and we give as little of our lives, time and money as we can back to God. What a disgrace! Repent!

This may sound strange, but I even miss the offerings we used to give in China. On numerous occasions the leader of a meeting would announce, "We have a new worker who is leaving tomorrow to serve the Lord." Immediately every single person would completely empty their pockets of everything they had. With that money the worker would buy a train or bus ticket and leave the next day.

Often this money was not just everything we had in our pockets at the time, but everything we owned in the whole world.

Just because you have a church building doesn't necessarily mean Jesus is with you. He is not welcome in many churches today. In Revelation 3:20 Jesus said, *"Here I am! I stand at the door and knock. If anyone hears my voice and opens the door, I will come in and eat with him, and he with me."*

Often this verse is used as an invitation for salvation, but actually the context Jesus was speaking in was very different. He was standing outside the door of the church in Laodicea, knocking to get in!

Of course not all Western churches are asleep! Of all the strong churches I have visited in the West I've noticed one thing they all have in common: a strong and sacrificial commitment to missions among unreached nations. I'm not talking just about local outreach, or even attempts to start churches in other cities in your nation. I'm talking about a heart to establish God's kingdom in the most gospel-starved and spiritually dark areas of the world, where nobody has ever heard the name of Jesus. When you start putting your time, prayers and finances there you will soon experience God's blessing on the work of your hands.

The Great Commission has not changed. There are many churches trying to create a heaven here on earth, but until the Western church obeys the Great Commission and takes the gospel to the ends of the earth, people are just playing with God and are not really serious about the truth. Many churches look beautiful on the outside, but are dead where it counts, on the inside. If you truly want to see God move, the two main things you must do is learn the Word of God and have the obedience to do what God tells you to do.

In Finland in 1999 I was asked to be one of the main speakers at a conference attended by about one thousand church leaders. The main speaker was a well-known American preacher. Every time he spoke it was about the love and goodness of God. During the prayer time everyone fell down on the floor and laughed.

After I spoke I commanded people to kneel down at the foot of the cross of Jesus, and they wept! Tears always come first before the Lord truly moves. He will never pour his blessing out on unsanctified and selfish flesh. The cross of Jesus must be at the centre of everything we do.

If you do these things you will see revival. Are you willing to give your all to God and to his service? *"Those who are wise will shine like the brightness of the heavens, and those who lead many to righteousness, like the stars for ever and ever."* Daniel 12:3.

Many Christians have also asked me why miracles and signs and wonders are so prevalent in China, but not so evident in the West.

In the West you have so much. You have insurance for everything. In a way, you don't need God. When my father was dying of stomach cancer, we sold everything we had to try to cure him. When everything was gone we had no hope but God. We turned to him in desperation and saw him mercifully answer our prayers and heal my father. We reasoned that if God could do that then he could do anything, so our faith grew and we've seen many miracles.

In China, the greatest miracles we see are not the healings or other things, but lives transformed by the gospel. We believe we're not called to follow signs and wonders but instead the signs and wonders follow us when the gospel is preached. We don't keep our eyes on the signs and wonders; we keep our eyes on Jesus.

Every house church pastor in China is ready to lay down his life for the gospel. When we live this way, we'll see God do great things by his grace.

*   *   *

One of the most difficult things I have struggled with in recent years is being away from my dear mother.

When she was in her early 70s my mother suffered a paralyzing stroke that made her lose consciousness. After conducting a series of tests, the doctors declared her condition hopeless and said she would never recover. I was told her death was imminent but I was in prison at the time and unable to visit her.

She was taken back to our home to die. The believers gathered around and prayed for her. Immediately, in front of a room full of people, she regained consciousness and began praising God! She recovered her strength and visited me in prison. She told me that if it were not for God's mercy I would never have seen her face again.

A few years later in September 1996, one year before I left China, I received a phone call while I was away preaching in a different province. I was told my mother had again suffered a stroke and was partially paralyzed.

I immediately left the meeting and caught a train to Henan. Arriving at the hospital, I saw my mother's facial muscles were badly contorted and she appeared pale.

My mother opened her eyes and in a whisper told us she wanted to be dressed in white funeral clothes, as she was going to meet Jesus. During that visit, however, the Lord clearly showed me her illness would not lead to death. I fervently prayed over my mother with great authority, rebuking the illness in Jesus' name. She felt strength flow into her body and she got up out of bed and walked around the room! Her face became normal. When the doctors came into the room they were completely speechless.

In the summer of 1998, after I had arrived in Europe, my mother became gravely ill for the third time. On this occasion, everyone was sure she was going to die. Even my own family had given up hope, and dressed her in her funeral clothes. They even purchased a coffin and had it delivered to our house.

I had been so close to my mother all my life. We had experienced so much together, good times and suffering. When I received this news I was on the other side of the world, preaching far away in Switzerland. I called my home in China and asked for the phone to be placed close to my mother's ear. I asked her, "Mama, are you listening? Jesus loves you, and he will heal you!"

As soon as she heard the words, "Jesus loves you", she got up out of bed and started to dance on the floor in triumph! Once again, the Lord spared her and brought her back from the clutches of death.

Finally, while I was in Germany on 5 December 2000, I received a call from China. My mother had passed into the presence of Jesus. I longed to go to her funeral, but I couldn't enter China without being arrested for all my past "crimes". I wept and thanked God for the mother he had given me and for the many struggles she had endured for the sake of the gospel. Like a sailing boat in a storm, she had been buffeted through years of trials and tribulations, but now she had safely reached the peaceful harbour.

I was comforted in my grief when I received a videotape

of the funeral. Hundreds of house church believers attended, including all the top leaders. Some brothers and sisters I hadn't seen for years – including many of the leaders mentioned in this book – came to honour my mother.

Attending the funeral was a great risk to the leaders, as the authorities were hunting many of them. Some had been on the run for years and their names are listed among the most wanted criminals in all of China. Yet they couldn't stay away. They all came back to Nanyang County in southern Henan Province to honour my mother in the place God had first touched us all those years ago.

At the funeral service Brother Xu stood up and said, "Although Brother Yun, his wife and his two children are not able to attend his mother's funeral today, all of us gathered here are her children in the Lord."

I thanked God for my mother. I remembered how he had reached down from heaven 26 years earlier and chosen to bless my mother, and then us, even though we were poor and despised, living in a small, insignificant corner of China.

I thought about how the Lord had moved so powerfully since that day, through our own family but also through thousands of others, so that today there are millions of believers just in Henan Province, and many tens of millions distributed throughout China.

I remembered how – when I was still just a teenager – my mother had prayerfully committed me to world mission. This was impossible in those days, when China's borders were firmly closed, yet in faith she believed God could do the impossible and her prayer was answered.

The biggest regret I have is that I never got to say goodbye properly to my mother. The last time I saw her was after my prison escape. I knew my family and I would not be able to return home for a long time. My mother's last words to me in person were, "Son, when will you return?"

I wanted to comfort her so I said, "Soon, Mama. Soon."

*   *   *

DELING: When we arrived in Myanmar we didn't have any preconceived ideas about what would happen. I knew if God wanted us to go forward then we'd go forward, and if he wanted us to stay there, we would stay. It was actually quite a good time for me. I had fellowship with brothers and sisters every day, and the children and I finally established routines in our lives after such a crazy few years on the run in China. Since 1996 we'd been asking the Lord to create a more peaceful environment, so that we might have a more normal family life.

When it looked as if we were going to be stuck in Myanmar for a while, Isaac and Yilin were enrolled in a local school. I feel our children really developed in Myanmar and I'm so proud of them. Isaac is a very smart boy. All we can say is that God has done something special in his life. When Isaac was in my womb, Yun was fasting for 74 days without food or water. For the first four years of Isaac's life his father was in prison. In a way, I believe the Heavenly Father fathered Isaac because his earthly father was suffering for Jesus, and God himself educated Isaac because he was not allowed to attend school for extended periods while Yun was in prison.

Teachers and students have humiliated Isaac, and he has been through experiences that few boys his age have had to endure. He has been on the run with us as we fled from the police, and he then crossed into a foreign country where he couldn't speak the language.

When we arrived in Myanmar neither Isaac nor Yilin could speak a word of Burmese, which is not similar to Chinese in any way. God helped them to learn the language remarkably quickly, and less than 18 months after arriving in the country Isaac was one of the top students in his school! He was even awarded a special honour. His name was published in the newspaper, which worried us, because we were not even meant to be in the country and were trying to keep a low profile!

After all Isaac has been through it's amazing that he is normal at all, yet today he can speak the Mandarin, Yunnanese, Burmese, Lisu, Jingpo and German languages! He's so smart because God personally educated him in response to our desperate cries for help. Isaac loves the Lord with all his heart. At his graduation from Bible school he stood up and announced, "I consecrate myself to serve God for the rest of my life."

Yilin is a special gift from God. She has a tender heart for the Lord, but also a fiery and strong personality. All she wants to do is serve Jesus. She has compassion for people and is willing to stand for the truth and never compromise.

Yun and I have been most blessed by the children God has given us.

CHAPTER TWENTY-SIX

A NEW KIND OF PERSECUTION

In September 2000, I travelled to Canada to begin an intense three-week speaking schedule. Meetings in different cities were arranged for each evening. I was excited at the chance to share what God has done in China with believers throughout Canada, and to encourage the Canadian church to become partners with us in taking the gospel back to Jerusalem.

The night before I flew to Toronto I received a vivid dream from the Lord. I saw myself inside a room in a church, preparing the message I was about to preach. I opened my Bible and discovered all my notes were missing. As I was thinking about where they might be, I took my wallet out of my pocket and placed it on my open Bible. Suddenly a rat appeared from a hole in the wall behind me. In a flash it ate my wallet and returned to its hole!

I felt that the attack was from an evil spirit in the form of a rat, rather than an actual rat.

In my dream, I was angry and found a long iron bar. I thrust it into the hole, seeking to kill the rat. I felt the bar strike the back of the hole and thought I must have killed the rat. I pulled the bar out of the hole and the rat came out also. The instant the rat came out of the wall it changed into a rooster.

The rooster crowed and jumped around, making a loud noise and thrashing its wings. I swung my iron bar at it. The moment I struck it on the head it changed into a seductive evil spirit in the appearance of a long-haired woman. She cowered and protested, "Why are you hitting me? I'm just a person like you. I don't understand why you're persecuting me. Please let me go!"

I replied, "I don't care who you are. You've stolen my notes and the wallet from my Bible." I tried to block the woman's access to the door so she couldn't get away. Knowing I was dealing with a demon and not an actual woman, in my dream I struck the woman and she fell to the floor unconscious.

Then I awoke.

I was puzzled at the dream so I asked the Lord to reveal its meaning.

After arriving in Canada I shared this dream with my co-workers and pondered what it meant. At breakfast I told my translator, "The Lord showed me that someone is trying to take the Word of God out of my hands, and is trying to steal financial support for the work of the house churches. I'm about to be attacked spiritually. When we stand up against it there will be two different demonic responses.

"First, like the rooster in my dream, we'll meet with a loud and aggressive reaction. Later, a seductive spirit will try to reason with us, pleading its innocence and trying to stop our ministry for the Lord through lies and deceit."

On the second day in Toronto I was scheduled to speak on a Christian television programme. After the interview a brother approached us with a printed article that had been sent to him by email. His face was pale and his demeanour serious. "Brother Yun," he said, "we need to sit down. I have some bad news to share with you."

Through our translator, the contents of the article – written by a Christian journalist in California – were read to me. The story had been sent around the world that very morning to thousands of readers. I'd never met the writer or even heard of him, yet, quoting an unnamed "Chinese informant", he proceeded to tear into me with a vicious attack.

He said my miraculous escape from prison in 1997 was a lie, that my claims of fasting 74 days without food or water in prison were fabricated, that my legs had never been smashed, and that I was not a representative or elder of the Sinim Fellowship.

There were two parts of the article that hurt most. It revealed my family was hiding in Myanmar, which placed them at great risk. I feared for their safety. Not only was I concerned that the Myanmar authorities would read the article and start searching for them, but the Chinese government would also love to have them sent back to China and punished.

I had been looking forward to spending Christmas with my family in Myanmar. The previous year (1999) was the first Christmas in thirteen years I'd been able to spend with my wife and children. I had been in prison for seven of those Christmases, and on the run from the authorities or otherwise indisposed at Christmas for five additional years.

Now, because the article publicly revealed my family's whereabouts, it looked as if I wouldn't be able to travel to Myanmar for Christmas. I was deeply upset.

The second part of the article that hurt was the accusation, "He is the most likely Judas who sold out the top-level leaders in the crackdown of 1999 . . . He has caused division and damage to the house church activities inside China."

When I heard these words my heart was pierced with grief. Ever since the Lord revealed himself to me in 1974 I had, by the grace of God, never betrayed any other believer in China. I'd spent many years being tortured in prison for the very reason that I refused to be a Judas to the body of Christ.

I thanked the Lord for preparing me in advance through my previous night's dream of the rat, rooster and woman.

Over the next few days our whole Canadian trip was thrown into jeopardy, as Christian leaders read the article and considered cancelling our meetings.

Within 24 hours, various Chinese house church leaders, including all the elders of the Sinim Fellowship, were notified of the situation. Signed statements from well-known leaders such as Xu Yongze and Zhang Rongliang were faxed out of China, stating that these accusations were completely groundless, and confirming that I was an elder and authorized representative of the Sinim Fellowship.

In the days after this attack, which appears to have been carefully timed to coincide with the start of our Canadian preaching trip, I struggled with this new form of persecution.

In China I had been used to beatings, torture with electric batons, and all kinds of humiliation. I guess that deep in my heart I had presumed that now I was in the West my days of persecution had ended.

I couldn't understand how someone who had never met me could write such a nasty article. I complained to my Christian friends, "Why don't these people call us and read the documents? I don't understand! Why don't they find the truth out for themselves? It's right here for them to see!"

My translator told me, "Brother Yun, these people don't want to know the truth. That's why they're not calling you or wanting to meet you. In China, Christians are persecuted with beatings and imprisonment. In the West, Christians are persecuted by the words of other Christians."

This new kind of spiritual persecution was no easier than physical persecution in China, just different.

I cried out in prayer, asking the Lord for his strength. I forgave the people behind this attack from the bottom of my heart and we continued our trip.

As we travelled to Winnipeg, Edmonton, and other Canadian cities the Lord moved powerfully and many churches and believers joined the Chinese house churches in prayer and partnership.

*   *   *

BROTHER XU: We were concerned when we heard that Brother Yun had been slandered and attacked while ministering in the West, so the elders of the Sinim Fellowship of house church leaders in China wrote this letter in support of him:

Brother Yun is a servant of God and is one of the five elders of the Sinim Fellowship of the house churches of China. The Bible clearly states, "Do not entertain an accusation against an elder unless it is brought by two or three witnesses." I Timothy 5:19. We hereby testify as a whole, how Brother Yun has served us as a witness to Christ's sufferings and is a faithful servant of the Lord. He is a soldier of Christ anointed by the Holy Spirit, a warrior for truth, a pioneer of the gospel in this age. His service has strongly witnessed the presence of the Holy Spirit.

In 1996 the Lord used him to start the Sinim Fellowship of the house churches of China. Not only is he one of the five elders, he is also a faithful, honest, truth-loving, reliable, pure and God-fearing servant of God. He has a good reputation outside the church, and is a good son, good husband and a good father.

We hereby witness how he often tries to have an attitude the same as that of Christ Jesus. This is why we are claiming that he is blameless before God. Praying with one accord, the house churches support the servant of God in his service around the world, and may he be a blessing to the house of the Lord from East to West. We can summarize his testimony in one word: "genuine".

The elders of the Sinim Fellowship and many co-workers earnestly pray and testify for him in the Lord, supporting all of his services in full and backing him up. As we have proclaimed, he has the authorization to fully represent the Sinim Fellowship throughout five continents (Europe, America, Africa, Australasia, and Asia).

May the Chinese and overseas churches who are members of the body of Christ work together as one and build up one another, so that the gospel of Jesus Christ will be spread all over the world quickly, even back to Jerusalem.

Amen!

*　　*　　*

YUN: There are many ways the Lord may lead a Christian during his or her life, but I'm convinced that the path of every believer will sooner or later include suffering. The Lord gives us these trials to keep us humble and dependent on him for our sustenance.

The Bible says in 1 Peter 4:1, *"Therefore, since Christ suffered in his body, arm yourselves also with the same attitude, because he who has suffered in his body is done with sin."* I believe when suffering and pain increases, sinning decreases. I've certainly not yet reached the point of being "done with sin". I still complain to the Lord when I suffer.

How we mature as a Christian largely depends on the attitude we have when we're faced with suffering. Some try to avoid it or imagine it doesn't exist, but that will only make the situation worse. Others try to endure it grimly, hoping for relief. This is better, but falls short of the full victory God wants to give each of his children.

The Lord wants us to embrace suffering as a friend. We need a deep realization that when we're persecuted for Jesus' sake it is an act of God's blessing to us. This might sound impossible, but it is attainable with God's help. That is why Jesus said, *"Blessed are you when people insult you, persecute you and falsely say all kinds of evil against you because of me. Rejoice and be glad, because great is your reward in heaven."* Matthew 5:11–12.

We can grow to such a place in Christ where we laugh and rejoice when people slander us, because we know we are not of this world, but our security is in heaven. The more we are persecuted for his sake, the more reward we will receive in heaven.

When people malign you, rejoice and be glad. When they curse you, bless them in return. When you walk through a painful experience, embrace it and you will be free!

When you learn these lessons, there is nothing left that the world can do to you.

God is my witness that through all the tortures and beatings I've received I have never hated my persecutors. Never. I saw them as God's instruments of blessing and his chosen vessels to purify me and make me more like Jesus.

Sometimes Western visitors come to China and ask the house church leaders what seminary they attended. We reply, jokingly yet with underlying seriousness, that we have been trained in the Holy Spirit Personal Devotion Bible School (prison) for many years.

Sometimes our Western friends don't understand what we mean because they then ask, "What materials do you use in this Bible school?" We reply, "Our only materials are the foot chains that bind us, and the leather whips that bruise us."

In this prison seminary we have learned many valuable lessons about the Lord that we could never have learned from a book. We've come to know God in a deeper way. We know his goodness and his loving faithfulness to us.

Christians who are in prison for the sake of the Lord are not the ones who are suffering. When people hear my testimony they often say, "You must have had a terrible time when you were in prison." I respond, "What are you talking about? I was with Jesus and had overwhelming joy and peace in his intimate presence."

The people who really suffer are those who never experience God's presence. The way to have God's presence is by walking through hardship and suffering – the way of the cross. You may not be beaten or imprisoned for your faith, but I am convinced each Christian will still have a cross to bear in his or her life. In the West it may be ridicule, slander, or rejection. When you're faced with such trials, the key is not to run from them or fight them, but to embrace them as friends. When you do this you'll not fail to experience God's presence and help.

When a child of God suffers you need to understand the Lord has allowed it. He has not forgotten you! The devil cannot snatch you away! Jesus made this beautiful promise to his children, *"My sheep listen to my voice; I know them, and they follow me. I give them eternal life, and they shall never perish; no one can snatch them out of my hand. My Father, who has given them to me, is greater than all; no one can snatch them out of my Father's hand." John 10:27–29.*

The first time I went to prison I struggled, wondering why God had allowed it. Slowly I began to understand he had a deeper purpose for me than just working for him. He wanted to know me, and I to know him, deeply and intimately. He knew the best way to get my attention for a while was to give me rest behind bars.

Whenever I hear a house church Christian has been imprisoned for Christ in China I don't advise people to pray for his or her release unless the Lord clearly reveals we should pray this way.

Before a chicken is hatched it is vital it is kept in the warm protection of the shell for 21 days. If you take the chick out of that environment one day too early, it will die. Similarly, ducks need to remain confined in their shell for 28 days before they are hatched. If you take a duck out on the 27th day, it will die.

There is always a purpose behind why God allows his children to go to prison. Perhaps it's so they can witness to the other prisoners, or perhaps God wants to develop more character in their lives. But if we use our own efforts to get them out of prison earlier than God intended, we can thwart his plans, and the believers may come out not as fully formed as God wanted them to be.

I'm often asked about the rights of pastors in China. A pastor has no rights, except the rights of a slave! Everyone in this world is a slave. They're either slaves to sin, or slaves of Christ. Our "rights" are in the hands of Jesus. We must fall on our knees in complete dependence on him.

Christians in China appreciate whenever believers around the world try to help them during times of imprisonment or persecution, but all efforts to help need to be bathed in prayer and rooted in God's will, otherwise it only seems to make things worse.

The world can do nothing to a Christian who has no fear of man.

CHAPTER TWENTY-SEVEN

A SUDDEN CHANGE OF PLANS

My wife and children had been living in Myanmar almost two years when finally, at the start of 2001, a plan was initiated to bring them out to Thailand and then to Germany, where we hoped to restart our life together. The German government granted permission for them to join me, and assured us they would receive the same refugee status as I did.

Because they were so long in Myanmar, a friend had helped us get Burmese ID cards. Numerous Chinese people were being rounded up all the time in northern Myanmar and sent back to China because they didn't have the correct identification. This was the last thing we wanted to happen to our family, because we were still wanted by the authorities in our homeland. We didn't think too much about it at the time, but later we realized our ID cards were not issued legally.

In February 2001, I flew into Myanmar for one last time. My family was excited and all preparations had been made for our departure. Deling, Isaac and Yilin were to fly to a town near the Thai border, where they would cross by land into Thailand. I was to travel on ahead and meet them there.

As with most things in our lives, our plans went awfully wrong!

Two nights before I was to leave Myanmar I received a vivid dream from the Lord. I saw my family and me leaving Myanmar. Isaac went on ahead. He was very nervous as he crossed the border, yet he passed through customs and left the country safely.

Next, in the dream, it was my turn to pass through customs. The official asked for my passport and told me to open my bags. He found my Burmese identity card and ordered me into an interrogation room. In the dream I saw the face of the customs official and also noticed the interrogation room was very poor and run down.

I awoke from my dream and saw it was just before five o'clock in the morning. I told Deling, "The Lord has shown me that if we are not careful we'll encounter trouble when we leave this country. We should pray more and ask the Lord to protect us."

I also told Isaac the contents of my dream and told him to pray fervently. He left later in the day, flying to the border town of Tachilek in north-east Myanmar. Deling and Yilin were to join him the next day, and together they were to cross the border into Thailand.

Incredibly, just minutes after Isaac's plane touched down, a war broke out in Tachilek between the Burmese military and the Shan Independence Army! Fierce fighting, shelling and gunfire erupted. All flights to Tachilek were cancelled for weeks. Isaac was cut off from us and there was no way to go to him.

The same day I'd received the dream from the Lord I shared it with the students at the Bible school where we were staying, and asked them to pray. With one voice the students all assured me, "Dear Brother Yun, there will be no problem! It's easy to cross the border. You have nothing to fear!" I started to feel confident that nothing bad would happen.

My wife, whom I thank God for giving an honest and wise heart, warned me, "You shouldn't be so positive about this. God has warned you and you must heed it. Make sure you leave your ID card with me. If you take it you'll surely find trouble."

I rejected my wife's advice and ignored the dream from the Lord. The previous few months had been a hectic time of ministry. I'd travelled to many nations and spoken in hundreds of meetings. My mother had recently died and I was still dealing with the grief and pain of her departure. I was burned out and needed a time of rest and refreshing.

In my sorry state, I had great confidence in my own "strength" and "abilities". The Lord needed to teach me a lesson and humble me. He taught me that if we trust in any kind of resource except him, we will fail. I had placed too much trust in my German passport. Deep down in my heart I somehow believed my passport would protect me from harm and help me overcome problems.

When I look back on what happened in Myanmar I fully realize one thing: God will never change his principles for any person. If you disobey his principles then you will surely fall into trouble.

Because I disobeyed the Lord, I fell into trouble.

The next morning I entered the customs hall at the Yangon (Rangoon) International Airport, before boarding my flight to Thailand. Immediately I started to feel uneasy. The scene before me was exactly the same as in my dream. The very same officer as in my dream looked at my passport and told me to open my bags. He saw my Burmese ID card and immediately his countenance grew serious. He took me into a side room and ordered me to wait. Straight away I realized I was in the same run-down interrogation room that the Lord had shown me in the dream.

Because of the outbreak of war in Shan State the airport authorities were on high alert for anything suspicious. When they found my false identity card, and realized I couldn't speak Burmese or even English, they presumed I was somehow connected to the Shan fighters. They paid no attention to my German passport because they were certain it was counterfeit.

As I waited in that lonely room my heart filled with grief and remorse and I began to repent to the Lord for my pride and disobedience. I cried out and sobbed great tears, and prayed, "Lord, I'm sorry I paid no attention to your warning. I now accept whatever punishment you have in store for me."

This was the second time I'd been arrested because I was burned out and my ears were closed to hearing the Lord's warning. My second imprisonment in China in 1991 also came about because I was burned out and trusted in my own strength. I didn't learn my lesson well.

If you are a worker in God's kingdom, or ever hope to serve the Lord, let me warn you from the words I wrote down in my notebook that day while I was waiting in the airport interrogation room. In large letters I wrote, "Beware! Beware! Beware! God's worker must never, ever disobey God's principles!"

Those Christians who have a public ministry are most in danger of falling into trouble, because they can easily be tempted to listen to the applause and praise of men. If you are a preacher, beware! You must cry out and ask God to help you listen only to his voice, not to the crowds of people who pat you on the back and place you on a pedestal. God's principles are often the opposite of our own. While we hope people will like and accept us, Jesus taught, *"Woe to you when all men speak well of you." Luke 6:26.*

Never be satisfied with God's calling or his gifts in your life. Be satisfied with Jesus Christ himself!

Many people hear God's voice calling them to catch fish for the kingdom of God. The disciples heard Jesus say, *"Let us go over to the other side." Mark 4:35.* They then rowed out onto the lake, taking *"him along, just as he was, in the boat." v.36.* Jesus was soon asleep, and a fierce storm arose.

As you go out in your ministry, make sure Jesus isn't asleep on your boat! You can try to row your boat or operate your ministry in your own strength, but you'll not get far while Jesus is sleeping. The disciples found that *"the waves broke over the boat, so that it was nearly swamped." v.37.* Wake Jesus up and make him the Lord and Master of everything you do! Too many churches and ministries have welcomed Jesus into their midst in the past, but today they are operating in their own strength and plans while Jesus sleeps in their midst.

Soon, three guards from the airport police entered the interrogation room and began to ask me stern questions in Burmese and English. I couldn't understand a word they said, which seemed to make them angrier.

They searched my bags and found some personal photo albums from my family's time in Myanmar, including pictures of an orphanage, of some friends, and some of rural scenes. These photos convinced the police I was an overseas spy or a reporter, and they started to treat me roughly. My passport showed I'd been in Myanmar eight times over the past two years. These eight visits had been to see my family, but to the police, this was firm proof that I was involved in illegal activities.

They also found a number of name cards of Christian leaders I knew. The next day several pastors throughout the country were interrogated by the authorities, as they attempted to find out who I really was.

As soon as the authorities realized my family had been living in northern Myanmar they started to search for them. The police told me, "We'll easily find where your family is hiding and they'll face the same punishment as you."

At that time I had no idea that my wife's and daughter's flights had been cancelled and all my family were still inside Myanmar. I told the police, "I assure you that my family is no longer in your country. They have already left for Germany where the government has officially welcomed them." When the interrogators saw how confident I was, they believed my family must have already left.

My hands were handcuffed behind my back and I was made to stand on one leg. From eleven o'clock in the morning of my arrest, to five o'clock in the afternoon of the next day – a total of thirty hours – they beat me severely with long sticks, and repeatedly kicked me. My arms and legs, back, private parts, and my neck and head were bruised and bloodied from being beaten mercilessly. Even when I changed the leg I was standing on they would beat me, shouting, "Who gave you permission to stand on your other leg?"

It was extremely hot and humid in that room. For thirty hours I wasn't offered a single drop of water or any food. My lips were chapped and my dry throat screamed for water, but none was given me. The few times I needed to go to the toilet the police wrapped a shirt around my head to conceal my identity from people outside the interrogation room.

As the long hours wore on I tried my best to stand on one leg as the police continued to vent their fury on my body. I tried to block out the pain and focus on the Lord Jesus. I thought of how my sufferings were in stark contrast to the sufferings of Jesus. The Lord was beaten because he obeyed God's will, whereas I was being beaten because I disobeyed God's will.

In one respect the beatings were not as bad as I have experienced in China because the Burmese do not use electric batons. Yet because I was suspected of being a spy during wartime, they didn't hold back anything. I knew if they continued I would surely be beaten to death, yet in my heart I felt it was not my time to go to heaven yet.

I cried many tears and my heart was heavy. From the depths of my soul I cried out, "My Lord, why have you forsaken me? Will you not use me any more? I'm so sorry. Please share your heart with me, Father."

Even as they beat me I repented of my sin, and waves of the Lord's forgiveness washed over me.

A picture flashed into my spirit from the Lord. I saw Moses tending sheep in the wilderness, all alone and with no one to speak to. I immediately understood that Moses had to be faithful tending his sheep in isolation, before God could trust him to speak to Pharaoh's court. In the same way, God wanted to see if I would be faithful in this foreign country where I could not communicate with anyone, before he would release me to speak before crowds of people in his name again.

I was greatly comforted. The Lord had not forsaken me.

After the beatings came to an end I was placed in a prison cell. The first thing I wrote in my journal was:

God, I thank you for your righteousness
God, I thank you for your faithfulness
God, I thank you for your mercy.

From the depths of my heart I praise and thank you.

*   *   *

DELING: When I was told Yun had been arrested again, I felt more guilty than when he was arrested in China, because even though God had warned my husband of impending trouble I had allowed him to carry his ID card with him. When he had been arrested in China we couldn't do much about it. But this arrest somehow seemed to be due to our foolishness rather than strictly for the sake of the gospel.

I'd been so happy that we were all leaving for Germany. For years I'd dreamed of us living together as a family again, with a measure of security in our lives.

Now, incredibly, our plans had been smashed to pieces at the last possible moment.

I believe this incident was the Lord's wake-up call to us because we thought once we arrived in the West our lives would be easier. He showed us that regardless of where we are, our lives will be difficult and we will encounter opposition.

We were unable to travel because of the outbreak of war along the border. Because of Yun's arrest the authorities knew our names and were searching for us. We were told not to try to travel on any transportation that required us to use our ID, as we would surely be arrested. Most likely, we'd be deported back to China, where we would face severe punishment for leaving the country improperly, in addition to problems resulting from Yun's prison escape and departure from China in 1997.

I could hardly believe what was happening. After waiting for years to join Yun in Germany, that dream looked as distant as it ever had. My husband was in prison. Nobody knew what would happen to him. Isaac was cut off from us in the midst of a war and we had no way to get to where he was on the border.

For two weeks we went on the run, praying nobody would ask for our ID cards. Yilin and I were placed in the back of a vehicle and driven a long distance across the country to an area near the Thailand border. Christian friends helped arrange for us to be led, on foot, across rugged mountains into Thailand. We were placed in a straw hut in the middle of the mountains, and ordered by the smugglers to stay inside, rest, eat, and wait for their return.

Each day seemed like an eternity in that little hut. We prayed a lot, but things were so intense that our nerves were on edge. We really knew we were in the midst of a fierce spiritual battle. Satan was throwing everything he could at us, all at once.

One night we were still awake after midnight when suddenly three Burmese men came and told us it was time to leave. They said we weren't allowed to speak a word, and forced us to remove our shoes and walk barefoot.

Only later were we told the men had been waiting for a moonless night to minimize our chances of being spotted by border guards. The noise made by squeaking shoes meant we had to discard our footwear.

The three men used long machetes to cut their way through a part of the jungle where nobody had ever been before. For hour after hour we crept along in the black of night. The whole escape was done in complete darkness. We never saw one person all night.

At one stage we had to scramble up a steep embankment alongside a waterfall. Several times we slid down and had to grab at branches and rocks to steady ourselves. All night I cried inside but didn't make a noise. I silently shared all my feelings with the Lord. It also happened to be my birthday.

Physically the whole experience was very difficult. As a result of the intense heat and suffocating humidity, sweat poured from our bodies until we were dehydrated and could sweat no more. Yilin cut her feet badly on the rocks, yet I was so proud of her. Not many ten-year-old girls could have endured the physical, emotional and spiritual pressure of our situation. The Lord sustained us.

In the middle of the night the Holy Spirit impressed on me a Scripture that I hadn't thought about for many years, from Isaiah 30:20–21: "Although the Lord gives you the bread of adversity and the water of affliction, your teachers will be hidden no more; with your own eyes you will see them. Whether you turn to the right or to the left, your ears will hear a voice behind you, saying, 'This is the way, walk in it.'"

You may remember that twenty years earlier in Henan, after I first believed in the Lord, on a number of occasions I saw a supernatural light showing me the correct path to take while I walked home from prayer meetings in the middle of the night. I hadn't seen the guiding light of the Lord for almost two decades.

Now, in the small hours of the morning in February 2001, soon after the Lord spoke this promise to me from the Book of Isaiah, I saw that same light directing me in the mountains along the Thailand-Myanmar border. The light wasn't constant, but appeared whenever I couldn't see which way I was supposed to walk.

Just before sunrise, after more than six hours of walking, we were told we'd arrived inside Thailand and our guides left us to return home.

We were in Thailand! We had few possessions, no shoes, and no documents. Our clothes were cut to pieces and our legs and arms were scratched and covered in dirt and dried blood. Yilin's feet were deeply cut and bleeding openly. I didn't know where my husband or son were.

Christian friends in Thailand came to where we were staying and picked us up. Isaac made his way into Thailand at a place much further north than we had entered, and we were reunited in the northern Thai city of Chiang Mai. Several days after that, the German embassy in Bangkok presented us with travel documents and we boarded a Lufthansa Airlines flight to Frankfurt, Germany.

Finally, after many trials, we were in the West!

Kind German Christians did everything possible to make us feel welcome. We moved into Yun's tiny apartment, but it wasn't the same without him. Our hearts ached to be together as a family.

After serving the Lord all these years I felt he had stripped us right down to nothing, so that he could launch the next phase of our lives.

CHAPTER TWENTY-EIGHT

A SEED IN THE GROUND

On the second day after my arrest the beatings ended and I was taken to a cell in a police station next to the airport. Much to their surprise, their investigation found my German passport was genuine, not counterfeit. They also discovered some documents in my possession from the Sinim Fellowship of house church leaders in China, declaring that I was their authorized representative. For the first time, they started to believe I really was a Christian pastor and not a spy!

While the letters from Sinim helped clarify my identity, they also caused the Myanmar authorities to alert the Chinese embassy that they were holding a Christian leader from their country in custody. Many Christians around the world had been alerted to my arrest by this time, and thousands of prayers went forth to the Lord, asking him not to let me fall into the hands of the Chinese government. Many feared that if China realized I had escaped from prison in 1997, I would be returned to China and executed.

A few days later the police station warden told me I had a visitor from the German embassy. The official asked how I was doing and brought me some food and clothes.

The very next day I was informed that representatives

from the Chinese embassy were coming to visit me at ten o'clock the next morning. I started to worry, and cried out to the Lord in prayer, asking for his will to be done.

When some Burmese Christian friends visited me later in the day I told them officials from the Chinese embassy were coming the next morning. Sensing the seriousness of the situation, my friends immediately went to the German embassy and notified them. The Germans knew my background in China and fully realized the danger if China got their hands on me again. The German embassy decided they would make sure they arrived at my cell before the Chinese officials the next morning, and would notify the Chinese that I was a German subject and that they were dealing with my case.

When the warden saw there was a struggle between two embassies over who should have access to me, he called the Chinese and told them it wasn't a good time for them to visit. They asked to reschedule their appointment.

I met with the warden and made it clear that I didn't want to see anyone from the Chinese embassy. The warden contacted the embassy and told them, "Yun thanks you for your sincere concern for his welfare, but because he is now a German citizen he prefers to deal with the German embassy."

The Chinese wouldn't give up however. They'd been told who I was and insisted on getting involved with my case. They tried to gather evidence against me to convince the Burmese authorities that I should be handed over to them. The Burmese were faced with a tough situation. On one hand they wanted to please the Germans, yet they also felt pressure from their giant northern neighbour.

By the grace of God, however, the Chinese authorities were not permitted to see me and I never received a visit from them.

Normally prisoners only stay in the airport police station cell for a few days at the most, but the authorities were confused about what to do with my case. I stayed there for one month. During this time I was allowed to have my Bible. I used the time to memorize the books of 1 Samuel, Esther, the Gospel of John, and Galatians.

In Myanmar no food is provided to prisoners. We had to buy our own from vendors outside the prison every day. We were allowed to shower for only two minutes, once every four days. This was always a welcome two minutes because of the extreme heat and humidity.

My Burmese friends told me I'd be set free after one month. Their prediction, however, proved to be incorrect. Instead of being released, I was transferred to the largest prison in Myanmar, in the middle of Yangon City. It houses ten thousand men. No words can adequately describe the conditions there. Many of the prisoners suffered from AIDS, and a large number had leprosy. The smell of rotting flesh invaded every corner of the dark, forsaken facility, where precious souls are left to die in silence.

One hundred prisoners were crammed into each cell. It was so tight that no one could sleep on his back. Each man had to sleep head to foot, side by side. We were packed like sardines inside a can. At night, if one prisoner moved too much or coughed uncontrollably, those surrounding him would beat him.

I've seen the inside of many prisons in China, but none came close to matching the terrible living conditions in this place. Yangon (formerly called Rangoon) is one of the hottest and most humid cities in the world. Every day the temperature was in the mid-to-high 30s Celsius (90s to low 100s Fahrenheit), with 85–90% humidity. We sweated continually in the steaming, putrid air. To make things worse, I wasn't permitted to have my Bible in this prison.

This may sound like a contradiction, but although I'd been arrested because I disobeyed the Lord's command, I also sensed it was his plan for me to be a witness for Jesus Christ to the desperate criminals there. It was for this reason God sent me into that hopeless place.

Before I left China in 1997 the Lord told me, "I will send you to a new place where you won't understand a single word of their language." This was exactly where I was now. My inability to communicate with the other prisoners was my biggest burden while in prison in Myanmar.

There were many hopeless men in my cell. One criminal, a convicted drug smuggler, had been sentenced to 387 years in prison! Others had received sentences of more than 160 years. Myanmar, being a Buddhist nation, believes in reincarnation. These extreme sentences, therefore, were designed not only to punish the criminals for the remainder of their present life, but also for the next several lives after that!

In a corner of our cell was a Buddhist shrine, with an altar and idols on it. The other prisoners heard I was a Christian pastor, and not knowing the difference between idolatry and the Living God, they made me sleep right beneath the shrine, thinking I would know better than most how to carry out religious duties.

Three times every day, between five and six o'clock in the morning, then from noon to 1 p.m., and finally between 7 p.m. to 8 p.m., all prisoners were forced to sit down in a Buddhist posture and pray and meditate in front of the idols in our cell. The government in Myanmar believes that making criminals pray to Buddha is the best way for them to be reformed. If any prisoner fell asleep during these times the guards savagely beat them.

Through another prisoner who could speak a little Chinese, I strongly protested to the guards, "I cannot worship the way you do. I am a Christian pastor. Even if you chain me up and drag me in front of these idols, I will not worship them and will not pray before them!"

One day while the other prisoners prayed and meditated to Buddha, the Holy Spirit gave me a simple tune,

Hallelujah, hallelujah, hallelu – jah
Hallelujah, hallelujah, hallelu – jah

As I sang, the Lord set my heart as free as a bird! Great joy flooded my soul. I could sense God was touching the hearts of the other prisoners. Even though they had no idea what the words of my song meant, a few of the other prisoners joined me. Soon they had broad smiles across their faces. This simple song started to bring happiness and peace to a room full of hardened sinners.

The prison warden came to me and said, "Singing is not permitted in this prison. You must cease at once!"

I answered, "I'm a Christian pastor. Jesus loves to hear people sing about him. Therefore, please understand my situation. Please allow me to practise my religion the way God prescribes."

By the grace of God my request sounded reasonable to the warden and he allowed me to continue singing.

Over the coming days all the other prisoners joined in singing "Hallelujah". Their grim faces turned to joy, and their suffering was alleviated for a few hours every day. The atmosphere in the cell dramatically changed. Because the other prisoners saw the presence of Jesus in me, they respected me as a man who knew God.

A small chapel stood in our prison compound. I was

allowed to go there when the other prisoners prayed to Buddha. There I met several Burmese Christians who had been sent to prison for different reasons. I was amazed to find that a number of my cell mates, including a Buddhist monk, started following me to the chapel every day, so they could hear me sing. They knew there was something different in my heart, and they were curious to find out what. When I knelt down to pray to Jesus, these men even knelt down next to me, hoping to receive some blessing from my God! Because of the language barrier I was never able to preach the gospel fluently to those men, but I know the Lord will find a way to satisfy their spiritual hunger.

Every few weeks the foreign prisoners were taken to a police station downtown for questioning. On our way back to the prison we were allowed to stop at a store to buy supplies for the Burmese prisoners. On one occasion I used my own money to buy more than 40 toothbrushes, dozens of bars of soap, and large sacks of food for my cell mates. For some of the prisoners who were nearly starving to death, this was the only food they could get.

Meanwhile, information about my case was very confusing. I hadn't been charged with any crime. Several times my Burmese friends assured me I would be released soon, but each day came and went without any change. I soon realized the outcome to my situation was in the hands of God alone. I knew I'd be released from prison as soon as my ministry in that place was completed, not a minute sooner and not a minute later.

On 9 April 2001, I was able to write a letter which was carried out to Christian friends around the world. I was aware that thousands of believers were praying for me every day. I wrote,

Dear brothers and sisters in Christ,
Thank you for your concern and prayers. My situation in
Myanmar depends only on the Lord, and I have completely sub-
mitted myself to his will. I deeply trust that my Lord has his own
time and holds my future in his hands because he is my Lord and
Saviour.

We cannot place our trust in the lawyers and judges here in
this country because they change their minds like the wind. I'd
rather submit totally to my Lord's care. Only the Lord knows my
tomorrow.

Living conditions here are even worse than in Chinese prisons
but I can sing and pray to my Lord freely every day. I know that
my Lord Jesus will find a way for me even if there seems no way.

Thank God I've led two prisoners to Christ. We've prayed the
sinner's prayer together. There are about 100 prisoners in my
cell and I am the only foreigner among them. Everyone knows
I'm a Christian pastor.

Please send my best regards to my family and all brothers and
sisters who are concerned for me. Keep praying without ceasing
because prayer makes all things possible!

Well, my friends, may my Lord give you joy and peace. I hope
to see you soon!
May God be with us!
Brother Yun

In the humid, filthy conditions, bacteria and diseases grew
and spread quickly. In our cell, one hundred men had to use
the same toilet. As a result a horrible plague struck, causing
many prisoners to die. Infection entered men's bodies
through their backsides and private parts. For several weeks
when the plague was at its worst, several prisoners died each
night. The disease felt like fire in the stomach. The afflicted
would roll around in dire agony before succumbing.

I was also infected with the terrible disease at this time, and was unable to digest any solid food for a month. Along with the other prisoners, all I could do was lie down and scratch all day. Parasites were rampant in my body. Sometimes I would look down at my stomach and actually see a worm moving under the surface of my skin. Occasionally its tiny tail could be seen sticking out through the pores of my skin.

It was a miserable time, yet I tried to maintain a cheerful spirit in the Lord. More than eighty per cent of the prisoners were afflicted. Finally, I grew so sick that I fell unconscious for five days. When I awoke I was in the prison hospital.

After several months in prison my day of sentencing finally arrived. My Burmese friends were certain I would be let off, possibly with a fine, and deported from the country. I didn't know what to expect but I placed my life in the hands of God.

I was handcuffed and taken from the hospital to the court-house. The judge reviewed my case, then, without any emotion, simply stated, "Seven years."

My Burmese friends and my lawyer were absolutely devastated. They'd never imagined such a sentence. They were speechless and looked at me with tears in their eyes. That day I was full of faith, and knew God Almighty was with me, regardless of the verdict. I bowed down before the judge's bench and said, through a translator, "I want to thank you, your honour, for granting me a visa to remain in your country for seven years."

With a wave of his hand I was dismissed and guards took me away, handcuffed, back to the prison hospital. When I told one cell mate the length of my sentence, he rejoiced for me and helped me gain a proper perspective. He was serving a sentence of 150 years.

In my heart I'd hoped God would allow me to go free quickly, as soon as I'd learned the lesson for my disobedience. I never thought I would receive such a long sentence. I complained to the Lord, "Heavenly Father, I have a wife and two children waiting for me. I'm sorry for disobeying you, but now can you please pour out your mercy on me and let me go home?"

When I look back, I clearly see that my time in prison in Myanmar really was a mission trip from the Lord. It was no accident that God had sent me into that dark place. There were so many desperate souls who needed to know Jesus.

I'd heard there were five Chinese men from Singapore in the prison, each having received a sentence of life plus 50 years for drug smuggling. They were all quite young, about thirty years old, yet had already been in the prison a few years. Another Chinese man from Taiwan, in his forties, had received life plus 100 years. Because these men could speak Chinese, I was eager to meet them and share the gospel with them in their hopeless situations.

Prisoners with life sentences were placed in solitary confinement, small dark rooms with little light or ventilation. Their isolation from the rest of the prison made it very difficult for me to have contact with them.

In God's provision, not only had I heard about those Chinese prisoners, but they had also heard there was a "Chinese pastor who loves Jesus" inside. They wanted to meet me as much as I wanted to meet them.

They found out I'd been admitted to the prison hospital. These men were so desperate to meet me and hear news about the outside world that they concocted a plan. They each feigned an illness, causing the guards to send them to the hospital for a checkup.

The moment I saw these men my heart was filled with the

Lord's compassion. They were like wounded animals, completely broken in their spirits and with nothing to live for. I couldn't help myself and hugged them tightly. I told them, "Dear brothers, you are blessed! The greatest pardon has already come down from heaven for you!"

They were excited, thinking I was trying to tell them their sentences were to be pardoned by the Burmese authorities. They hoped some international court had managed to secure their release.

I continued with tears in my eyes, "Brothers, I know nothing about your situation with the earthly authorities, but I've come here to tell you that Jesus Christ is the true and eternal Judge. He offers his life for you. He is the Lord of forgiveness."

They replied, "We all grew up in families that believed in Buddha, but he has never helped us. How can we receive Jesus?"

I shared the gospel with them and said, "When you die you will not suffer any more, but you will receive eternal life in Jesus. Only Jesus can save you!"

One of the men fell to his knees and held onto my ankles. In his desperation he cried, "Oh pastor, please teach me how to be saved!"

At that exact moment, the prison hospital guards interrupted us. They shouted, "You're not allowed to discuss religion here!" and ordered the men to leave my room.

I was so frustrated because there was so much more they wanted to say, and so much more I wanted to tell them about Jesus. I prayed God would give us another opportunity to meet.

All prisoners serving life sentences wore red uniforms. I asked my lawyer to bring me a red shirt the next time he visited. I hoped if I wore the same colour of clothing as those men, then maybe the guards wouldn't watch us so closely when we met together.

The next time I saw four of these prisoners I asked, "Do you really believe Jesus died for you on the cross?"

They firmly replied, "Yes!"

I asked, "Are you ready to turn away from idols once and for all, and receive Jesus as your Lord and Saviour? Do you believe his blood can cleanse you from all sin?"

Again they answered in unison, "Yes! We believe."

We prayed together and they received Jesus into their hearts. They crossed over from death to life. I knew there was no time to lose so I led them all into the bathroom, where there was a tap and sink. I asked each one to bend over and place his head under the tap, and I baptized them in the name of the Father, Son, and Holy Spirit. I told them, "Some men live free in this life, only to face an eternal prison in hell. You're in prison in this life, but from today your names have been written in heaven and you are free!"

Before I'd finished baptizing them a guard came rushing into the bathroom. He shouted, "What are you doing?"

I shouted back, "Don't worry! I know what I'm doing! I'm a servant of the Most High God!"

The guard just stood there speechless.

I told the four new believers, "From now on, you have the authority to pray for the other prisoners and tell them of the wonderful salvation you've received."

By the Lord's grace I was able to lead twelve prisoners to Jesus, including a man from Taiwan, Yue Minyu, who was serving a life sentence plus 100 years for drug smuggling. He told me he had previously served time in prison in Taiwan, where the seed of the gospel had first been planted in his heart by a visiting prison ministry team.

I took every opportunity to teach the new believers basic

Bible stories and how to pray. Because of my illness I stayed in the prison hospital for almost two months.

After I contracted the dreaded plague that swept the prison, I lay unconscious for five days in hospital. Even after I recovered I suffered regular fevers, headaches, high blood pressure, and severe gastric pain. Only later did I discover that God had a plan in allowing me to get sick. Not only did it give me an opportunity to share the gospel with the Chinese prisoners, but if I hadn't been transferred to the prison hospital I would have been sent immediately to a prison labour camp in the countryside to complete my seven-year sentence.

On several occasions the doctors came to inspect me to see if my health had improved enough to leave the hospital. The days before they visited I felt fine, yet when they came to inspect me I suddenly suffered from high blood pressure, or gastric problems, or came down with a fever!

God's grace was with the new Christians in prison and they grew in their understanding of him. Through song I taught many Bible passages to my new brothers in Christ. Because we were speaking and singing in Chinese, the guards didn't realize we were discussing the Bible. In fact, the guards and doctors seemed to enjoy our singing. These prisoners' lives changed dramatically, as only Jesus can do. From being men full of hate and anger, they became full of love and mercy. They reached out to prisoners in hospital who were close to death, spending their own money to buy them food and bring them comfort. They prayed for the sick, and did all they could to share the gospel with them. Each man also prayed fervently for their families in Singapore and Taiwan, asking God to have mercy on them.

They also told me they were praying daily that I would be released from prison, so that I could continue my ministry.

I cry whenever I think of those men and how the grace of God reached them in their desperate situation. We grew close in a short time and experienced true brotherhood. I've tried every way possible to have Bibles taken into the prison for them, but so far all my efforts have failed. I continue to cry out to God to provide his Word for those men.

Some people go through their whole life free on the outside but prisoners in their hearts, enslaved to sin and bondage. These men face the most miserable existence possible inside prison, but on the inside they are as free as birds gliding over the mountain tops! They love Jesus with all their hearts. *"Therefore, I tell you, her many sins have been forgiven – for she loved much. But he who has been forgiven little loves little." Luke 7:47.*

These were wonderful days filled with God's presence, and to be honest, I didn't even feel that I was in prison. I hardly even thought about the seven-year sentence I'd received, for each day was so full of joy and life. Those seven years to me seemed like the seven years Jacob had to wait for Rachel, *"So Jacob served seven years to get Rachel, but they seemed like only a few days to him because of his love for her." Genesis 29:20.*

My family was now living safely in Germany. I wrote to my daughter Yilin, "I'm sorry I can't be with you right now, but your daddy is on a special assignment for the Lord in Myanmar. As soon as I've finished the task the Lord has for me I'll come to see you."

Immediately after my seven-year sentence was announced I decided not to tell my family how long I'd received, at least for a while. I knew they were struggling in the West without me, and didn't want to break their hearts with the news they wouldn't see me for another six-and-a-half years.

Earlier, about a month after my arrest, the Lord had impressed this Scripture on my heart, *"I tell you the truth, unless a grain of wheat falls to the ground and dies, it remains only a single seed. But if it dies, it produces many seeds. The man who loves his life will lose it, while the man who hates his life in this world will keep it for eternal life." John 12:24–25.*

As I meditated on these verses, I started to think about my time on the farm in Henan, and how it took about seven months for a seed of wheat to appear above the soil after being planted in the ground. I felt the Lord was showing me that I would need to be "in the ground" (prison) for seven months before he would release me.

Jesus taught me many lessons when I was a seed buried in the prison. I have found the Christian life is not glamorous to the flesh. When a little seed is put into the ground it is not comfortable. It lies in the dark isolation of rough soil for months, suffers in the frozen ground of winter and the heat of summer, and is even covered with stinking manure and fertiliser. Only after it has silently endured all these trials is the seed ready to spring to life and produce a harvest that will feed many.

When a seed is buried in the ground it has no choice but to wait patiently for God's time for it to spring to life. In the same way I knew it was completely futile to trust in human efforts to get me out of prison. Instead of trusting in human-rights organizations to apply political pressure, I knew my future was completely in the hands of God only, and I would get out only when his time had come.

One day the prison warden came to me and said, "A representative from the German embassy is here to see you. Get dressed and go down to the gate."

As I walked towards the gate where visitors waited to see prisoners, the lady from the embassy saw me and shouted,

"Today I have good news for you! You are being released! The moment you sign this release form you're a free man. You'll need to be a little patient and wait inside the hospital for a few days while arrangements are made to take you to the airport, but from now on you are a free man!"

I signed the form and returned to the hospital, bubbling with joy. As soon as I reached my room I took off my prison uniform and threw it on the floor. The guard didn't know about my release and angrily threatened to punish me. I laughed and informed him, "I'm no longer your criminal! I'm free to go!"

I feel so sorry that many Christians live in bondage even though Jesus has signed their release form with his own blood. When you've been set free, you should act like it!

After I'd been sentenced to seven years, the German embassy had asked the Myanmar government to have mercy on me and send me out of their country. The German authorities said they would take responsibility for getting me back to Germany, where my family awaited me.

By the grace of God, their petition was granted.

Three days later, at eleven o'clock in the morning of 18 September 2001, I was handcuffed and taken by immigration officials to the Yangon International Airport. They were very kind and courteous to me, in stark contrast to how they'd treated me when I was first arrested!

At the airport several staff from the German embassy and some Burmese friends greeted me. One of them was a man named Ding Kai. In prison he was one of my Burmese cell mates. I had shared the gospel with him but he didn't make a commitment to Jesus at the time. He was released soon after I met him. He told me, "If your God helps you get out of this prison, then I will start to follow him on the same day you get out."

When they knew I was set free, my Burmese friends called Ding Kai and told him the news. When I arrived at the airport he ran to me and hugged me. We knelt down on the floor and prayed together for him to receive Jesus as his Master. By God's grace I was able to lead three men to Christ in the last few days in Myanmar.

I boarded a plane to Bangkok, Thailand. News of my release had already reached the ears of Christian friends, who gathered in Bangkok to see me. When I saw them I said, "My work in prison is finished, so Jesus brought me out. I was sent there by Jesus to share the gospel with those who'd never heard about him, and many were saved."

We linked hands in a circle, bowed our heads, and thanked the Lord for his goodness and mercy.

He is truly the Living God!

Many Bible scholars say that the number seven represents God's perfection. I'd been sentenced to seven years in prison, but the Lord didn't agree with that human sentence. In his perfect plan, I was released after seven months and seven days.

On the flight from Bangkok to Frankfurt I was accompanied by a friend who had travelled to Thailand so that he could welcome me out of the prison. A few hours into the flight he asked me, "Brother Yun, were you able to hear any news at all from the outside world while you were in the prison?" I answered, "Not a word."

"Here, I have something to show you," he said.

He gave me several Chinese newspapers from the previous week. At first, I didn't understand what I was looking at. There were pictures of an aircraft flying into a tall building.

I read the articles and learned that exactly a week before my release, on 11 September 2001, the world had been changed dramatically by terror.

*   *   *

DELING: As the weeks wore on into months, with still no sign of my husband's release, my faith weakened and I grew more and more frustrated.

I had dreamed of the day when Yun would welcome us to Germany and show us around the country that had warmly accepted him four years earlier. He had waited for us while we were in Myanmar for almost two years. I never expected that we would now be in Germany waiting for him, while he would be in prison in Myanmar.

We all struggled in Germany, although local Christians did everything possible to help us adjust. At first none of us could speak German. The food and culture was strange to us. I had never before had to get money from a machine by putting a plastic card into it and pushing numbers! Everything was so strange to me.

As the months went by I slipped into a deep depression. I cried out to the Lord for an answer.

One night I received a dream. I saw various numbers and saw that Yun was being released from prison. The numbers added together came to eighteen. I wrote "18" in my diary and told my children I expected their father to be released on the 18th.

One morning I received a call, telling me that Yun was to be released on the 18th of September! There had been so many false alarms and disappointments during this imprisonment that I didn't want to believe it until I knew he was safe, despite the dream I'd received.

Then, on the 18th, I received a call from my husband. He was standing in Bangkok airport, getting ready to board a flight to Germany. God is good!

CHAPTER TWENTY-NINE

A FUTURE AS BRIGHT AS GOD'S PROMISES

At six o'clock on the morning of 19 September 2001, my aircraft touched down on the tarmac at Frankfurt. It was almost exactly four years since I had first arrived in Germany in 1997.

When I first left China I thought my family would soon follow me, but the Lord had other ideas. There was much more he wanted to teach us and lead us through before bringing us together as a family in the same place.

After going through customs I walked out and found not only my family waiting for me, but more than a dozen German believers! We hugged and laughed. Even the German evangelist Reinhard Bonnke – whom God has used to lead millions of souls in Africa and other parts of the world to Jesus – came to the airport to welcome me! I was greatly honoured.

My wife Deling was glowing with happiness and my children bubbled with excitement. It was a wonderful reunion from the Lord.

We went home to the town where I'd been given a small apartment to live in by a Christian mission. I didn't have much furniture or even a bed, but Deling and the children had lovingly stayed in that apartment, not wanting to find a new place to live until we were all together again. As soon as we entered our home we shut the door and knelt down and worshipped together, tearfully thanking the Lord for his goodness and faithfulness. I raised my arms to the Lord and sang,

> *I cannot prevent tears of joy from filling my eyes*
> *For the Lord's hand has led me out of the prison*
> *I cannot help but follow him wherever he leads*
> *For his nail-scarred hands enable me to overcome.*

In the weeks after my release from prison in Myanmar it became apparent that my health had suffered. My system was infected with parasites and worms as a result of the plague and the dirty food and water we'd been forced to eat and drink. Worms started exiting my body through my skin, and I itched all over. The first thing my wife did was take my clothes and boil them, to kill the parasites trapped in my clothing. The Lord helped me to recover my health slowly. This was a good time for me to slow down and have quality time with my wife and children. Finally, Deling's request for a more settled family life started to come to pass.

Deling and I have now been married for twenty years. Our marriage is far from perfect, but I can honestly say it is growing richer every year. Deling is the best friend I have in the whole world. Twenty years ago she was just a young lady when I said to her, "God has chosen me to be his witness and to follow him through great hardships and the way of the cross. I don't have any money and am always being pursued by the authorities. Do you really want to marry me?"

She answered, "I will never let you down. I will join with you and together we'll serve the Lord."

Deling's promise has been tested many times, yet she has been completely faithful to the Lord and to me. I have spent about seven of our twenty years of marriage in prison, and have been on the run for many additional years.

Deling is a wonderful wife and mother. She's much smarter than me, and always reminds me of my weakness when she sees me getting too busy or putting too much confidence in my own abilities. She has a quiet spirit, and can never be found gossiping or making trouble in the church. She also has a great gift for worshipping the Lord in song. At one meeting in China I was eager to preach but the people told me, "We've heard plenty of your preaching already. We would rather hear Deling sing!"

Now that my family is together outside China, it doesn't mean we'll stay away from our homeland forever. We didn't flee the country by our own efforts in a bid to live an easier life. We left China because God clearly told us to. He then confirmed it by opening a door for us to leave.

Now that we are out, we're still as busy as ever preaching the gospel and facilitating the Back to Jerusalem movement. Yet we know that being led by the Holy Spirit brings many unexpected turns. Jesus told Nicodemus, *"The wind blows wherever it pleases. You hear its sound, but you cannot tell where it comes from or where it is going. So it is with everyone born of the Spirit." John 3:8.*

If we truly claim to follow Jesus then we must do so without imposing any conditions or self-made plans. If God tells us to go back to China one day, we will. It's as simple as that. Some people may say, "Well that's stupid! Don't you know you're a wanted criminal and you'll be arrested as soon as you arrive?"

We're not called to live by human reason. All that matters is obedience to God's Word and his leading in our lives. If

God says go, we'll go. If he says stay, we'll stay. When we are in his will, we are in the safest place in the world.

*   *   *

DELING: After twenty years of marriage, I know my husband's heart. His heart and his faith are solid. He's very open and forward. He has no fear of man. Everything he has in his heart he just speaks out. So in that way I never have to second-guess him. What you see with him is exactly what you get, no more, no less.

I respect him for his love and commitment to God. I know him very well in this way, but yes, there are other ways I don't know him so well because circumstances have meant we've been apart for most of our married life. The worst thing is that he has seldom been around so I've basically raised the children by myself.

It hasn't been all bad news however! Our lives have been filled with hardship, great suffering, and long periods away from each other, but also with great victories and experience of God's deep love and grace for us.

I haven't been very lonely because of the children. They've been with me and have been a great comfort to me. The biggest cross and most pain I've had to endure is not from poverty or persecution from unbelievers, or from loneliness. The hardest thing has been when the church started to spread false rumours about my husband. To this day I don't understand why some brothers could be so devious in spreading lies about a brother who so honestly tries to serve the Lord and love people.

Yun often tells me, "We are absolutely nothing. We have nothing to be proud about. We have no abilities and nothing to offer God. The fact that he chooses to use us is only due to his grace. It has nothing to do with us. If God should choose to raise up others for his purpose and never use us again we would have nothing to complain about."

When I was younger I saw God as a mighty healer who did something for me, but after all these years of valleys and painful trials Jesus has become an ever-present friend who is with me all the time. He has gone from being an historical God to being a living God to me today. I've fallen short many times during these trials and testings, but he has always been faithful. Whenever I've asked him to help me he always has.

Jesus is everything and we are nothing.

* * *

YUN: When I think of what the Lord has for me in the future, I'm excited! These are great times to be alive for Jesus! The Holy Spirit is moving mightily throughout the earth and it's a great privilege for us to be involved with reaping the harvest in these last days.

I believe the main focus of my ministry will continue to be the Back to Jerusalem movement. What started as a small trickle of missionaries leaving China has now become a steady flow, and soon I believe a mighty torrent of workers will leave China's borders with the gospel.

I continue to have the opportunity to speak in many churches and meetings around the world. My message to the Western church is to get back to basics in order to hear again the voice of Jesus speaking to you.

Then I want to challenge not only the Western church, but believers all around the world, to join hands with us in partnership to train and equip workers for this mighty harvest; to establish God's kingdom not only throughout China but also all the way back to Jerusalem.

A new church era has begun.

I believe the West's role is to be partners with us so that together we can get the job done.

We're not looking for handouts, but partnership.

I don't know exactly what the future holds, but I do know who holds my future! Since the Lord saved me as a teenager it has been an exciting ride! I've never known what was waiting around the next corner.

One day I may be killed for the sake of the gospel in a Muslim or Buddhist nation. If you hear this news, please don't grieve for me, but grieve for the millions of precious souls who are enslaved by Satan without any gospel witness. Death is not the end for a servant of God, but just the start of indescribable everlasting life in the presence of Jesus.

If you hear I have been called home to heaven, please go on in my place with the gospel, preaching and discipling the people groups of the world until Jesus comes again.

My Lord Jesus is the most wonderful friend you can ever have. He has been so loving, patient and kind to me over so many years and through so many valleys.

Many people have said to me, "Yun, you must really love Jesus." You need to realize that any love I have in my heart for Jesus is only because of his love for me. *We love because he first loved us.*" 1 John 4:19.

Jesus is truly worth knowing. He is worthy to receive our whole lives. If you do give him your life, you'll surely never regret it.

Will you follow him?

You can receive the latest information on Brother Yun, fresh updates on the Chinese house churches and the Back to Jerusalem Movement, and ways to pray for and support the advance of the gospel by the Chinese church by logging on to this website: www.backtojerusalem.com

Paul Hattaway is Director of Asia Harvest, a ministry committed to serving the church in China through:

- training
- Bible printing
- supporting church planting

See www.asiaharvest.org for more details.

INDEX

*The authors and publishers wish to thank John Robins who kindly
prepared this index.*